'I Am Sorry'

Indian Bureaucracy at Crossroads

‘I Am Sorry’

Indian Bureaucracy at Crossroads

Dr. P.K. Agrawal, IAS

&

N. Vittal, IAS (Retd.)

Former: Central Vigilance Commissioner

Manas Publications

Delhi-110092 (INDIA)

Manas Publications
(Publishers, Distributors, Importers & Exporters)
4402/5A, Main Ansari Road,
(Adjacent Bank of Baroda)
Darya Ganj, New Delhi - 110 002 (INDIA)
Ph.: 23260783, 23265523:, 23842660 (R)
Fax: 011-23272766
E-mail: manaspublications@vsnl.com
www.manaspublications.in

IInd Impression 2008

ISBN 81-7049-214-9
Rs. 495/-

Typeset at
Manas Publications

Printed in India at
R.K. Offset, Delhi
and Published by Mrs Suman Lata for
Manas Publications, 4402/5A, Main Ansari Road,
(Adjacent Bank of Baroda),
Darya Ganj, New Delhi - 110 002 (INDIA)

Preface

We have been hearing adverse criticism of the bureaucracy for the last thirty years as a part of this organization. We found that the bureaucracy is not so bad. There are various problems in this organization. If one doesn't pay even the lip sympathy towards this organization, the organization also becomes deaf and opaque to such criticism and complaints.

In this book, an attempt has been made to peruse bureaucracy in India in its correct perspective with complete objectivity and impartiality. Earlier it was contended that the bureaucracy mainly consisted of Indian Administrative Service (IAS) and other senior officers. After 57 years of independence, the gamut of bureaucracy has increased like anything. Even the apex service IAS has lost the reins of control of the bureaucracy under pressure of the political executive. Secondly, lower level bureaucrats known as street level bureaucrats in the USA or inspectors in India have created havoc with public. They are the first contact points of public with the administration. They are beyond redemption. As a result, the antagonism of public has been increasing day by day. Thirdly, the size of the bureaucracy has increased so much that it is very difficult for the top level to bring any positive reforms in the middle and lower rungs of the bureaucracy. As a result, everybody expresses helplessness. But the public is not prepared to listen to this. This is also due to increased consciousness in the public regarding their rights. The behaviour of officials at the crucial point of interaction between the bureaucracy and public is far from satisfactory. The British raj legacy of feudalism still persists. Secondly, the bureaucrats in the Indian society feel that they are better placed than their counterparts in the society. Thanks to their long complacency, inaction and inefficiency, the private or informal sectors have overtaken them. They have already been left much behind and will be further left behind if they do not improve themselves with the time. Any society or organization which doesn't change with changing time, is rendered obsolete or redundant. It is high time that the bureaucracy in India reads writing on the wall. In the age of liberalisation of economy and information technology, no society or polity would tolerate a bureaucracy that doesn't improve its efficiency with the increase of their pay, perquisites or allowances and with the increase of manpower. In fact, beyond the optimum manpower, it tends to be inefficient as it becomes more engaged or concerned to look after its own home front i.e. service matters of its members like pay, allowances, provident fund, social securities, pension etc. It is rightly stated that India has to pay more pension than salaries to her employees. The work or employment has to be output or result oriented. The purpose of doling out employment through bureaucracy is no longer relevant in the present day context. If any country resorts to it, it will be left behind in the race of development and will always be begging for help or aid from other countries or international organizations.

Yet it is futile to criticise bureaucracy without placing pros and cons. It is a bad fashion to call bureaucrats as 'babus' as the press does palpably to appease people who are generally fed up with the functioning of the bureaucracy. It is high time that the press should introspect as to how much *they* are involving themselves for welfare of the public and the country or are simply working at the behest of their capitalist proprietors or to increase circulation of the paper or magazine they are working for. Similarly, it is high time that public too does a self-analysis as to how *they* are discharging their own duties towards the system and the society at large. If every person violates law, no system can correct the heap of ills generated in the society. As a result, the bureaucracy is becoming indifferent. The bureaucratic organisations have started serving for themselves for example, the hospitals are for doctors and hospital employees, railways are running for railway officers and employees and so on.

The employees of a particular department or organisation forget that if they perform or work hard on their own seats, their personal needs will be met elsewhere because other persons across the window will similarly be well equipped to serve them. Therefore, one should do his own job faster and should give better service or output to avoid trap into the vicious circle. The public has also to remember that they should not pressurise their relatives or friends in bureaucracy for undue favours to them. This will of course generate ill-gotten money which will be spent on conspicuous consumption and in final analysis, all will be paupers. On the other hand, they should condemn and socially boycott a corrupt and indifferent employee even if he happens to be their relative or friend. Thus to awaken bureaucracy, the society has also to awaken herself. More the criticism of bureaucracy, more it becomes sullen and complacent. However, true and fair criticism will be a catalytic agent for reform in bureaucracy. It is, therefore, essential to start the process of reform in bureaucracy.

The bureaucrats have a problem that 93% members of bureaucracy are Class III personnel i.e. Clerks and Class IV employees i.e. peons. They constitute a solid vote bank of political parties. Accordingly, political bosses look for them and they look for their support. There is no check on it. The employees' unions are now becoming militant. The senior bureaucrats find it difficult to control them.

This book contains variety of articles so that it may provide an integrated view of the bureaucracy in India. Wherever, the articles couldn't be procured from the eminent contributors, the editors themselves have written a few to fill up the gaps. The article of Parkinson has been borrowed and is included in the book since no book on bureaucracy can be said to be complete unless it has a humorous touch of Parkinson. Similarly, the case study of Gujarat violence has been contributed by two eminent writers so that it may be an eye-opener for the government and such incidents do not repeat further which may be termed as shame on bureaucracy. Similarly, an article on privatisation has been included to understand the role of bureaucracy specially in India in the light of privatisation of goods and services.

We are grateful to the eminent bureaucrats and contributors of articles to the book. Most of them were not only bureaucrats but they have equally good public image and the Indian public have faith in them. The bureaucracy has done not so badly after independence inspite of political and administrative constraints. The country has achieved self-sufficiency in foodgrains. The population below the poverty line has come down from 60% to nearly 25% inspite of swelling population. The farmers have more or less got their land records. Land reforms measures have been implemented to some extent inspite of fractured 'political will'. The country has self-sufficiency in steel and coal production and is marching ahead for self-dependence in oil and fuel gas production. There is unprecedented spread of higher education. As a result, the young engineering graduates could conquer the Information Technology field and made India the super power in the field of I.T. Similarly, in the sector of Space and Nuclear Technology, the country is self-contended. This was possible because in the Deptt. of I.T., Space and Atomic Power, there has been consistently no minister in charge except the Prime Minister who had given full autonomy to the scientists or bureaucrats who are capable of desired performance, given due opportunity. Similarly, successful conduct of elections in India for more than fifty years is a pointer to the success of bureaucracy. Thus, the Indian bureaucracy is capable of performing if it is given due opportunity to perform.

We are sure that the book will give an insight into the working of the Indian bureaucracy and set its agenda for future.

Dr. P. K. Agrawal
N. Vittal

Contents

The Contributors

Dr. P.K. Agrawal, writer of thirty-two books, an Indian Administrative Services(IAS) officer with D.Phil(Law) & MBA degrees, at present, Principal Secretary, Department of Women & Child Development and Social Welfare and Department of Jails, Govt. of West Bengal, Kolkata (India).

N. Vittal, IAS (Retd) was Central Vigilance Commissioner, India. He did remarkable and dynamic work in removing the corruption from govt. departments. Wrote several books including '*Fighting Corruption and Restructuring Government*' and '*Information Technology: India's Tomorrow*'.

Sagar Agrawal, B.Tech. in Computer Science and Information Technology, working as Software Engineer in M/s. Infosys Technologies Limited, Bangalore.

P.C. Alexander, ex-Principal Secretary to the Prime Minister of India, ex-Governor Maharashtra, at present Member of Parliament, Rajya Sabha.

P.S. Appu, Fellow, Harvard University; former Director, Lal Bahadur Shastri National Academy of Administration, Govt. of India, retired IAS Officer.

Pradip Bhattacharya, IAS officer, International HRD Fellow, Manchester University, at present, Principal Secretary to Govt. of West Bengal and Director, Administrative Training Institute, W.B., Kolkata.

M.N. Buch, Chairman, National Centre for Human Settlement and Environment, Bhopal (M.P), retired IAS Officer.

Subesh K. Das, IAS officer of 1982 batch, West Bengal Cadre, Scholar of Cornell University, USA, working at present on convergences and divergences in employment relations.

M.K.Kaw, ex-Secretary, Civil Aviation & Education, Govt. of India, retired IAS Officer.

Harsh Mander, I.A.S. officer of 1980 batch, former country representative of Action Aid who resigned from the IAS on the issue of Gujarat riot.

C.N.Parkinson, famous writer on bureaucracy who is synonymous with humorous representation of bureaucracy all over the world.

Major General S.K.Sen VSM, Army Postal Service, 1968 batch.

CHAPTER

1 A Survey of Bureaucracy in India

Max Weber described the rational legal organisation as bureaucracy. Weber never thought that this organisation would ever become so much powerful in times to come. Even socialistic states could not do away with the bureaucratic system. The bureaucracy didn't wither away but it caused the USSR wither away under pressure of socialist bureaucracy. The political elite who tried to finish it, themselves were lost in oblivion. The bureaucratic system has inherent power to change governments what to say of rulers. This has swallowed even best of democratic or autocratic governments. It is like unruly horse for rulers. Therefore, a successful ruler is one who can ride this horse carefully and can drive it fast. Despite all efforts to prune it, it is expanding day by day with the blessings of its worst critics like Parkinson. Even decentralization of administration through municipalities and panchayati raj bodies in India has not helped to minimize its size and power. Bureaucracy thus, is accepted as a necessary evil.

After independence of India in 1947, the Indian economy had to be rebuilt to fulfil the long-cherished expectations and hopes of its people. As a result, the concept of the Indian State from the regulatory state was changed to the mother state i.e. the state caring for its people and catering to their needs from the field to the kitchen. The people also had lot of respect for the public administration. But in the eighties, the government sector started crumbling under pressure of demands. At the same time, the private sector continued to perform reasonably well. This was the scene world over. The strongest socialist bureaucracy in the

USSR was also run over by the market forces. However, the same market regime adopted it in a changed form, which suited it. Thus, during the nineties, interference from the state lessened. The government confined itself to the role of a facilitator or a regulator. This process of change also blurred the role of administration and management and both were known as one and the same. Yet, the legacy of public administration continued to rule the roost. By this time, it was already well entrenched in telecom, posts, electricity, water supply, conservancy, health services, education, environment apart from regulation of land and law and order. But its performance went down substantially. Therefore, it becomes difficult for popular governments to support their choicest instrument i.e. public bureaucracy.

The Economy Committee (1948), Parliament's Estimates Committee (1951), The Administrative Reforms Commission (1966-70), Economy Administration Reforms Commission (1985) and host of others recommended a cut down in the size of the bloated bureaucracy.

All these efforts have been in vain during the period 1967–1991; the number of ministries in the Central Government went up from 18 in 1947 to 20 in 1952, 35 in 1979, 60 in 1987 and 71 in 1990.

No less drastic has been the increase in the size of the public bureaucracy. The second, third, fourth and fifth Pay Commissions reporting in 1959, 1971, 1984 and 1997 respectively have given the census of government employees for these years as 17 lakhs, 29 lakhs, 37 lakhs and 40 lakhs.

The expenditure on the salary bill of the civilian employees of the Central Government increased from Rs. 1468 crore in 1974-75 to nearly Rs. 3000 crore in 1981-82. At present (2004), it stands at a staggering amount. It means the instrument is an end in itself. Bureaucracy is there to feed itself and serves no other fruitful purpose. Development can be done if the funds are left over after meeting the wage bill of employees. The increase in the size of state level bureaucracy has been equally staggering. Some State governments have been left with only to pay salaries to their employees.

The governments have assumed excessive functions like the Central Government has about 2000 functions. It is believed that the state instrumentality in India should not indulge in works or activities, which primarily belong to other organs of the State. But none could check the expansion of the bureaucracy in India. Bureaucracy in India has infinite capacity of frustrating any reform; its resistance is resolute and firm and requires, above all, a vastly superior political will and vision to overcome it.

This has been possible because after independence, leaders like Shri Vallabhbhai Patel had faith in basic sincerity, integrity, and the efficiency of public bureaucracy, as they were confident that it was the educated, enlightened and modern-outlook bureaucracy which could take the nascent nation on the path of progress after slavery of about a thousand years. It is debatable whether bureaucracy performed satisfactorily or not. However, there is no denial of the fact that the public bureaucracy in India, as compared to the bureaucracy in other countries did not perform so badly. The public bureaucracy had been performing these jobs exclusively: Policing, Prisons, Defence, Adjudication, Maintenance of law and order, Management of land, Health, Education, Emergency Services, Money supply, Roads, Maintenance of standards, Regulation and Inspections, Revenue collection, Welfare services, Public utilities, Communications, Transportation etc.

But the public image of the bureaucracy has hit an all time low in India. A survey conducted as part of the National Election Study 1996, reveals that the bureaucracy and the police were relegated to the last two positions in the index of popular trust in institutions (Yadav 1996-2000). The survey revealed that out of a maximum score of 100, the Election Commission secured 62, State Governments and Judiciary 59, Local government 58, Central Government 57, Public representatives 40, Political parties 39, Bureaucracy 37 and Police 28.

Atal Behari Vajpayee, the Prime Minister while addressing the National Development Council meeting held on February 19, 1999 said:

> "People often perceive the bureaucracy as an agent of exploitation rather than a provider of service. Corruption

has become a low risk and high reward activity. Frequent and arbitrary transfers combined with limited tenures are harming the work ethics and lowering the morale of honest officers. While expecting discipline and diligence from the administration, the political executive should self critically review its own performance".

The Planning Commission in its 10th Five Year Plan document talks of bureaucracy, which never earlier gave so much emphasis on reforming the delivery system: "A civil service renewal programme which improves public satisfaction therefore, has to be an essential component of effective implementation of development programmes".

In the area of Civil Service reforms, the Government faces three critical challenges. It must enhance the productivity of the Civil Service and make certain that each employee is performing socially relevant tasks. It must ensure the long-term affordability of the Civil Service, and it must enforce procedures for rewarding and promoting merit, disciplining malfunction and misconduct, to strengthen accountability and performance equality. It has become necessary to reshape the bureaucracy so that it performs its core public functions and develops new ways of ensuring that critical economic and social services are provided directly or indirectly. A new work culture will have to be evolved at all levels of the staff.

Components of the Indian Bureaucracy

The Indian State has three organs i.e. Legislature, Executive and Judiciary.

Executive in India is vested in the President. But the Indian Constitution has not recognized the doctrine of separation of powers in its absolute form but the functions of different parts or branches of government have been sufficiently differentiated and consequently it can very well be said that the Indian Constitution does not contemplate assumption, by one organ or part of the state, of functions that essentially belong to another. The Constitution has built in system of 'checks and balances' so that one organ does not become despotic to even overrun the democratic form of government where the people are at the roots. The sovereignty in India thus, lies in the people who have given Constitution to themselves as per Preamble of the Constitution. Thus, the Constitution is the Supreme Code, the Bible, the Vedas or the Ramayana, which will regulate the functioning of all organs of State including the executive. Rule of law is one instrument provided in the Constitution to prevent misuse of power. In States, the Governor is the head of the bureaucracy. Thus, all officers or staff under the President or Governors by and large constitute public bureaucracy in India. The executive power of the Union extends to the matters with respect to which Parliament has power to make laws, while the executive power of a State extends to matters with respect to which the Legislature of the State has power to make laws. But so far as the concurrent list is concerned, ordinarily the executive power is vested in the States. But in exceptional cases, the Union Parliament can prescribe functions to the Union Executive.

The President appoints Prime Minister and other members of the Council of Ministers and they hold their Office during the pleasure of the President. They are collectively responsible to the Parliament and the people. The President makes rules for transaction of the business of Govt. of India. He has the power to grant pardon, reprieve, respite, commute and remit punishments given by the courts or judiciary.

The President also has the power to summon, to prorogue and to dissolve the Houses of Parliament. He has the power to issue ordinances when the Parliament is not in session. The Governor has similar powers in the States.

But no organ of the State has exclusive power in their jurisdiction. There is a system of checks and balances beautifully woven in the framework of the Constitution so that one organ of the State doesn't become despotic to transgress or overrun the interests of the people.

For the executive or public bureaucracy, the biggest check is law itself and if any member of the executive violates it, he is liable for action before a court of law. Then there is the writ jurisdiction of the Supreme Court and High Courts, whereby the executive can be directed to desist from a particular course of action or conversely directed to perform a particular function. They can also review any action through PIL (public interest litigation) in the broader public interest. The Legislature, to whom the Ministers are responsible, can call the Government to account through discussions, resolutions, adjournment motions, budget debates, questions, and no-confidence motions. If need be, the Legislature can even oust the Government. The Ministers are part of the Legislatures and in fact the Prime Minister is the leader of Parliament and the Chief Minister is the leader of State Legislature. Similarly, the executive controls conditions of service of the legislature and the judiciary. The judges of High Courts and the Supreme Court can be impeached by the Parliament. The members of Parliament or the State Legislatures have been declared as 'public servants' by the judiciary and are accountable. They are like any other citizen of the country, liable before any court of law for their conduct outside the House. The independent judiciary is the safeguard against arbitrary exercise of powers in India. However, these checks and balances by themselves do not give the other organ of the State the power to interfere in the working of any organ including the executive or to place it in a subordinate position.

But this presumes that the particular organ of the State is functioning in its allotted field without arbitrariness or mala fide. No organ of the State should and is supposed to interfere with day-to-day functioning of the other organ of the State.

The public bureaucracy generally is of pyramidal structure with four levels but it has now extended upto six levels. The public services can be generally classified into four categories:

1. Senior officers—executive and administrative,
2. Junior officers or inspectors—administrative and field work
3. Clerical services
4. Helpers or peons

Earlier, the services used to be heavy on the bottom but gradually these are becoming top heavy due to time bound promotions without the criteria of merit or efficiency. Secondly, due to modern technological innovations, the requirement of peons or helpers is reducing day by day. Just after the independence, the public services were created just for giving employment. Therefore, employment at the menial level served the purpose of distributing gains of the system or 'raj' to maximum people by providing minimum of salaries. But the public services no longer are serving that purpose except through reservations where the persons belonging to socially backward classes i.e. Scheduled castes, Scheduled tribes, Backward classes or economically backward classes get into public services.

The Economic Administration Reforms Commission (EARC), in its report on Economy in Public Expenditure (1983) has also recommended that the pyramidal structure with a very wide base and a narrow apex coming down from the British days is no longer appropriate. Under present conditions, fewer posts at lower levels and more posts at higher levels would lead to greater economy and efficiency. It also recommended:

(ii) Each new activity need not be the occasion for the creation of a new agency, additional activity should be entrusted to an existing agency.
(iii) Government's working methods and procedures need to be reviewed with a view to minimizing duplication, over-centralization, and excessively high-level clearances.
(iv) There should be only one preliminary examination of a proposal before a decision, and this should not be at the lowest level but at the lowest appropriate level at which the kind of examination which is necessary can be carried out.
(v) A re-examination of the multiplicity of different services, some sharing common professional backgrounds and skills, might indicate possibilities of economy. The possibilities of merging certain services (e.g. various Accounts services, etc.) may also merit consideration.

Fifth Central Pay Commission (1997) observed that the expansion of the Government was disproportionate to the increase of work level. It generally recommended as below:

(i) Ascertain tasks that need not be done by Government,

(ii) Pass on tasks to State Governments/local bodies,
(iii) Transfer certain tasks to corporate entities in public sector,
(iv) Contract out tasks to the Private Sector,
(v) Transfer some entities to the Cooperative Sector, and
(vi) Convert some institutions into autonomous bodies,
(vii) Reduction in number of Ministries and Departments,
(viii) Introduction of officer-oriented system of Governments,
(ix) Avoidance of delay and level jumping,
(x) Multi skilling,
(xi) Computerization,
(xii) Office automation,
(xiii) Creation of a paperless office, and
(xiv) Changes in office systems and the management.

The Expenditure Reforms Commission in February, 2000 recommended:

1. A cut of 10% of the staff as on January 1, 2000 to be carried out by the year 2004–2005.
2. A screening committee should be set up for the purpose.
3. There should be a total ban on creation of new posts for two years
4. Surplus staff should be made eligible for a liberal Voluntary Retirement Scheme. Ex-gratia amount will be paid in monthly instalments covering a five-year period.
5. Those who do not opt for Voluntary Retirement Scheme and are not redeployed within one year, will be discharged from service.
6. Top group officer opting for Voluntary Retirement Scheme will not be required to seek approval for commercial employment after retirement.

In fact, all the recommendations of the Fifth Pay Commission to trim the bureaucracy were not implemented but the pay-hike was implemented resulting into the basic bankruptcy of the Central Govt. and the State Governments. This could not perhaps be done due to fragile political and administrative will and fear of pressure of government employees' unions and organizations who had in the past and still are capable to put the governments to ransom. Now, the Supreme Court by banning strikes, has come to rescue saying that the government employees are in trust of public money. Therefore, they have no right to go on strike. It was realized that the bureaucracy was introduced to serve the system, but very soon it turns the system to serve itself.

Luckily, liberalization in economy and setting up of panchayati raj institutions all over the country have come as timely relief.

The Panchayati Raj which ushered in on the recommendations of the Balwant Raj Mehta Committee report (1957), after several ups and downs, has finally got constitutional recognition and firm base after the 73rd and 74th amendments in 1992 adding new Chapters IX and IXA in the Constitution of India.

The panchayati raj institutions for most of the part, utilized the existing machinery of the bureaucracy by way of deputation or working in addition to their government duties. On the other hand, governments got a large number of functionaries at the village, block and the district levels who were quite knowledgeable in local affairs and were sincere and devoted to the cause of local people. Unlike the members of the Legislative Assemblies or Members of Parliament, these elected representatives-cum-panchayat functionaries were honorary workers. Thus, the system of panchayats had the same system of collective responsibility of the Cabinet but panchayat representatives were available as ministers, without pay and allowances and worked as workers, officers, inspectors or even clerks of the panchayats and in turn served the people at the grassroots. Thus, a great size of rural bureaucracy has been created by a stroke of an amendment in the Constitution. This has largely helped and will further help to reduce ever-growing size of public bureaucracy and thereby will result in reduction of non-plan expenditure to a large extent.

Achievements of Bureaucracy in India

Before independence, the bureaucracy was introduced by the British because they considered the civil services essential to the functioning of the parliamentary democracy. They considered them neutral and loyal to the king and will ensure the sovereignty of law. Later on, it was expected that the senior civil servants of ICS (Indian Civil Service) will follow the tradition of the British

Civil Servants and will ensure smooth running of the administration in India. ICS personnel were grown as the British civil servants in the Indian colour or British wine in the Indian bottle. Their job was also to integrate administration in diverse situations in India. Gradually, they had grown sympathy with the indigenous non-violent movements based on the tenets of the democracy. The leaders of freedom movement were impressed with their way of working. The Service fulfilled its primary function of making the apparatus of government work, which was mainly confined to revenue collection and maintenance of law and order. The same Service helped the country to cope with the communal holocaust and transfer of powers from the erstwhile rulers. Gandhiji had his own ideas to introduce panchayat system and that was introduced in few States. Pt. Jawaharlal Nehru who was in hurry to bring about scientific and socialistic innovations in the country, did not like both of them. He wanted more commitment from the bureaucracy to public governance. However, in the backdrop of inadequately educated mass of leaders, the bureaucracy led by the IAS (Indian Administrative Service) as successor of ICS continued their journey uninterrupted for the welfare of the nascent nation. Their achievements can be recounted as follows:

(i) *Central Government:* The civil servants worked as servants of the people while their predecessors in service including ICS represented the authority of the colonial power;

(ii) *During 1950 and 65:* The bureaucracy showed remarkable progress in achieving goals of development. They adopted the Community Development Programme combined with National Extension Service in 1952. About 500 BDOs (Block Development Officers) in each block in the country became the focal point of development. Side by side, the panchayati raj bodies were associated in developmental work. Cooperative bodies also equally grew to associate themselves extensively in the development movement. About 50% rural families were covered by the cooperative network of societies. The cooperative societies made available seeds, fertilizers, pesticides and credit facilities.

During 1965 and 80, the strategy was of Green revolution. The seed, water-fertilizer-technology under green revolution was responsible for significant rise in output of foodgrains and the famine became a thing of the past. The country achieved self-sufficiency in foodgrains in due course of time. Through major irrigation projects and the Command Area Development Authority programme, irrigation was widely provided. Then, came the idea of land reforms and decentralization of power and resources. For that purposes, Small Farmer Development Agencies were formed.

The period from 1980 to 90 is known as poverty alleviation period. These measures like Antodaya, IRDP, white revolution (milk & egg revolution) assisted by the nationalized banks gave fillip to the rural employment programmes of different types. Programmes of self-employment aimed at improving the productivity of small and marginal farmers and rural artisans. The Khadi and Village Industries Commission assisted the rural and cottage industries to grow in a big way. Food for work and other employment generation schemes eliminated hunger from the rural areas. As a result, the number of people below the poverty line were reduced from 2/3rd to less than 1/3rd of the population of the country even with respect to ever growing population. While attending to the development of rural areas, the infrastructural development was neglected in the fields of power, transport, road network, education, health services etc. This affected the industrial development adversely which came to contribute a major share to the economy similar to other parts of the contemporary world. The public bureaucracy adapted to the liberalization approach since 1991 but were not successful. In the meantime, a large network of public sector industries was already built up which provided steady development to the nation free from exploitation. Later on, these public sector enterprises also became burden on the exchequer and indirectly on the people. On the other hand, the private sector became very successful globally under the leadership of the West. The Nehruvian approach collapsed. But this time, the Central Government had already built up basic infrastructures in steel manufacturing, coal mining, and power. Even the IT industries were promoted through the Deptt. of Electronics. This, it cannot be said that the regime of 'licence raj' had all failures. It had its glaring achievements in the fields of higher education which was almost provided free of cost from the State. This promoted scientific and technical advances including in the field of space, biomechanical industries, scientific and industrial researches and Information Technology sector. The educated bureaucrats had interaction abroad and brought new technologies and approaches to the country. Therefore, it can be safely said that what we see today, the public bureaucracy has a large contribution in this. In the 21st century, however, the role of the public bureaucracy is going to be limited as private sector and private entrepreneurship have stepped ahead of them. Thus, the bureaucrats have to play a role of facilitators and promoters and not actors because of adequate spread of education and consciousness among the people of India. Now, India has more than 100 million as its makers.

However, two major shortcomings were growth of corruption and ever-bulging foreign loans. For most of times, foreign loans, though essential were taken to please the political bosses, who wanted to rule the country on the basis of their personalities rather than through association of people on a large scale.

The Indian bureaucracy has shown notable success in conducting free and fair elections in the largest democracy of the world. Without any separate staff, specially recruited for the purpose, the normal bureaucratic machinery has carried this entire burden on its shoulders. Elections in India have been conducted with a high degree of efficiency, acumen and sense of responsibility. All foreign visitors and experts have appreciated role played by the Indian bureaucracy in this regard. The District Administration has played crucial role in maintaining law and order and was the key instrument in development inspite of lack of financial and personnel resources. The Government of India has also taken a major initiative to popularize the Indian culture in India and abroad.

Achievements by State Bureaucracy

(i) *West Bengal:* The bureaucracy duly led by the Left Front Government since 1977, has implemented widespread land reform measures and power has been transferred to the panchayats. Now, both are working in close unison with technical and educational expertise from the bureaucracy and local know-how from the local representatives for the good of the people of the State.

(ii) *Gujarat :* The public bureaucracy has followed the general psyche of the people of Gujarat and is output oriented. In early years after independence, panchayats and cooperative societies specially milk cooperatives have played major roles in making Gujarat as the most developed State in India attracting maximum direct foreign investment.

(iii) *Maharashtra:* The public bureaucracy was helpful in the development of cooperative societies in the field of sugarcane. It has also led the State on the path of modern advances in the fields of industries, services sector etc. As a result, Mumbai, its capital, has developed as Financial Capital of the country.

(iv) *Tamilnadu:* The bureaucracy of Tamilnadu has been consistent inspite of political upheavals after every five years. They have kept the administrative machinery intact and are running administration with sincerity and honesty. As a result, Tamilnadu is emerging as a major industrially advanced State in the country specially in the textile sector.

(v) *Karnataka:* The bureaucracy of the State has shown due openness and has converted Bangalore city as the hub of IT Services globally known as the Indian Seatle. As a result of heavy export revenue, city of Bangalore and the State as a whole is now on the path of prosperity which earlier used to be sole prerogative of four metro cities.

(vi) *Kerala:* The State has achieved 95% literacy. The health and education facilities available in the State can be compared with the best anywhere in the world.

(vii) *Uttar Pradesh:* After initial progress of the State, the State has gone down due to widespread corruption and feudal style of working of bureaucracy. The political instability has given the blow to the ailing bureaucracy. As a result, the state is crumbling under hostilities of castes, creeds or religion. One can only hope that the biggest state of the country awakens from its slumber because without its progress, progress of the country will be meaningless.

(viii) *Madhya Pradesh:* Initially it was a backward State. The bureaucracy in the State was given lot of autonomy. It has well laid down decentralized administrative system upto tehsil level. The people are good and amenable to reforms. Now, the State has come among the progressive states due to persistent and sincere leadership by the enlightened bureaucracy.

(ix) *Rajasthan:* The public bureaucracy is also afflicted with feudal set up in the State. The public is loyal and obedient to the State. The administration has done its bit to improve literacy and to do away with social evils. However, inspite of lot of tourism potential, the State has still to achieve expected level of progress. Of late, due to natural changes, the State is getting normal rains and is likely to jump to the frontline category of States.

(x) *Punjab:* The State is very rich. It is surplus in production of foodgrains. This is due to hardworking people of Punjab. The bureaucracy had however, played yeoman's service to the State to bring about normalcy after militancy years in Punjab in nineteen eighties. The bureaucracy could hardly make impact to eradicate corruption and religious fanaticism in the State.

(xi) *Haryana:* The State is a prosperous State. It contributes lot of surplus foodgrains in the Centre's kitty. It has good industrial potential being close to the National capital city of Delhi. However, bureaucracy has failed to tackle corruption and casteism in Haryana.

(xii) *Jammu & Kashmir:* The State of J&K has been suffering from militancy for more than two decades. The State has been made dependent on central aid. Bureaucracy could hardly play its role to fruitfully utilize central grants to bring the trouble-prone State to the mainstream of national life. However, bureaucracy has properly demonstrated its mettle and strength to bear with terrorism and fight against armed militancy in J&K.

(xiii) *Bihar:* It is the most backward State in India. The bureaucracy couldn't exert vis-à-vis the politicians. There were exceptionally high-ranking bureaucrats but they could not prevent the downslide of the State. However, the bureaucracy has still maintained its framework, which can act, in emergent situations. Overall there is hardly any achievement of bureaucracy worth mentioning in case of Bihar.

(xiv) *Jharkhand:* Jharkhand is a newly created State. The bureaucracy is trying to come out of its poor legacy of Bihar administration. Good results are expected.

(xv) *Chhatisgarh:* The State is a surplus State. The bureaucracy has yet to learn to work as efficient staff and officers have not opted for Chhatisgarh State. Over and above, initial rule of Congress Party could not contribute properly to place the bureaucracy on the main track.

(xvi) *Uttaranchal:* The State is trying to come out of her bad legacy of corruption, nepotism and red-tapism of U.P. bureaucracy. Better results are expected.

(xvii) *Orissa:* The State is a backward State. The bureaucracy is also self-centred. There are top ranking bureaucrats in the State. Now, the political elite has become conscious. So far, hunger has been overcome in Orissa inspite of adverse reports in the press. This is the single biggest achievement of the bureaucracy in Orissa.

(xviii) *Andhra Pradesh:* The bureaucracy is an enlightened one. It has also got support from the political leadership from time to time. As a result, A.P. has become leader in the field of production of rice, fish, grapes, eggs etc. whereas it used to be a State of scarcity. This is one example of success of administration.

(xix) *Goa:* It is one of the most prosperous states in the country. Though tourism industry was initially criticized, the same has brought prosperity to the State. It is a forerunner in the field of health facilities and peaceful law & order situation.

(xx) *Delhi & other UTS:* Administration of UTs have always been good as it has less of political interference. The UTs have surplus Central grants and have locational advantages for industrial development.

(xxi) *North Eastern States:* The States suffer from problem of local versus outsiders. The bureaucracy could still not win the hearts of people. They couldn't utilize central grants properly. As a result, the people are dissatisfied and alienated. Corruption has increased and militancy has flourished. However, bureaucracy has been fighting militancy with utmost neutrality and sincerity and has developed requisite infrastructures.

(xxii) *Assam:* The State is affected by militancy. The bureaucracy is equally afflicted with corruption. However, administration has done a lot to develop infrastructures in the State.

Miscellaneous Achievements

Some of the Central Public Sector undertakings have done very well. The Central Govt. has been running the railways efficiently round the clock without interruption. Indian Oil Corporation, ONGC and other Oil & Gás companies have turnover more than Rs. 1 lakh crore per year which is more than 5% of the total GDP of the country. Some other PSUs like SAIL, BHEL, Nationalised Banks have been doing fine. Posts & Telegraph services have been pulling on similarly. Bhartiya Sanchar Nigam Ltd (BSNL) has been providing extensive telephone services all over the country including remote and inaccessible areas successfully and is standing as a rock against exploitation by private service providers. However, Electricity Boards in the States have been limping. An intervention of private sector is being worked out as an alternative. But it is not known how many years more, it will take.

Most Important Achievement: One of the greatest achievements has been the timely and positive response of the bureaucracy during natural calamities like flood, drought, earthquake or cyclone. The greatest achievement of the public bureaucracy in India is its success in maintaining national integration. Fissiparous tendencies based on race, caste, religion or language have been surfacing from time to time but these have been nipped in the bud. The secular framework of the polity has become so much firmly entrenched in bureaucracy that it will take twenty to thirty years to change it. Latent national integration can be visible when there is some danger or threat to the national security. It can humorously be seen during cricket match or other international events of games and sports. Secular thread is so well woven, that no political leadership can afford to defy or tear into it. It is the great measure of success of administration of India that by and large, the nation of a continental size has been able to move together.

Limited Role of Bureaucracy: During the two decades, after independence, the Indian bureaucracy was allowed free hand to deliver goods to the people. During the decade from 1971–1980, the political interference started. In the decade 1981-90, the political leadership only believed that the bureaucracy should toe their line and they wanted only the committed bureaucracy. This process started during emergency (1975–77) and surfaced formally during eighties. As a result, the development was skewed. The exchequer got depleted. And privatization became as only alternative during nineties. This is continuing into the first decades of the 21st century alongwith panchayati raj institutions. The bureaucracy will have to wait for two more decades for its turn to show its performance once more because by that time, the private sector and panchayati raj institutions might meet the same fate which the bureaucracy is meeting at present. At this juncture, it is futile to blame the bureaucracy for all ills in the society.

The total size of the Indian Economy during 2003-04 in terms of GDP was roughly Rs. 27,29,300 lakh crore per annum. The private sector contributes 75% of the GDP and 25% is contributed by the public sector. If defence, railways and public sector units are excluded, the size of the economy affected will be much less i.e. 13% of the Central Government's Expenditure. The size of budget of Railways will be around Rs. 15,259 crore. The contribution to GDP from PSUs of oil sector is around Rs. 1.5 lakh crore. Therefore, out of Rs. 6,82,250 crore, the GDP handled through bureaucracy comes to Rs 6,82,250 – (Rs.65,330 + Rs.15,259 + Rs. 1,50,000 + Rs. 2,30,559) = 4,51,691 i.e. Rs 4.5 lakh crore (appx.) which comes to about 16.5% of the GDP.

Thus, the impact of the public bureaucracy on the Indian economy will be around 17% . This includes about 5% officers and staff posted with panchyati raj bodies directly or indirectly after 1992. If it is taken that the Judiciary is able to make impact to the tune of 10% and the Legislature can influence the economy to the tune of 10%, the left out field is fairly large segment of 60% of GDP where the private organized, unorganized or informal sector are operating at present in the country.

Employment in Public Sector

	1983	*1988*	*1994*	*1999-2000*
As a % of Total Employment	5.43%	5.6%	5.19%	4.88%
As a % of Organized Sector	68.55%	71.25%	69.15%	69.05%

So far as the employment in the Central Government is concerned, it increased from 17.37 lakh in 1957 to 29.82 lakh in 1971, 37.87 lakh in 1984, 41.76 lakh in 1994 and then decreased to 40.67 lakh in March, 1999. Thus, the employment in Central Government increased at the annual rate of 3.9% between 1957 to 1971, 1.9% between 1971-1984 and 1% between 1984-1994.

The employment rate decreased @ (-) 0.72% during 1994-99. This shows that the deceleration in employment in the Central Government during 1994-99 is at a higher rate than the decelaration in employment in the organized public sector as a whole (Organized Sector includes business and government organizations). In most countries of the world, public sector employment accounted for 1/5th (20%) of the total employment of the world. During the year 1990. Australia had 22.8%, Canada 19.7%, France 22.6% U.K. 19.2% and USA had 14.4% in 1989 public employment.

In India, it is much less as the bulk of employment (93%) is in unorganized sector of agriculture and self-employment in various sectors of the economy. Organized sector employment (including both private and public sector) has constituted around 7 to 8% of the total employment over the last 20 years.

As percentage of population in 1991, there were 120 public employees for every 1000 members of population in France, 81 in the United States, 80 in the United Kingdom and 40 in Japan. In case of India, the figure was 21.7 for a population of 1000 in the year 1994.

As a percentage of total population, the size of Central government work force in India in 1999 was 0.4%. The total employment in public sector (including Central government), State Governments and all the organizations/undertakings of government in 1999 as a percentage of total population was 1.93%.

It shows that the destiny of India is unnecessarily shown as fully dependent on the functioning of the bureaucracy. In fact, the figures indicate otherwise.

I distinctly remember, that my family and most of the families in my neighbourhood and even farmers, never used to refer to the government servants as helpers upto nineteen-sixties. They were treated as agents of exploitation. It is only by the successive politicians in government who created an unnecessary psyche of dependence of public on government to win votes. They raised expectations of people based on resources which did not exist. The Indian culture teaches everybody to follow self-dharma (Swadharma) and to abstain from other dharma (Paradharma). But now a days, everybody points out fingers on another person without his self-introspection as to how much he is contributing to the nation building. Of course, it cannot be denied that the public bureaucracy has a solemn role to perform as they are paid from the hard earned money of public. But that is not all. Even, the private sector hold its fortunes as trustee to the society. They draw funds from public. Let everybody perform his duties well and contribute to the nation's well-being.

As the expenditure on public bureaucracy is increasing day by day, their role is shrinking in the same proportion. It is the logical corollary that the size of the public bureaucracy should be decreased in future. Due to implementation of the recommendations of the Fifth Pay Commission, the total civilian salary bill (excluding TA) has gone up from Rs. 18,094 crore in 1996-97 to Rs. 32,834 crore in 2000-01 ie. an increase of Rs. 14,740 crore. The cumulative effect on State Governments will be around Rs. 17,500 crore (appx). The popular governments cannot carry on this burden too long as they have other commitments towards people to discharge. Therefore, the country is looking forward to create wealth and employment in the following important emerging sectors of the Indian Economy.

1. Food Processing Industries;
2. Small Sector Industries;
3. IT Sector (By 2008, the turnover of IT sector will be around $80 billion of which $50 billion will be from its exports);
4. Housing and Real Estate Development; and
5. Tourism Sector.

It is shocking that even the private sector industrialists, political leaders or press spokespersons do not accept their own social responsibilities and blame bureaucracy for each and every ill of the country. Let everyone give his best wherever he is. The country will automatically reach the peak of its glory.

References

Dubhashi, PR. *Essays in Public Administration*; NBO Publishers' Distributors, H-39, Green Park Extension, New Delhi-110016; 1985, pp. 376.

Mehta, Vinod (ed). *Reforming Administration in India*, by Indian Council of Social Science Research; HarAnand Publications Pvt. Ltd., D-9 Anand Niketan, New Delhi-110021; 2000, pp. 460.

Ludwig Van Mises. *Bureaucracy*; B.R. Publishing Corporation, 4222/1, Ansari Road, Darya Ganj, New Delhi; 2002, pp. 128.

Magazines periodicals etc.

Jha, Nikhilesh. "Rightsizing the Government: the Indian Experience", pp. 13-41, *Management in Government*, April-June, 2002. A quarterly journal published by Deptt. of Administrative Reforms & Public Grievances, Sardar Patel Bhawan. Govt. of India, New Delhi.

CHAPTER

2 Indian Bureaucracy in Historical Perspective

—Dr. P.K. Agrawal

There was the system of kingship. The king used to serve his public like his sons. The bureaucracy or army was unorganised and they were generally called during need. Whatever small bureaucracy was there, it was a part of king's household. However, duties of the king and his servants are narrated in ancient scriptures as follows in order of priority:

1. Protection of public/country, 2. Welfare of public, 3. Timely payment of wages to employees and armed forces, 4. Collection of revenue with tact, 5. Ideal conduct by the persons in authority by way of observance of dharma or show of bravery, 6. Sufficiency of foodgrains, 7. Safeguard to women, children and the helpless. 8. Appointment of intelligent and diligent persons as associates, 9. Patronage to the business, 10. Watch on enemies, friends and neutral through secret agents and representatives.

During Rama's period, king was also a part of bureaucracy. So is the case now-a-days. Tulsidas's *Ramacharitmanas* says that the chief should be like the mouth, which alone does all the eating and drinking, yet maintains and nourishes all the other limbs with discretion [Doha 315, *Ayodhyakand*].

Similarly, Bhisma in the *Mahabharata* says that the king should take care of his public like the pregnant lady takes care of her child in womb without caring for herself [*Bhismaparva, Mahabharata*].

Tulsidas further says that mean spirited is the servant who seeks his own advantage by placing his master in an embarrassing situation. A servant's interest lies in setting aside all selfish pleasure, to do his master's service and not to be greedy. He should not exceed the brief of his master or duties assigned by him [Doha 267 (3 & 4), *Ayodhyakand*].

Similarly Vibhishana tells Ravana, "Oh king ! There are many who will always tell you sweet things. But when it comes to the relevant, helpful, bitter truth, there are few sayers and even fewer teachers" [*Valmiki Ramayana*]. Kautilya supported the superior rights of king but criticised anti-people kings.

We find that there was sudden departure of authority from the king to the minister or advisors during the reign of Akbar and Sher Shah Suri during the Mughal period. Akbar put Todermal to carve out definite administration of land.

After the Britishers came to India, they brought the semblance of bureaucracy beginning in Warran Hastings' regime through the Regulation Act, 1772. He created the office of Collector on 14th May, 1772.

The Weber's concept of political neutrality had already formed part of the British Civil Service which later became operative in the Indian situation. Weber held that bureaucracy was an integral part of every planned and organised group activity called administration and that it was not restricted to any particular system, colonial or capitalist, socialist or communist. The idea of loyalty to the emerging concept of state or the public good, as distinct from service to the king, was slowly engaging people's mind. The Weberian view of bureaucracy did not apply to the Indian situation for the greater part of the British rule. Democracy was of course introduced as late as in 1935 in the provinces. Civil servants became subject to ministerial control. But the presence of imperialism made this control more formal than real. The Secretaries to Government reported to their Governors and the Governors in their turn to the Viceroy over the heads of the Minister. They sometimes quarrelled. The British Government in India remained a bureaucracy until the formation of the Interim Government in September 1946 when the balance tilted in favour of democracy for the first time.

Macaulay 's Report mooted the idea of a generalist administrator —'all rounder' to those who liked the idea and amateur to its critics. They were moving from job to job within the service, was capable of taking practical view of any problem, irrespective of the subject matter on the basis of his knowledge and experience in government (Fulton Committee Report). Cornwallis after Warren Hastings introduced ICS collector's system. They were known as 'Mai Baap' (mothers & fathers) in the districts. He was the patriarchal district officer in whom the British Empire had full faith and confidence. In 1919, there were 1029 ICS officers: 48% of the ICS officers worked at the district level, 15% in judicial posts, 27% at the state headquarters and 11% in the Government of India. The district was the basic unit of administration in colonial India. He was the pivot of the administration combining revenuer, magistrate and general administrative duties. He was coordinating, supervising controlling and directing all the component parts of the district administration towards achieving goals set by the British empire.

The British, while defining the district as the unit of administration, were merely building on the foundation of the Mughal administration. The British retained Akbar's revenue division of the country into 'Subas', Sarkars, Parganas and Mahals. Under the British, the ICS officer who was in charge of the district had as much power as that of a Mughal subedar or fouzdar. Thus, the story of bureaucracy in India of Weberian model starts from Akbar's time. However, after the independence and specially after 1992 amendment of the constitution, the bureaucracy in India is going to turn full circle which will also imbibe some of the features or characteristics of vedic and epic system of administration.

The Britishers controlled through ICS men in control posts at all levels throughout British India. However, the IAS successors of ICS could not hold on as they failed to deliver goods. Only in one third public sector enterprises, IAS could be Managing Director or CEO. The IAS were frequently transferred making their tenure less than one year on a post on the average.

During emergency, 1975-1977, the credibility of the IAS was badly eroded. The public didn't like them to be committed to the ideology of the political party but wanted them committed to the ideology of the constitution for which they are bound by oath before taking up their job. The mainstay of the IAS in District

Administration as Collector also got eroded. The collector had lot of political pressures and had to involve in local issues. In the Secretariat, the Ministers came to exert more authority in the name of their direct accountability to people. As a result, steelframe of the Indian bureaucracy or administration received cracks now and then. The Prime Minister and Chief Ministers no longer consulted the Secretaries separately. They heavily depended on their Ministers as they didn't have charisma or statesmanship which was held by personalities like Pt. Jawaharlal Nehru and many others in the States. Thus, IAS got slowly cut off from the policy making. The politics and political consideration became uppermost as the governments changed frequently.

The IAS had to manage his minister as well as his subordinate staff and officers. The political parties had by this time entered into staff union and instructed their minister to toe party line. As a result the work of the top bureaucrats became very difficult. He had to manage the minister as well as to control his subordinates who were indirectly or invisibly affiliated to his master. The corruption entered into the political mainstream. Thus, there was a crisis of faith in the echelons of bureaucracy. The bureaucracy thus, became directionless.

However, the well entrenched institution of District Administration kept the administration of the country going. From the revenue collector and head of administration in district, he became head of mini-secretariat of the Government. All works of Government were converging in him and he efficiently kept the flag of administration flying in colours. As and when, panchayat institutions were introduced, he was actively involved in their administration. Such is the faith reposed by the Indian people in the unit of administration of India known as district administration. The collector has following main jobs:

1. The Collector has power to appoint Class III (Gr. C) and Class IV (Gr. D) employees. He is the State Public Service Commission in the district.
2. The Collector in most States has power over postings and transfers of employees in Class III & IV services.

3. Food & Civil Supplies is under him. He maintains supplies of essential commodities. So also relief in calamities and rehabilitation work are also under his sole control.
4. He is head of law and order machinery and District police is under him as he is the head of civil government in the District. He writes Annual Confidential Report from Supdt. of Police to the Inspector level offices in few States. He has power under the Code of Criminal Procedure to issue order u/s 144 Cr.PC and various preventive sections to maintain peace and tranquility in the district. He has power to evict encroachers from Government land.
5. He is nodal officer of all the developmental activities schemes in the district which are not assigned to Panchayat bodies. In many States, like West Bengal, he is the Chief Executive Officer of Zila Parishad whereas he has a major say in affairs of panchayat bodies. He controls BDOs and thus he has a say in the affairs of grassroot panchayat bodies also. He has vital say in all rural development schemes like Jawahar Rozgar Yojana, Pradhanmantri Rozgar Yojana, IRDP, ITDP, NREP, RLEGP.
6. As a collector, he is the head of land matters in the district.
7. Other departments/sections under him are land acquisition, arms licences, motor vehicles, protocol, treasury, elections, welfare of SC & ST, criminal prosecution etc.
8. He is the chief coordinator of affairs of family planning, industries, youth welfare, sports, water supply, social welfare, etc.

This institution has helped maintain stability in the country inspite of instability at the State or Central level due to coalition governments from time to time. Like the joint family system and self-governing system in villages have provided stability in the Indian social fabric for centuries, the district administration headed by District Magistrate & Collector, mainly an IAS officer provided political stability in country. Even the great P.M. Pt. Nehru used to sit in UPSC to select new recruits to the IAS in interview boards. He encouraged middle class to come to IAS. Upto 1970, the steelframe of IAS ruled the roost. But this steelframe became gradually weak in 1980 because politicians learnt how to use power of transfer and writing performance appraisal reports of senior bureaucrats. During the emergency in 1975-77, the myopic cleverness of the politicians became the ruling philosophy and ever since then each day has only pulled the bureaucracy lower. In the name of committed and socialist bureaucracy, one man rule of Mrs. Gandhi was prevailing. She was not allowed to rule freely due to caucus within Congress. So she wanted to control Congress alone rather than the decentralized system in the party. In such a party, it was very difficult. As a result, she encouraged corruption and her cronies. People of India did not bother as they believed that the ruler was right so far she or he could ensure them all good things in life. And she had the background of winning the decisive war against Pakistan in 1971 dismembering Pakistan into Pakistan and Bangladesh. She was projected as Kali. In fact, she was the most powerful personality the Indian politics has ever seen. She could even afford to fire the Chief of the Army. The persons who had met her, can recollect that she was a powerful person. But her charisma soon got diluted and she imposed emergency during 1975-77 which resulted in excesses by bureaucracy including police. People remembered earlier repressive British rule. Soon she was dethroned. S.V.D. Government headed by Morarji Desai came into power. He hardly could stay for two years due to internal bickerings and this experiment of coalition government failed. Shah Commission gave report to take stringent actions against bureaucrats who committed excesses which further demoralised the already fragmented bureaucracy.

The politicians, recklessly interfered in the working of bureaucracy and patronised the lower bureaucracy to cow down the senior bureaucrats through political manoeuvring. They created unions in government offices who paid more heed to the political bosses rather than to their bureaucratic bosses. It resulted into indiscipline and lack of work culture in the bureaucracy. Other states tried to follow West Bengal experience where the left wing unions dominated the office scene supported by ministers or their representatives or party representatives in the district. The Left Front Government had control over their unions and knew the Laxman rekha for doing so. As a result, good work was done in West Bengal but in other States including Central Government, it got converted into indiscipline. The great strikes organised by the Central Government employees demonstrated that '*steel-frame*' of bureaucracy could no longer control their home fronts. Even police action proved ineffective. It was partially due to the reasons that the senior bureaucrats gradually started surrendering to the political masters for small gains and due to fear of transfers. But the bureaucracy, in spite of their loyalty towards one party maintained its high tradition of neutrality, efficiency and devotion to duty in Tamilnadu, Gujarat, Maharashtra and Karnataka.

Other States overlooked the fact that in West Bengal, the control of the bureaucracy is for the broader party purpose. The ministers live very simple and relatively honest life. It is also a fact of the day that the bureaucracy alone cannot run the public administration unless it is supported by the party cadres at the grassroot level. Otherwise, opposite political parties will exploit all actions of bureaucracy for their ulterior political motives by misguiding people. Thus, in a large country like India, the public bureaucracy and the political support have to go hand in hand. Bureaucracy cannot bind such a big country together on its own.

In 1980s, the bureaucracy received challenge from the technocrats and specialists. They put forth the viewpoint that they should be allowed to head the departments which were engaged primarily in technical jobs. But the technical people while heading the department or organisations independently failed to their internal technical bickerings and as a result they failed to deliver output. They were not apt in the art of managing big public sector undertakings or semi-government bodies like thermal or hydro-power stations etc. They also collapsed. As a result, during 1990s, the technical CEOs had to be removed even from the purely technical departments or bodies. State Electricity Boards which were once considered stronghold of the power engineers were worst performers and had ultimately to yield to the top management by the IAS and other senior bureaucrats. The technical people, they could never agree to a point. Therefore, I.A.Ss were called to arbitrate and take decision. Thus, it can be safely presumed that IAS are the natural rulers of the country.

Shri Rajiv Gandhi would be remembered as a young PM with innovation. He introduced computerisation in bureaucracy at a stroke of pen inspite of opposition from all quarters and similarly brought panchayati raj in existence.

Had he lived, he would have done away with ills of bureaucracy due to arbitrary transfers, postings and recruitment based on nepotism and corruption. He made some genuine postings through computer. The people loving status-quo were very much scared of him. But the leaders with solid public mandate are loved by bureaucracy and they can only bring about reforms in bureaucracy posted in far flung areas of the country. During the five years regime of Shri Narasimha Rao as Prime Minister, the bureaucracy was again moving on the basis of old tradition only with innovation of liberalization of economy.

The hegemony of the IAS over the country's administration was successfully challenged by the software giants like Infosys, TCS and Wipro. They earned so much foreign exchange and employed so many young boys and girls that it would have taken years for the bureaucrats to plan and execute. That too, the icons of IT industries did like yogi without any help or patronage from the government. But bureaucracy did not obstruct their efforts. It is said that the bureaucracy has delayed the liberalisation process in the country in 1990s. But the bureaucracy alone is not to be blamed. The Members of Parliament take lot of time to pass any new initiative or law. After passing the law or regulation, invariably it is challenged in court's of law who take their own time before it is implemented in the field. But the sad story has a silver lining. The rapidly liberalized economies of South-East Asian tiger countries soon collapsed. But the slow liberalisation in India put the liberalisation on sound footing as the liberalisation has to be accompanied by distributive justice. The large country like India cannot afford it without public support. This is a chance justification. However, the greatest malice of the Indian bureaucracy which crept into it in 1980s and 1990s cannot be justified by any logic. Omissions to perform and delays caused are equally culpable to punishment. However, due to good performance of IT sector, bureaucracy is sitting complacent with the happy situation of the Indian economy and is trying to take a credit along with the politicians for its success.

The first decade of the 21st century will observe litmus test for initiatives taken by the Central and State bureaucracies. The Central Government is going to dislodge itself from the recurring burden of its public sector units. The inefficiency of PSUs should not be financed by the hard-earned money given through the revenue. The Central government will also give assistance to the States, henceforth based on efficiency. The political masters by law will be restrained to spend money beyond the permissible limit as they had been doing in past ruining the economy of the country. Even the Prime Minister will be brought under the ambit of Lokpal Bill. Therefore, gods in politics or bureaucracy will have to shirk off their privileges or special protection. In free economy, none should enjoy protection or privilege. Then only, they will realise the pangs of public and will try to make India worth living equally for all.

The Chief Minister of Andhra Pradesh Shri N. Chandrababu Naidu behaved like Chief Executive of the State. He was more prompt in decision making than any of his counterparts in the private sector. Through his programme of *Janma Bhoomi*, he had taken the administration to the doorstep of people. In West Bengal, law has been passed to nominate members of opposite political party if none is elected in panchayat bodies so as to ensure working of panchayats in true democratic spirit. Gujarat Government is working like private enterprise to write off all his loans so that it may have more funds for development projects. Govt. of Madhya Pradesh is experimenting with government at the district level. Chief Minister of UP personally pays surprise visits to schemes and punishes delinquent officers on the spot. Chief Minister of Tamilnadu is standing like a rock against support to terrorism. Chief Minister of Kerala has vowed to clean the public life whereas Chief Minister of West Bengal is spearheading the movement to recreate work culture in West Bengal. In Maharashtra, fight against organised crimes has been brought as state focus whereas the Karnataka Government has decided to make Bangalore as no. 1 city in the world in the IT sector after Silicon valley. In Punjab, bureaucracy is led to fight against the widespread corruption. Even, the ex-Chief Minister was not spared. Small states like NCT Delhi and Goa have demonstrated how they can function more efficiently than the best managed private sector units.

The public bureaucracy has not yet shown its hidden hostility towards panchayati raj bodies as there is political will and constitutional mandate to establish them and to ensure their proper functioning. Bureaucracy has gone out of way in West Bengal, Gujarat, Maharashtra, Kerala and Karnataka to allow free growth of the panchayati raj (P.R.) institutions. In fact, all the Collectors in All India meet convened by the then Prime Minister Rajiv Gandhi suggested for formation of P.R. bodies and their active functioning in rural areas for rural development works to overcome corruption and lethargy in implementation of rural development schemes worth more than Rs. 15,000 crores every year in the country.

It is correctly said "a good administration is better than the best constitution". Ex-Prime Minister Smt. Indira Gandhi used to say that "rules are for the people and not the people for rules."

The bureaucracy has spread its wings very far. Even the apex level bureaucrats are not able to control the lower level bureaucrats from the inspector level to the clerks and peons. General public generally comes in contact with these people who are sitting in front seats of the office. They still do not possess the attitude of assistance to the people for whom they are serving. This has created a bad image of the public bureaucracy. The people feel themselves as part of administration and they cannot tolerate such behaviour to the taxpayers or voter. The superior officers are failing to control and supervise the lower level officials. The method of departmental proceedings to control them is very tedious and time-consuming. The affected person can easily take shelter of the court of law and win sympathy of the court by showing only their part of the story. There is none to speak for the poor and dumb government. Secondly, the superior bureaucrats have either failed to lead the lower ones by way of their conduct or by showing their higher skills in the art of working. As a result, the public is growing indifferent towards the bureaucracy. One can only hope that the dissatisfaction or unrest of the public may not burst one day overrunning the fortress of bureaucracy built on the principles of clean and welfare government.

A caste-based democracy is a kind of cancer in the Indian body politic which has surfaced in many states, particularly in Bihar and U.P. in an ugly fashion. It is being kept in check by the higher echelons in rule-oriented bureaucracy whose administrative culture theoretically permits serious deviation from the universally recognised norms of public administration. The higher echelons of the bureaucracy, however, are not all-pervasive or immune from the corroding influence of political, social and sectarian pressures on rational administration.

Apart from caste factor, which became very obvious after emergence of Laloo Prasad Yadav as the Chief Minister in Bihar in 1990 and DMK in Tamilnadu. The reservation factor gave a fatal blow to the already limping bureaucracy. To gain votes, reservations were allowed upto 68% in Tamilnadu. Without harmonising with the efficiency of the system, employment and not the efficiency in bureaucracy became the motto or catchword. Thus, the top bureaucrats of IAS numbering only about three thousand in the country, could not tackle the ever-expanding size of bureaucracy. Further, frequent contempt cases by courts like the Vasudevan case demoralised the IAS. In 1990s, brilliant students of IITs started entering into IAS but they too, were soon demoralised and started running to foreign countries for jobs.

The courts like public, cannot appreciate that the lion cannot rule in the jungle if its teeth have been taken out. No bureaucracy in the world has worked in such difficult situations as the top level Indian bureaucracy has done and is working. Initially, it had to tackle people's hunger and poverty. Then, it had to surmount the arbitrariness of its political masters with respect to the system by indulging into wild postings and transfers making it as industry. Thirdly, it had to change its complete orientation to market forces from its regulatory working up in 1990. The senior bureaucrats have demonstrated their mantle in international bodies and on foreign deputations. They are preferred for jobs by U.N. Bodies over all other bureaucrats in the world.

Now, the bureaucrats are struggling to ensure timely payment to its work force as all State Governments more or less are financially bankrupt. At the same time, they cannot expel or terminate an assistant or a subordinate officer. The procedure of departmental proceedings provided by rules is more cumbersome and time-consuming than the judicial process in India. If he indulges into it, he can probably do no other work. In the process, he will be first proceeded departmentally himself.

The worst thing has occurred that the dream or mission of the bureaucracy has been tarnished that they have to do for the public and the nation as per the Constitution. They are sometimes insulted and demoralised by their political masters in private and in public and sometimes by the Courts. The senior bureaucrats specially in IAS or IFS etc. service or in some other specialised jobs join the bureaucracy for serving the country and people. If that is gone, then none can control the steep downfall which will be bad for the country. This demoralisation is seen among young officers sometimes. The IAS who were posted in the Election Commission of India as Election Commissioners or Chief Election Commissioners have shown that they have the proper mantle to take on the politicians of the country. The reform process of elections started from Seshan as Chief Election Commissioner, India and continues even today. Earlier CECs who were from judicial services, could hardly make impact on election process to ensure transparency and freedom from malpractices like rigging etc.

I am sure that the system will take care of itself if it is allowed to work free within the prescribed limitations. Then, accountability will be there for output. Then they will take the country in 21st century ahead of other nations in the world. It is hoped that the bureaucracy will show its agility once more and help the country to leap forward.

CHAPTER

3 Image of an Indian Bureaucrat

—Sagar Agrawal

As per dictionary meaning, a 'bureaucrat' is a government official responsible only to his departmental chief.[1]

The meaning stinks of the narrowness and parochialism in the bureaucratic organization. In fact, the bureaucrats starting from the times of the creation started to control or regulate the affairs of the society when the things or population started increasing.

Even God of death Yamaraj employs Chitragupta to record deeds or 'karma' of human beings to give them award or punishment.

The first bureaucrat employed by Adam was a man to record births and deaths of human beings and number of animals belonging to each group of people. Then Kautilya needed bureaucrat to prepare and maintain the records of rights of village landholders in the 'nibandh'(register) of a village.

After Todarmal settled land disputes, Akbar requested him to control the corruption among the officials (Muquddam). Later on rajas exploited the cultivators in league with amins and Karnam.

The English required their own system with people in governance of their colour and thinking who could be instrumental and helpful in their exploitation of the India's people and her resources.

---

[1] *Chambers Twentieth Century Dictionary*, Ed. by A.M. Macdonald, published by Allied Publishers Pvt. Ltd. Calcutta-700 072. Year 1981, p. 172.

Mahatma Gandhi gave a jolt to the traditional bureaucratic system when he asked them to abhor the foreign marking and to do the duty for the country as per requirement of their inherent Indian culture and 'Swadeshi'.

The present-day bureaucrat owes this dilemma or dichotomy. The Constitution of India in 1950 further became a third pillar of his ideology. A bureaucrat is labouring under these three differing ideologies, i.e., his own, his employer's thinking and ideology and the ideology enshrined in the India's constitution.

When Rabindranath Tagore, during pre-independence period, approached a bureaucrat, he found him immersed in file work. Since morning to evening, he had no time to lift his head less to attend a person and least to gaze at the nature or the world around. He taunted him as heartless and emotionless if not lifeless being. Moreover, he is always busy without business. However, Sardar Patel wanted to make him an independent and neutral person so that by change of government, the nascent nation would not suffer and the government could run more or less on a stable basis. He found him true guard of democracy in that respect. In fact, the politicians of that era adjusted with him generously though he had to beat and heckle them as agents of the British Government or Empire, but then, maintaining the faith of his patron unlike in Pakistan, he saved the country from going into the hands of army in India. But Pandit Nehru wanted bureaucrats committed to the ideology of socialistic development as per Mahalonobis model of development. Yet he did not fail much in the estimate of Pt. Nehru. But all of a sudden it was discovered by Smt. Indira Gandhi, the then Prime Minister of India, that bureaucrat was not properly committed to the ideology of the party and could not duly implement her election manifesto.

Thus, this trend combined with inner contradictions as envisaged by Marx and conflicts such as between bureaucrats and specialists or technocrats, public versus private, demoralized the bureaucrat. He became a ship without a rudder.

The society regarded him in high esteem as he was the educated person and one of the most resourceful elite of the society. His family and friends held him in high esteem as the 'babu' of the British rule whose pen was mightier than the sword. After the independence, the Indian Society had the socio-cultural onslaught from the West and there were lot of demands of wealth or goods put on this poor 'babu' by his peers and family. They refused to appreciate his position that he was a simple servant of the regime. In this melee he found himself churning between the fear of security of service and projection of image as the 'power centre'. As a result, he chose a path of easy gains or the path of least resistance which is shown by the acquisitive and materialistic society.

In this ideological tug of war, the present-day bureaucrat has made the following image of himself:

His self-image: This is one of self-assurance, subordination and fear for the termination of the job, lack of confidence towards family affairs, subordination to his projected image—the way in which he thinks, the world sees him. The closer he is to his self-image, the better and more secure he can feel about it. Pseudoism breeds psychological disorders.

Today's Indian Manager is more concerned with (a) happiness, contentment and peace for himself and his near and dear, (b) achieving goals set for himself, (c) a 'goodman' image, and (d) self-actualization. Spiritual values have decidedly taken a back seat, though stark materialistic western values like success, prestige, power and money have not yet made any major inroads into his life. His elitist origin, which could have proved a handicap in relationship with the work force because of social distance and the value gulf, is no longer so because he had acquired a value system tinged with concern for genuineness in human relationships, a humane attitude, devotion to task, concern for being diplomatic coupled with a deep regard for other people's feelings and interests. What an Indian manager seeks from the work situation is job satisfaction, credibility, competence, creativity, truthfulness and achievement/success. His ethical value system is somewhat blurred; in the abstract, he holds strongly to positive ethical values, whereas in concrete situations which are difficult and threatening, idealism gives way to pragmatism. Nonetheless, the country's interests are very much at his heart.

"In value relation, the Indian manager stands somewhere midway; he has been able to realize his value moderately.

Perhaps, this is a healthy discontent, for, in the arena of chaotic industrial life today, it is seen that he is prone to take a proactive rather than reactive stance; act rather than react, confront rather than withdraw, assume responsibility rather than apportion blame. May be this provocative stance is the unconscious instrument through which greater value realization will become a reality for him.[2]

His projected image: The image is that he is always very busy in work. The work eats away all his vitals of life. He tries to do many good things but due to adverse social environment, he is not able to deliver the goods. The political system lets loose all the hell on him and mars his bona fide intentions too.

He looks sullen, bossy, supercilious and disorganized. He often indulges in self-criticism. He blames the Government and would be anxious to show that he is overburdened with work. As a result, he compares himself unfavourably with others.

He often fails to consider reactions or needs of others. Sometimes he is demanding attention even by being controversial. This behaviour can be an imposition—even offensive. Self-possessed people do not need to try that hard. They are not threatened by others and have no urge to overpower others. There is a room for others to express their individuality, too, a sense of give and take.

He is inundated with stereotype image in the media. Rather than considering his strengths and weaknesses through self-examination, he adopts a ready-made image. If he otherwise poses, others will mistrust him.

He keeps on dressing as he was doing when he entered the service. Old habits die hard and it is easy to take this aspect of his image for granted. Times are ripe for him to consciously engage himself in image building or image management. The opening up of the skies and the subsequent transformation of the world into a global village has pushed the trend further. The stylish and up-to-date managers are more successful than others. He should not only be thorough but should look also thorough and

---

[2] Course Material for MBA (MS 3-1) by Indira Gandhi National Open University, School of Management, 1991, p. 33.

overbearing. If he doesn't do his image building and also doesn't use media for this, he will be left behind in the race and will be treated as second grade manager in the society as compared to managers of MNCs (Multi National Corporations) and other successful private companies. This will be very frustrating for him and will reduce his efficiency and productivity.

As a result, conflicting signals are received and others get confused. He is immaculately groomed, but if he opens his mouth and speaks insolently, the illusion will be ruined and others will sense inconsistency.

His appearance, behaviour and environment need to reinforce his efficiency, creativity or concern for others.

When one meets the other, the former seeks involvement, and identification with the latter, asserts his individuality, seeks to assess other's individuality.

In the melee, the public servant establishes his separateness.

One meets a public servant when he is sure that he is friendly and approachable. Some public servants, are accessible/ threatening/lively/timed. He may respond by appearing receptive, respectful or bored when the other person/visitor is nervous by way of rapid eye contact, fidgety movements and hunched posture, he may give the impression of being relaxed, using an open gaze with a slight smile, and expensive body language with little distracting movements.

Each one of us has a system of values, which comes into play when we form a first impression of another person. When those values and beliefs are irrational and extreme, we become prejudicial. The order in which we notice characteristics of another person is as follows:

Colouring, gender, age, size, facial expressions, eye-contact, hair, build, clothes, movement. If a person racially, sexually or on the basis of caste is prejudiced, then his irrational attitudes will notice immediately that the other person is of a race or sex that he is afraid of (because prejudice develops from fear and ignorance) and will be blind to qualities.

He looks scrubby and indicates through posture and body language that the cannot be bothered to talk to public. Then public dismiss/disdain him also. Something remarkable will have to happen to make the public servants change their minds. That is all-round motivation.

His received image: The way in which others really see him is important. This is generally at odds with his projected image. It may be because he has not spared the time and effort to consider how he is presenting himself.

Unless public servants wish to isolate themselves, they should seek to involve themselves with other people and find shared values and experiences. If they do not find some common area of understanding, then the relationship will progress no further.

As an old person making a first impression in someone younger, he needs to consider that the other person may feel respectful, rebellious or that he is out of touch.

This person is in power in India generally. But he has to endeavour a lot to come up against impenetrable prejudice from the other person, that he can do nothing to change.

People who are very self-conscious are painfully aware of their shortcomings. They imagine these shortcomings to be considerably worse than they are. This hightened sense of inadequacy may cause them to blush, to appear defensive, to remember their physical and intellectual limitations. They may find it impossible to sit still in a chair or may stumble over their words. Some people compensate for feeling self-conscious inside by projecting a very different image to the outside. But others judge him as arrogant and inconsiderate.

Among them, extroverts find speaking in public and meeting new people easier than introverts.

He should think less of the effect, he is making and more about what he is doing.

Sometimes they are warm by shaking hands or by making contacts through touch; some have apprehensions and they never talk to strangers.

He likes talk of surroundings or people to open conversation.

Women to be extroverts, they try to be more attractive.

Men can improve their understanding of others and develop interpersonal skills; women can learn to improve the way they convey self-possession and power. They can learn from each other.

"The visual impact predominates", says, Davies, quoting the finding of a professional psychologist, to the effect that 55 percent of the impression you make depends on what people see (your posture, facial expression, dress, body language etc.), 38 percent on what they hear (the tone and pitch of your voice, clarity of speech etc.), and only 7 percent on the actual words you utter which in any case could have been written for you by someone else.[3]

"Unfortunately, in a tradition bound bureaucrat, the ceremonial dress still could not be changed and continues to be Bandgala jackets or black or white trousers even in the hot months of Delhi. For lady officer, the dress code still could not be firmed up." [4]

Image at work: One of the all times famous bureaucrats Late L.K.Jha says that the bureaucrat sits on file. He sleeps over reminders and eats his words.

Shri T.N. Seshan, an ex-bureaucrat calls the highest public service of India as 'I am sorry' service.

A bureaucrat speaks a lot and listens or hears a little. He forgets that he has two ears and only one mouth. Great communicators are always great listeners.

Any behaviour which indicates one's concern with himself (fidgeting with hair, his nails, adjusting his clothes), rather than attending to the speaker, is distracting. He hastens with defensive body language (arms crossed, hands in front of face), he does not appear particularly receptive. The best listeners forget about themselves and focus on what they are receiving.

In meetings, a public servant is at his best. The attention is strayed and generally judgments about other people present are made in haste.

A public servant is prone to choose to take breaks, sometimes long, for calls of nature, refreshment, to stretch his legs and to allow brains to recharge.

---

[3] Phillip Davies, *Your Total Image: How to Communicate Success*, published by J Piathus Books, London, 1988, Distributed by UBS, India.

[4] Deshmukh, B.G. *A Cabinet Secretary Thinks Aloud*, Bhartiya Vidya Bhavan, Mumbai-400 007, 1998, p. 194-95, pp. 196.

The officers have sick building syndrome. This unnecessary noise and light is harsh and tiring. The home office is sometimes more effective for disposal of confidential matters.

One's work accessories like watch, briefcase, diary, folder, pen and desk accessories also describe some haphazard story, Good quality furniture, pen and leather bound diary indicate to others a certain regard for quality and for tradition.

Choice of design, paper, typography also indicate one's image.

Few among bureaucrats as workaholics only function efficiently for a certain number of times. It is better to do efficient work for seven times then take sometime to do physical activity than to work inefficiently for ten times. The exercise will help him to build energy. If he improves his body images which he likes to assert as individuality or distinctiveness, he is likely to feel a lot more confident in interviews, meetings and presentations.

Once the cult of red tape comes in, the bureaucrats become united. A bureaucrat does two jobs successfully i.e. keeping his family happy alongwith providing good education to his children and maintaining the status quo in his office.

India has moved one hundred years in last ten years. Now, the perception of service is different. Now, the younger bureaucrats are much more educated, more modern and use better technology for monitoring, information and communication. Inspite, there is mistrust in the bureaucrat by politician and public alike. Neutrality has become a victim. Fortunately, there is growing realization among public that it is the political executives who are really at the helm of affairs. More decentralized administration through panchayats at each level and municipalities will strengthen this and channelize the discontent of public in a more purposeful way. The lateral entries of political executives in future can help in further strengthening this public confidence building and making politicians solely accountable to people. Then, the bureaucrat will be an ally to the politican'.[5] Volatilization through caste feeling or Mandalisation or politicisation of bureaucracy in India will only destroy the last leg of Indian Polity. "If the

---

[5] Pradhan, R.D., IAS (retd.) Ex-Cabinet Secretary and Ex-Governor, Lecture at TMTC, Pune on 4-02-1994.

administration is not efficient, then politicisation, along with corruption, may, in fact, be the lubricant that makes it work".[6] Even the British bureaucracy which was an ideal civil service to uphold neutrality and efficiency is slowly becoming corrupt. "Atrocities against scheduled castes have actually increased by putting scheduled caste officers to oversee atrocities against harijans. The means to stop caste persecution is not to appoint scheduled caste officers but competent ones, even if they belong to the so-called higher castes. Further law and order constitutes one indivisible whole. One cannot save Muslims and specific castes while allowing crimes to flourish everywhere else. The criminal friends of the ruling party must be dealt with firmly as well. However, the bureaucrats have always accepted the leadership given by the political executive. They look forward to their own leaders only in case of insecurity or as a part of defence mechanism. A challenge is also thrown to the Indian bureaucrat by surging multinationals and their high-fly executives. An open challenge is thrown by World Bank and IMF to the Indian bureaucrats and the political executive whether they can translate the gains from outside help into the typical Indian situations or become docile to them. They have also a golden opportunity to use the comfortable foreign reserve situation (more than $100 billion in January, 2004) to take the country ahead of other countries in the world specially using the world leadership of India in Information Technology sector and put India in the category of the developed nations by the year 2020—a target placed by Shri A.P.J. Abdul Kalam, President of India in 2003—who is the first and the foremost public servant of the country.

[6] Vithal, BPR, *Depoliticisation*, Administrative Staff College of India, 1991.

CHAPTER

4 Ethics in Administration

—**Brig. Shekhar Sen and Pradip Bhattacharya**

Whither the Bureaucracy?

Whither the bureaucracy? This is a question that is becoming increasingly pertinent as the days go by. Has the civil service been able to live up to the expectations of the people for whom it was appointed to serve? Has it followed the role that the constitution bestowed upon it or has it usurped a role for itself, which gives it more powers and privileges and a redefined value system that is conveniently flexible? The answers to these daunting questions are depressing. *The bureaucracy has more or less failed the people as public servants and has also failed their political counterparts as straightforward advisers on policy formulation.* A few idealists who tried to live up to their designated role have either been sidelined as inconvenient, or have fallen by the wayside in utter desperation, or have jumped on the juggernaut of rumbling inefficacy in sheer resignation just to survive. W.B. Yeats, in *The Second Coming*, said:

> *"Turning and turning in the widening gyre*
> *The falcon cannot hear the falconer*
> *Things fall apart, the centre cannot hold,*
> *Mere anarchy is loosed upon the world,*
> *The blood-dimmed tide is loosed, and everywhere*
> *The ceremony of innocence is drowned;*
> *The best lack all conviction while the worst*
> *Are full of passionate intensity"*

That is what exactly has happened to our bureaucracy. The best, the right-minded people, people with the right values, people that are conscious of their designated role, "lack all conviction" because of a totally hostile ambience, while the worst, i.e., the sycophants, the corrupt and the power hungry, "are full of passionate intensity." So, what must truly be done?

Perhaps one most important step to be taken is to view critically the existing relationship between the policy maker and the policy implementer, i.e., the politician and the civil servant. Unfortunately, the executive arm follows the diktat, said and unsaid, of the political head. Where the political head is committed to public welfare and takes to heart the oath he swears to uphold the provisions of the constitution, the executive arm has no option but to follow suit. Where the signals are otherwise, as documented at length in TN Seshan's anguished speeches, "Rishvateva Jayate" replaces "Satyameva Jayate."

Over the last few years, scam after scam has inundated the country, in each case the bureaucrat following closely the desire of the political executive. In the fiftieth year of independence, the special session of the Parliament was content merely to take note of the profoundly disturbing Vohra Committee Report which speaks of the mafia network, "virtually running a parallel government pushing the state apparatus into irrelevance", of "a politician-bureaucrat-underworld nexus", and of even judiciary falling prey to the mafia which has caused "a sense of despair and alienation among the people." It speaks of a "disastrous combination of high skills and absence of ethical sense and moral values." *The CEC as if in continuation reported that 180 out of 425 MLAs of UP Assembly had criminal records. The Economist too wrote that rascals ruled West Bengal.* The Vohra Committee, among other things, noticed a steep rise in deaths in police custody, rapes, public lynching, crimes against women and children. It also warned that people are becoming totally alienated from the Government machinery.

The common man has no way of knowing whether the Supreme Court's directive for government to submit an action-taken report regarding the Report has been complied with. These are danger signals for us to see, if we wish to unfortunately, history is, as ever, an unfashionable topic and those who rule—the legislative, the executive and the judiciary—have no time for such "ancient" matters. Gibbon, analysing the causes of the fall of Roman Empire, had highlighted the following:

- Concentration of power in the hands of one ruler for whom there was no constitutional term of election;
- A widening gap between the rich and the poor, a pampered soldiery;
- Defence cuts and a rundown of military forces in spite of massive taxation;
- A failure of the army to meet its commitments;
- Suppression of the middle classes while the rich pursued the life of luxury and avoided shouldering the responsibilities of government;
- The alienation of a bureaucratic central government from the people;
- A breakdown of law and order.

These reduced Rome's resistance to external aggression. At least some obvious similarities with the Indian situation will, one hopes, raise a hint of discomfort, if not alarm. The three arms of the Indian state—legislative, executive and judiciary—are indeed the salt of the earth. "But if the Salt has lost its savor, wherewith shall it be salted? It is thenceforth good for nothing, but to be caste out, and to be trodden under feet of men."

But the situation did not come about suddenly. It developed over long years and the bureaucracy is squarely to be blamed for this pass. Manohar Subramanayam, an IAS officer of 1958 batch belonging to UP cadre, says, "*In our kind of democracy, a politician and his money cannot be separated. The lay public is not important. I was naive enough to assume that my responsibility was only to the people I served and to my professional peers.*" One sees in this statement that the understanding of the stated role of the civil servant has been described as mere "naiveté"! Is it tongue-in-cheek or seriously stated? If stated seriously, then we are in trouble. Yeats' statement, the best lack all conviction, is reinforced. Manohar Subramanayam comes out with another very perceptive statement underlining the reasons for the failure of the civil service, "*Our generation has failed because while we did educate ourselves about the intricacies of administering our country, we did not ever try to educate our political masters. Instead we let them do as they pleased and if they did something abjectly wrong, we only made sure that our involvement was minimal...*" Therefore, civil service not only lacked conviction, it allowed wrong things to multiply and perpetuate without raising any conscientious objection and initiating corrective action. Thence began a tradition of abdication and passive acceptance while developing the masterly art of saving one's own skin. The inevitable followed. Subramanayam observes, "*We were making sure that we did not rock the boat, but while doing so we overlooked the fact that the boat was beginning to leak. Today the boat has a hole and we all bemoan the fall in standards.*"

These therefore were the views of an insider who had been at the helm of administration for a long time. Some outside agencies too, over the years, concerned themselves with the predicament of the politician-bureaucrat relationship.

The Administrative Staff College of India conducted a series of programmes, which brought out very forcefully the IAS officers' major concern regarding their utter dependence on political executives for their performance. Therefore, in September 1986, the ASCI organized a politician-administration interface in which four Ministers, eight Secretaries and eight Additional Secretaries participated. Some of these civil servants were technocrats. Some members of public, selected at random, were also involved. This programme projected some revealing images of politicians and bureaucrats.

Images

Political Executives

- I rise to meet people's aspirations through Government action
- Leadership qualities
- Pragmatic, hardworking, shrewd
- Ambitious, publicity-conscious
- Accessible and warm to the people
- Belief in people's power

- Anxious for quick results
- Populist view and soft options adopted

Public Administrators

- Intelligent, experienced, hardworking
- Just and fair, disciplined, conscientious, adaptable, courteous
- Rigid and conservative, rule-bound but flexible when it suits
- Snobbish, self-opinionated

Technocrats

- Professional experts, knowledgeable
- Narrow perspective
- Carry a sense of not getting their due
- Egoistic and less adaptable
- Result-oriented

Public

- Growing awareness of rights
- Patiently suffering but becoming restive
- Pessimism for future
- Aware that they can change the Government but do not see it as a solution to their problems
- Simple, emotional, prone to exploitation
- Increasingly subject to casteism, regionalism, communalism
- Robust common sense
- Inherently patriotic
- Considers money most important
- Desires clean, honest and responsive administration treating them with dignity as equals
- Expects remedies to his lot

Some of the impressions gathered from the discussions were:

- Politicians generally felt that many administrators were pleasant but few gave wholesome though unpleasant advice
- In any exercise during the course, leadership role was automatically assumed by the politicians
- Civil servants did not listen to technocrats.

These images and impressions were more or less substantiated by a Values Survey conducted by the Indian Institute of Management, Calcutta, of civil servants vis-a-vis corporate sector. It revealed that:

- Relationship with superiors and subordinates is worse in civil service
- 95% civil servants feel that man is just a combination of needs. 66% of others agree
- 45% civil servants believe conscience has to be suppressed to achieve success. 15% of others accept this.
- 50% civil servants believe society must change first before the individual can undergo value based change. 92% of others believe management principles and public administration philosophy are universal and do not need any input from one's culture heritage. 80% of the others agree
- 50% of the civil servants believe that an extrovert personality is the foundation for effective decision-making. 15% of others agree
- 75% civil servants believe that excellent professional management needs to concern itself with moral issues. 96% of others believe this.
- 70% civil servants believe that major traditional family values are irrelevant today. 23% of the others agree.

Generally speaking in practically all critical surveys, opinions, etc. of the Civil Service, some common trends can be discerned. It is commonly believed that civil servants have no vision beyond self-advancement. They have no self-control and depend entirely on external control. They have no self-generating strategy of change for oneself and for shaping the environment. The file is a personal zamindari. And finally, they are presently starting at total intellectual, emotional and spiritual stagnation. The value-base of the service has consequently become quite hollow.

But there is a problem. And that problem has been posed by an eminent trainer of our time. Is it at all possible to inculcate "correct" values? Preaching flops because of the chasm between precept and practice in our country. Secondly, is "our" values system better than "theirs" (the new generation)?

In UK the Cabinet Secretary sees his main job as making sure that civil servants do what the Ministers want, not as guarantors of government propriety, ensuring that ministers did not use the civil service for party-political ends. Permanent Secretaries sign agreements with their Ministers regarding their personal objectives taking into account government's collective interests, not just that of their own departments. The relationship is of a CEO to a ministerial Chairman. And finally, does a good, workable, culture-neutral value module exist? If not, then how do we create one?

The 1996 Conference of Chief Ministers initiated a change in policy stressing charters of citizens' rights, accountability of public servants, transparency in administration, etc. This was followed by a workshop, held on 20 Nov 1996, on effective and responsive administration in which all Chief Secretaries of states participated and decisions were taken which would have transformed the negative image of the bureaucracy. Most importantly, it was decided that a Charter of Ethics and Civil Service Code must be promulgated based on secularism and equality.

Bureaucracy is a bad word. Nathaniel Hawthorne, in a marvellously perceptive passage on the Customs House officer in *The Scarlet Letter*, called salary drawn from the government "the Devil's Wages". He wrote, "Whoever touches it should look well to himself, or he may find the bargain to go hard against him involving, if not his soul, yet many of its better attributes; its sturdy force, its courage and constancy, its truth, its self-reliance and all that gives emphasis to manly character."

It thus becomes obvious that all is not well with the civil service. The ambience is negative, the attitude is indifferent and the morals down in the dumps.

The question, "How to handle the intrepid politician?" always pops up like a jack-in-the-box. Indifference, abdication or surrender seem to be the ruling characteristics of the service. A lot of effort has been made to identify the causes of the failure of the bureaucracy and to find out ways and means of improving the performance of the civil servants. But nothing seems to have made any impression and the negative image and performance continue. Is there therefore anything that we are overlooking?

Problems and Criticisms

Problems facing the IAS are many. A senior member of the IAS holds that the IAS today has become a part of the problem, not of the solution. Officers are more interested in private welfare at the cost of the society. The noble image that the IAS projected in the earlier days has taken a severe beating over the years. The IAS used to be considered a saviour of the people from the rapacious clutches of the lower bureaucracy. Now they are perceived as a parasitical force, as corrupt as anyone else. They are alienated from the public. The standard of their performance is declining. They have become inaccessible, hostile and insensitive. They oppress the poor, are no longer accountable to the people and do not exhibit an attitude of service. One of the main criticisms against the service is that it has started grading jobs, pretending jobs with business connections and not jobs involving the poor. It is no longer comfortable working for the poor in whole areas.

Other reasons for deteriorating standards are not far to seek. Secrecy, cumbersome procedures and unnecessary controls are some of the maladies that have removed the service further away from the people.

The internal bureaucratic culture is also changing fast, hastening the downward roll. Posts have proliferated tremendously and that has demoralized the service. Powers have reduced. Many posts have been marginalized. All this has resulted in cut-throat competition and loss of camaraderie. Politicians have not lost any time in exploiting the situation, playing one against the other. These have also resulted in lack of professionalism. The civil service is now reluctant to tender unwelcome advice for fear of transfer. Major problems are handled ineptly. There is no effort to even update knowledge and skills facilitating proper policy formulation and implementation. Innovativeness is lacking. There is reluctance to take decisions and dilatory tactics are being adopted in taking decisions. On the other hand, there is a sense of belonging to an exclusive club, which motivates the civil servant to take too much from the system, contributing very little to it.

The external political environment is also not conducive as the structure of rewards and punishment has undergone a sea change. Earlier, there was a clear concept of desired behaviour. The civil service itself used to decide rewards and punishments. Now, no one is sure anymore about the desired behaviour and decisions regarding rewards and punishments are usually taken by the politicians. As a result, traditional civil service values of neutrality and integrity are sacrificed. In the emerging new political environment, the entire control over the civil service has shifted to the politicians. And since politicians gradually over the years have become divorced from general welfare and are now more concerned with sectarian interests the civil service too has followed suit, to please the political masters. The consequent low expectation of the people therefore has become a fait accompli. The politician uses executive power for personal gains. So does the civil servant. The civil servant has no market value or employability since he does not acquire any professional or technical competence and remains a mere generalist. If anyone is given any alternative employment ever in the private sector, it is more for his high connections than the professional competence. Consequently, he knows that he has to survive and cannot afford to challenge the politician in the new ambience. In a model where the politician is casteist, corrupt and harbours criminals, can the civil service be efficient, responsive and change-oriented? In addition to all this, the inefficient delivery system of the civil service has led to the growth of political populism and sectarianism to win votes.

Impartiality, Social Justice and Rule of Law

Some of the other major conclusions of the Chief Secretary's conference were:

- Loyalty should only be service to the public and to the rule of law.
- Move towards a citizen-centred administration stressing transparency and scrutinizing performance against publicized standards of service, mandatory disclosure of all development schemes and approvals.
- Citizen's Charters for all service institutions.
- Effective grievance redressal at all levels.

- Fullest decentralization of service delivery.
- Ensure participation by stakeholders in schemes affecting them
- Simplify procedures, amend obsolete laws.
- Cleanse the civil service through exemplary and speedy punishment.
- Improve performance appraisal, support subordinates in sincere performance of duty, in resisting illegal pressure.
- Civil Service Board to regulate transfers and promotions.
- Ombudsman for grievances of officials.

However, all were forgotten with the change of government at the centre. The Bible puts the entire matter in a striking eidetic image without need of the buzz words, like "transparency", "accountability", etc.: A city that is set on an hill cannot be hid... Let your light so shine before men, that they may see your good works.

The Judiciary also framed a similar resolution on 7 May 1997. A Five Judge Committee of the Supreme Court issued a 16-point Restatement of Values of Judicial Life focusing on ensuring credibility, be above criticism, be free and impartial. The aftermath of that resolution is not known, except that it does not appear to have received wide circulation in the judiciary itself. In 1997, the officers of the 1961 batch of the Indian Administrative Service met at Mussoorie and drew up another set of resolutions which the Cabinet Secretary circulated to all Chief Secretaries on 21 November 1997. This Mussoorie Resolution called upon the civil service to consecrate itself to the sacred endeavour to foster India's spirit of harmony, tolerance and respect for diversity, strengthen its civilizational uniqueness by cultivating:

- Integrity, professionalism, dedication.
- Impartial implementation of rule of law.
- Tightening efficiency to provide better quality of service cost-effectively and promptly. Focus on results and not the procedures.
- Fostering a culture of continuous improvement.
- Probity, political independence, leadership, excellence, dynamism, openness, productivity.
- Mutual respect between political leadership and civil service.

- Enable citizens to organize and express their needs and the public service to respond to them.

On the one hand, we have the Cabinet Secretary circulating the platitudes of Mussoorie Resolution self-consciously and self-righteously adopted by the officers of the 1961 batch of the IAS during what is termed, not very serendipitously and with telling naivete, a "retreat." If might have been instructive if, while retreating they had taken a look at what a ruler merely twenty years old, had to say when swearing in the Principal Secretary of the State, if familiarity with Sardar Patel's advice had produced its usual consequence ("Today my Secretary can write note opposed to my views. I have given that freedom to all my Secretaries. I have told them, 'If you do not give your honest opinion for fear that it will displease your Minister, please then, you had better go.' I will never be displeased over a frank expression of opinion."). Queen Elizabeth I, swearing in Sir William Cecil, stated: "This judgment I have of you that you will not be corrupted by any manner of gift and that you will be faithful to the state and that without respect for my private will you will give me that counsel that you think best." that probably says it all!

Our training gives us the technique. But how much of social awareness and vision does it give, or the ability and minds realize these and sustain the visions? Hence, our training, along with professional competence should also be able to give social responsibility.

This takes us to the second responsibility of the civil servant—the responsibility to others. Bureaucracy has been vested with many powers both formal and informal. Use of those powers depends upon the philosophy of the state. In a democratic state the philosophy must direct the civil servant to have a concern for the people because this power comes from the people of the country, through the constitution. So, the power must be used to bring welfare and fulfillment of the aspirations of the people.

The concept has a parallel in Indian mythology in the legend of Vaivasvat Manu. Having become tired of an anarchic situation in the country, people approached Vaivasvat Manu to administer the country. They vested him with all the powers required and provided him with the resources with which he could maintain the administrative machinery. He did it to the satisfaction of the people and the concept of kingship was born—a king who is created to protect the people and look after the well-being of the people. In *Raghuvamsham* (1/18), Kalidasa states: "The State took taxes from the people only to ensure their own prosperity in return, like the Sun takes moisture from the earth only to give it back in thousand fold measure." Therefore, the civil servant who gets all his powers from the people must use those, not for self-aggrandisement but for the welfare of the people.

Concept of Power Leads to Concept of Service

The principal job of the public servant is to serve the public with dignity, freedom and responsibility. In their approach to the job the mood and spirit of service must exist. To a civil servant, a member of the public who comes to him with a problem must not be seen as an intruder but as a fellow citizen who has come to him for help because he has the power to help him. The power does not make him a demi-god but merely one who is returning a favour done to him. Unfortunately, the opposite is the case—people who come for help are not helped and are considered as intruders. NC Saxena (UP 1963), Union Rural Development Secretary and Planning Commission Secretary, was forced to comment, "There was a time when people looked up to the IAS Officers as their savior. Slowly they have become part of the problem, not the solution." He goes on to say that they must have genuine concern for people. Interestingly he observes that IAS officers consider those jobs as good ones which are business and power-oriented. The poor-oriented or development-oriented jobs are considered bad jobs. This attitude can change only when the concern for people, and not self, becomes the principal concern for the civil servant. In a democracy, the bureaucrat is paid to help people. And that help has to be given with *Shraddha*, not as a favour; help with a sense of duty and responsibility, help with respect. It is not alms that are being given. It is a right, a claim that is merely being restored. If giving with Shraddha is the aim, then it must be given speedily. Delay means neglect and neglect can never signify *Shraddha*.

In a democratic society where people are important, the civil servant is required to take up social leadership. On occasions, to establish transparency of administration and sympathy for the oppressed classes, the civil servant has to act as a social activist. People have a right to information. They are entitled to know how the administration is being run and the fashion in which their fate is being decided. People must be empowered with information for that administration must be open and there should be transparency. If not, then other agencies, like the NGOs, will grow up to fight for the right and become popular with people. Aruna Roy and her Mazdoor Kisan Shakti Sangathan fought for transparency in Land Records administration for information of the people. She won the struggle and now has a lot of credibility with the people. But was the fight necessary? Why should there be secrecy in administration? Is it because knowledge is power and sharing that power with the people would dilute the importance of the civil services? It seems to be so otherwise why should everything in Government be Top Secret. Secret, Confidential, Restricted etc.? The entire gamut of roles enforcing secrecy should be reviewed. The Chief Vigilance Commissioner's ordinance against secrecy, the Law Commission's recommendation for repealing at least 1400 laws enforcing secrecy, underline the need for removing secrecy and making administration open. If administration becomes open, then it will be easy to handle, cumbersomeness will be removed, credibility of the civil service will rise, imaginative sympathy at all levels will make the government empathetic and responsive. And the young civil servant can take on the role of a social activist who will be credible, approachable, responsive and popular. People have aspirations but they cannot express. The civil servant would help people in expressing their aspirations. Public opinion is the bedrock of democratic polity. The civil service can help forming, developing and channeling that public opinion thereby having a different kind of power, a power rising out of openness and supported by popular will. Free expression of thought is also essential for building up pressure for radical reforms. The civil servant can be a very effective change agent in that process by using his power effectively, instead of being an indifferent bystander.

The civil servant also must be a change agent. He can be the medium through whom desirable changes can be brought about. Hopefully the momentum of change will pick up in the coming years and not die down. Judicial activism has started in a big way. Some information channels are being opened up to the people as in case of Andhra Pradesh. But much more needs to be done. At least some of the basic things must be done immediately; there must be stability of tenure for a minimum period so that the bureaucrat gets a fair chance of being able to do something useful. There should be openness in administration also in matter like transfers, cadre allotment, etc. The tax returns also should be available for public scrutiny in case of any doubt about the integrity of the executive. Size of the civil service should be reduced to make every post count. A minimum standard of performance must be prescribed at organizational and individual level to ensure a minimum standard of efficiency of the civil servant.

Implications of Civil Service

There is no doubt about the quality of the people who enter the service in terms of education, mental readiness and ability. The mental readiness grows out of the education one receives before he enters the civil service—"the Elite" who become equipped mentally to an extent to handle the responsibility and power that go with the position as an administrator. The training that is imparted to the civil servants equips them with the techniques of administration. But does it, at any stage, impart to them the right kind of value system that makes them socially conscious and responsible? Perhaps it is at this point that the basic problem lies, lack of a definite value system for the civil service.

What does the civil service imply? The nomenclature, civil service, has the word, "service" in it. That is a pointer. The definition "public servant" too has no ambiguity. Then why should there be a desire to have autocratic privileges? The concept of service does not normally enter a civil servants' scheme of things. Therefore, this concept of service has be internalized even as he enters the service. One of the reasons of the downward slide in the attitude and performance of the civil service must be, therefore, internal. The civil servant must look inwards to see if there is any scope for improvement. May be then he will find solutions to his external problems also because a strong and reinforced personality normally can exercise control over the external factors.

By definition the civil servant carries two burdens: the self and the others who depend on him. He must train himself so that his native talent is developed, intellect, will and competence are reinforced and the required professional skills are sharpened. He must develop a democratic personality, which persuades him to have a healthy concern for others, not as a slave or a master, but as an empathetic co-traveller who has the power to help others. It has freedom of action that is tampered by a sense of responsibility. This is possible if he has a dynamic personality as against static one. A static personality is characterized by inaction or action that only serves the self. A static person is only interested in his salary, career, family and personal convenience. A dynamic person does not bother very much about these but is interested in work, serving others and generally growing up by keeping his eyes and ears open.

P.S. Appu (IAS Bihar 1951) classified the IAS officers roughly into three categories. In his opinion, 35% of the Civil Service in the early '50s consisted of such officers. In the late '90s this 35% sadly become 10% . We have the examples of Sardar Patel and V.P. Menon on the question of the merger of the states and later, of C. Subramanium and B. Sivaraman on the question of 1ADP. In the second category, Appu places people who work according to the book, postpone decisions and would prefer to take no decisions to avoid committing mistakes. This group comprised 60% of the service in the '50s and has come down to 40% in the '90s. And finally he places such people in the third category who are unscrupulous, use power arbitrarily and abuse their power for personal gains. He further says that only 5% of the civil service consisted of such people in the '50s but in the '90s the percentage increased to 50%. A dismal picture indeed! One may question the veracity of the statistics (some participants did raise a point of doubt during some courses) but generally, the classification and the trend cannot be questioned. We need more people in the first category, which is the category of men with dynamic and democratic personality.

Secondly, the bureaucrat must enjoy his work. He must have a sense of pride in whatever he is doing and enjoy doing it. This joy cannot come from selfish motivation. Selfish motivation gives one only frustration and ennui, which finally results in a nervous breakdown. Joy comes from satisfaction of a job well done and a target achieved. One has to develop work-interest in others.

Thirdly, one has to have vision, *Drishti*. People have problems. A civil servant cannot be everywhere to personally see the problems. But he must have the ability to visualise those problems and only a person with empathy is able to see a projection of those problems. Futuristic planning can only be done by being able to envision the problems of the multitudes. Knowledge never has an opportunity of becoming wisdom as he never internalizes this knowledge and puts the knowledge into practice. He operates from his static self and consequently the knowledge he has, becomes impotent and useless. TS Eliot wrote:

> *"Endless invention, endless experiment.*
> *Brings knowledge of speech but not of silence.*
> *Knowledge of words, and ignorance of the Word.*
> *Where is the life we have lost in living?*
> *Where is the wisdom we have lost in knowledge?*
> *Where is the knowledge we have lost in information?*
> *Men both deny gods and worship gods. Professing first reason.*
> *And money, and power and*
> *What they call life, or Race, or*
> *Dialectic...*
> *an age which advances*
> *progressively backwards"*

We have failed to convert knowledge into wisdom. To convert knowledge into wisdom, so essential for obtaining a dynamic personality, it is essential to rise to the level of *Buddhi*. At this level, it is possible to combine executive efficiency with social efficiency and transform brute efficiency into humanized efficiency. This requirement of the two-fold efficiency persuaded the founding fathers of the Indian Administrative Service to adopt another powerful concept of Gita, *Yogah Karmasu Kaushalam*, as the motto of the service. It means that yoga should be the technique of doing work.

What is Yoga?

Yoga literally means Yukta (united) with self. To understand the implication of the motto, we have to see the full verse along with the two preceding verses:

> *Yogastha kuru karmani sangang tyaktva Dhananjaya /*
> *Sidhyasidhyoh samo bhutva samatvang yoga uctiyate // 2/48*
> *Be steady in yoga, Arjun, do whatever you must do; give up attachment, be indifferent to failure and success.*
> *This stability (samalva-buddhi) is yoga. (P. Lal's translation)*
>
> *Durena hyabarang karma buddhiyogat Dhananjaya /*
> *Buddhau saranamanviccha kripana phalahetaba // 2/49*
>
> *Selfish work is inferior to the work of a balanced uncoveting mind; shelter yourself in this mental stability (samatva buddhi), Arjuna. Harassed are the seekers of the fruits of action. (P. Lal)*
>
> *Buddhiyukto jahatha ubhe sukritadushkrite /*
> *Tasmadyogaya yujyaswa yogah karmasu kaushalam // 2/50*
>
> *With this mental poise, you will free your self from good deeds and ill deeds. Devote yourself to this yoga; it is the secret of success in work.*

This mental pose is *buddhi*. The buddhi or "intelligent will" as Sri Aurobindo calls it, is not affected by good work or bad work or with their result. Buddhi guides one to be united with the higher self. And therefore this buddhi is yoga and yoga is the skill of performing, remaining united with yoga. Meaning of yoga is made clear by Krishna in verse 48. The samatva-buddhi or stability is yoga. Swami Ranganathananda describes yoga as "the path to achieve a fullness of personality development. That, when transferred to work, helps one to achieve all-round excellence in performance." Elsewhere he says, "Yoga is the philosophy of life and action capable of ensuring individual and collective welfare. It makes one work without discrimination and with equality achieving samatva (Justice). Yoga gives one the power of concentration, single-minded devotion, full control of mind and body and increases insight and understanding."

Dr. S. Radhakrishnan says, "He is rid of selfishness and therefore is incapable of evil ... yoga is evenness of mind in success or failure, possessed by one who is engaged in the performance of his proper duties, while his mind rests in God." Work is also explained in verse 49. Any work is not work. Selfish work is inferior to the work of a balanced and uncoveting mind (buddhiyoga or buddhiyukta mind). Therefore, one must take shelter in this mental stability. Work therefore is not as important as the buddhi of the worker. If the worker is endowed with buddhi then whatever he does is bound to be relevant. Buddhi is intellect, which is capable of making a choice between relevant and irrelevant and chooses self-realization as the only guiding principle. Changes can be brought about. These could be physical changes, spiritual changes, attitudinal changes or intellectual changes. Swami Vivekananda said, "They have come to think that they are born to be trodden under the feet of the wealthy. They have to be given back their individuality." It is the civil servant, by being a good change-agent who is near to the people, can bring about the vital change in attitude, by giving them back their individuality. He should be able to educate the people, conscientise them as Paulo Freire would like to say and turn them into responsible dynamic citizens. It is not only the rights that they should be made conscious of; they should be made aware of their duties too. A balance between the rights and duties must be struck. For far too long we have underlined the fundamental rights which, no doubt, are necessary for human growth and a healthy socio-political order. But these cannot become strong and positive without a consciousness about duties. Someone said that for a long time now, we have only looked at the statue of liberty. Someone should now make a statue of responsibility!

Then there is the concept of collective will. It is the collective will of the people that creates the State. It also activates the State. There is no doubt that the collective will of the people is a tremendous power. The collective will of forty million British ruled 300 million Indians. The British had the collective will. The Indians did not. The civil servant must recognize this and build this collective will by reaching out, developing it and giving it a direction. N.C. Sexena said, "The Indian political system is highly resilient to public opinion. Full expression of thought will lead to building up of pressure of informed opinion so necessary for radical reforms." The civil service is a powerful agency for energizing the rest of the human resources.

This then is the implication of being a civil servant. He has a responsibility towards his own self, of developing and strengthening his civil service personality, which consists of professional competence and social consciousness. And secondly, he has a responsibility towards others who depend on him for their well being, by being empathetic, by being able to help with shraddha and by being a dynamic centre of social change and by energizing public will.

An Alternative: Focusing on Self

For all this, there is a need for a darshan, a vision, (which can loosely be called philosophy though darshan is much more than philosophy), which would give a sense of direction. Darshan is seeing life steadily and as a whole. That is why *Mandukya Upanishad* calls it Sarva Vidya Pratistha. Darshan of the administrator however depends on the philosophy of the state. If the state is feudal or colonial, then the civil service also adopts a darshan, which suits the rulers. In that situation, only intelligence and will are required. In democracy, it has to be people-centred in addition to intelligence and will. There has to be an additional ingredient, social consciousness.

It is very fortunate that civil service in India does not have to look for a darshan elsewhere. It is available in our own ancient literature. *Gita* provides us with a direction. As Lt Col G.L. Bhattacharya has very perceptively observed. Gita contains instructions for men of responsibility. It distinguishes between a small darshan and a large darshan. Small darshan is for small people who have only himself and his family to look after. His sphere is limited. But for men of responsibility it has to be a large darshan, because he has to look after the interests of a large number of people, sometimes, the entire nation. His own self and family are insignificant. It is the difference between a small lamp and a large lamp. A small lamp lights up a very small area but a large lamp lights up a very large area. The civil servant is like a large lamp. His area of responsibility is very large. Therefore, his darshan also has to be large as it covers an entire population. This darshan then helps him in the transformation from a static to a dynamic person—the transformation of a man with a small limited sphere of activity involving only self and family to a man with a much larger sphere of activity involving the people of the nation. Like in Arjun's case, the ultimate destruction of the warrior class and the resultant evils that would visit the society. All this fear caused his inaction. The administrator too has fears—the fear of transfer, fear of retribution and all the small fears concerning his self and family. All these result in depression as in the case of Arjun and finally, inaction. A person with a large darshan, with dynamism, is not daunted by these small fears, because he puts priority on the welfare of people above the welfare of self.

This *Darshan* can come about only when *Buddhi* is used

Buddhi is another concept in Gita, which implies enlightened intelligence and knowledge. At the level of ego, self, (small darshan), knowledge and intelligence are self-centred and limited, being at the mercy of instincts and impulses. But at the level of Buddhi, knowledge becomes wisdom. It makes one creative, resourceful, humane, and sympathetic. With the application of Buddhi, we increase wisdom as much as knowledge. Bertrand Russell said in *Impact of Science on Society*, "Unless men increase in wisdom as much as knowledge, increase of knowledge will be increase of sorrow."

But it does not happen this way in reality. Our civil servant is very well read. His knowledge is immense. But this corpus of actors determines the action. It makes a person wise enabling him to shed both *sukrita* (good deeds) and *duskrita* (ill deeds), leaving only one alternative with man i.e., self-realization. Therefore the *buddhiyukta*, hopefully, our civil servant, will have the capacity to shed choices, adopt yoga which will make him incapable of taking evil action and enable him to strive for self-realization by doing his duties successfully, through yoga.

It becomes obvious why these few words were chosen as the motto of the service. The founding fathers dreamt that they were laying the foundation of a public service for independent India, which would be able to combine work efficiency with insight and social awareness by working through yoga. That would ensure justice for all, the maximum concern for people. And it was perhaps also expected that these Yogastha people, the civil servants, would also not hanker for possessions and power! What finally is aimed at is the concept of *Rajarshi*, enshrined in Chapter 4 of Gita. A public servant should be like Gita's Rajarshi. A Rajarshi is a combination of the qualities of Raja, a king and a Rishi, a sage. Raja is one who shines in responsibility *Ranjata Virajate*. He also pleases, *ranjate. Mahabharata (Shantiparva)* describes the king thus: *Ranjitascha prajah sarvastenarajeli shabdayate* (one who pleases his subjects is called a Raja). His qualities are power and efficiency. On the other hand the principal quality of a sage is his wisdom. A Rajarshi therefore has the power and efficiency of a king and the wisdom of a Rishi. His efficiency and energy enable him to perform and his wisdom, his darshan, guide him in that performance of duties. The civil servant must be able to become a Rajarshi—a combination of power, efficiency, professionalism and wisdom to achieve welfare of people. If the administrator has a small darshan, he becomes static, a burden. With a large darshan, he is Rajarshi, a dynamic force with wisdom and the sense and capability of taking responsibility of the masses. Obviously extraordinary effort is required to achieve this extraordinary energy and this synthesis of power with responsibility, strength of character, clear thinking, dedication and practical efficiency.

And the secret of secrets, the essence, is in the last verse of Gita:

Yatra yogeshwara Krishno yatra Partho dhanurdharah /
Jatra srivijayo bhutirdhruba nitirmatirmama // 18/78
"Where Krishna, lord of yoga, is,
Are victory, success, prosperity and law,
I am convinced of this." (translation by P. Lal)

We too are convinced of this; if the civil servant can transform himself into a Rajarshi, then doubtless he will have the qualities of both Krishna, the master of yoga, with the energy of vision and calm spirituality and Arjun, wielder of the bow, with the energy of intense action and efficiency. This will also ensure the achievement of *lokasangratha* of which Gita says in chapter III

Sakta karmayavidyanso yatha kurvanti Bharata /
Kuryatvidvangsthaasaktaschikirshulokasangraham // 3/25

The wise man must act even as the work-obsessed toll does
But shedding selfishness and pursuing knowledge // (P. Lal)

Lokaraksha implies that people without wisdom work for self. Wise people work for others, *Lokasamgraha* is holding together of people in the way of dharma. How does one do that? Just before this verse Krishna speaks about setting an example— "I do not need to work but still I do just to set an example for other people to follow, because people to follow, because people will always imitate a superior, following the example set by his action." (21–23/3). Therefore, the civil servant must set an example for people that increases his credibility and while doing work uses state-power for the fulfilment of the desires of the people thereby pleasing them. All this will work towards the achievement of the ideal of lokasamgraha, which is in any case one of the responsibilities of the civil servant.

The civil servant therefore has an onerous task before him. He has to prepare himself for a very difficult but a very significant role in society. He has the politician to handle. He has various lobbies and vested interests to face. Above all, he has his own. Buddha, while lying on his deathbed, was asked by Ananda, his disciple,

"Lord, after your departure who should we go to clear our doubts?"
Buddha said, "Atmano Deepo Bhava" (Be like a lamp; be a light unto thyself).

Thus, the responsibility of training the civil servant lies with the civil servant himself. He has to strengthen himself and empower himself with such energy of the inner self that he can rise above all adversities and crises of conscience and be of great ability and help to society.

CHAPTER

5 How the Bureaucracy Functions in India?

—M N Buch

The Constitution of India, in its Preamble lays down the four foundation pillars on which our Republic rests. They are: **Sovereignty,** which means that we shall not bow our head before another power. **Socialism**, which means that we shall try and secure an economy and polity which promotes equality for all. **Secularism,** which means that the state while protecting all religions, will neither lean towards any nor promote any, and **Democracy,** which means that it is the people who will decide who will govern us and how. The Preamble further mandates that this Republic and its government will promote social, economic and political justice and liberty of thought, expression, belief, faith, worship, equality of status and opportunity and a spirit of fraternity, which ensures the dignity of the individual and unity and integrity of the nation.

The Republic, like any other country, has to be governed, with the governance of India being guided by the provisions of our Constitution and its Preamble. The scheme of things is that there is separation of power between the legislature, the executive and the judiciary, the first being the determinant of policy and the watchdog over how government functions, the second being the implementer of policy and the third being the forum of adjudication of disputes between citizen and citizen, state and state, state and the citizen and, further, being the final arbiter to decide on whether the Constitution is being followed or not.

Where there is equilibrium there is no conflict between these three organs of the state. Dispute arises only when one of the organs tries to dominate the other two. However, the resolution of any conflict in this behalf still lies within the domain of the judiciary.

Where our Constitution is different from the constitutions of most other democratic states is that the executive itself is constitutionally divided between that which is elected and, therefore, deliberative and that which is appointed, is permanent and is responsible for the implementation of the decisions of the elected wing of the executive. This distinction is important, in fact vital, as I shall try and demonstrate in the course of this paper. Under Article 53 and 154 of the Constitution the executive power of the Union and the States vests respectively in the President and the Governor of the state, which functionaries are required to exercise these powers through officers subordinate to them. In exercising their powers the President and the Governor are aided and advised by the Council of Ministers appointed under Article 74 and 75 in the case of the Union and Article 163 and 164 in the case of the States. The Council of Ministers frames policy, decides on what legislation to pilot through the legislature, makes rules and regulations and generally lays down the guidelines for the manner in which the officers who are required to exercise the executive powers will function and perform. The permanent officers, however, while performing these functions are required to even-handedly apply the policy framed by a Minister, to act according to law and to be totally impartial and fair when dealing with the people. Put another way, whereas the policy of the government will undoubtedly be based on the political ideology, goals and programmes of the party in power, in its implementation there will be no favour shown to followers of the party and no disfavour to those who oppose it. If there is a law then the officer responsible for implementing it or enforcing it will act according to law and not take orders from politicians. The politicians are always free to change the law, provided the legislature agrees.

This is how the system functioned up to 1967, which I consider a watershed year in Indian politics. In 1967 in states such as Haryana and Madhya Pradesh, soon to be followed by others, governments were toppled by the purchase of legislators. I use this word 'purchase' judiciously because the support of the legislators was bought with actual payment of cash. Suddenly Members of Parliament and the State Legislatures, in particular the latter, found that they command a price. Obviously those who are in power or aspire to it can only pay this price by milking the state and this was not possible unless the civil services were suborned. The instruments of transfer, plum postings for the pliable, harassment of those who did their duty and the general creation of an environment in which the civil servants are made to feel unsafe, was used to subvert and subjugate the Civil Services. The tragedy is that the services succumbed to this pressure.

The Constitution of India is unique in that it is perhaps the only constitution, which makes a special provision for the Civil Services. The Armed Forces do not find such mention except in Entries 1, 2, 2(A) and 4 of List 1 of the Seventh Schedule. The Seventh Schedule only gives legislative competence to Parliament and the State Legislatures—by itself it does not create the Armed Forces nor does it create constitutional rights and safeguards for the armed forces, who have to depend on laws of Parliament both to come into existence and to function. Part XIV of the Constitution, however, from Articles 308 to 314 in Chapter 1 and Articles 315 to 323 provides safeguards to services against an arbitrary action against them. Article 312 creates the All India Services, of which the Indian Administrative Service, the Indian Police Service and the Indian Forest Service are now in existence. This provision of the Constitution is unique because it creates Services, which will serve both the central and the state governments in a federal set up. In all other democratic federations the centre has its services and the states their own. The Services in India not only have the protection in the matter of appointments and in disciplinary action, but they have further protection of Administrative Tribunals set up under Article 323-A of the Constitution, which exercise powers of the High Court in all disciplinary and other service matters. So far as the constitutional and legal protection of the Civil Services are concerned, it is of a very high order in India. It is to the eternal shame of the Civil Services, especially the three All India Services, that even in their normal functioning they have given in to political pressure, including the pressure to show favours, to apply the law selectively, to use their offices to earn illegal money for themselves and for the politicians and to use the authority of the state against the opponents of the party in power. In effect, this means that one of the important component elements of government, the permanent executive, is increasingly failing to fulfil its constitutional role and duties, which is seriously affecting good governance in India.

What precisely are the mechanics of government in India? Because democracy is the guiding principle of government elected bodies are constitutionally mandated at all levels of government, ranging from the central government down to the lowliest gram panchayat. That is why we have periodic elections to Parliament, State Legislatures and the urban and rural local bodies. It is appropriate that people at all levels should not only have the right to select the rulers but also the right to decide how these rulers will govern. In principle, democracy is a system in which there is both election and accountability built in. So far as elections are concerned, despite all the perversions, which have occurred, by and large we have an adequate system of checks and balances, which ensures that the elections are reasonably fair and impartial. I make this statement despite the horror stories we hear from states such as Bihar about booth capturing, rigging, etc. My own suspicion is that where parties are reasonably well-balanced electoral malpractices of one party cancel out those of another and, therefore, the end result is almost the same as if the malpractices had not occurred. I remember what was said to me by an eminent ex-soldier who stood for election (I deliberately refrain from naming him in public). He said that one of the parties in opposition to him had told him in confidence that it had captured certain booths and would get cent percent votes in its favour at these polling stations. When the ballot boxes were opened the party found to its horror that it had not even obtained a single vote because obviously the ballot boxes had been replaced. The party could not even complain that it had captured these booths because that would have earned it instant disqualification. Suffice to s. y that, give or take a little, India has a well-established electoral system, which is reasonably efficient and functional.

Elections are the first step in the democratic process. The people elected have thereafter to govern and that, too, wisely. Are we being well and wisely governed? For the first twenty years after independence the answer would be a resounding yes. We had a leadership which had come through the crucible of the independence movement and not only did it bear no hatred for the British but it was also confident of its own legitimacy and its ability to govern. It did not destroy the institutions it has inherited from the British, though it democratised them. The leadership clearly understood its bounden duty to promote the welfare of the people, not only in terms of the Preamble but also in terms of the Directive Principles of State Policy, especially Article 38, which reads, "State to secure a social order for the promotion of welfare of the people—(i) the State shall strive to promote the welfare of the people by securing and protecting as effectively as it may a social order in which justice, social, economic and political, shall inform all the institutions of the national life, (ii) the State shall, in particular, strive to minimise the inequalities in income and endeavour to eliminate inequalities in status, facilities and opportunities, not only amongst individuals but also amongst groups of people residing in different areas or engaged in different vocations." It was an exciting time to be alive in India between 1947 and 1967. I joined the IAS in 1957, i.e., mid-way through the process. I felt exhilarated at being given an opportunity very early in life to actively participate in the effort at nation building. We took over from the British, a country, which, as per most indicators of development, was primitive, and we very quickly proceeded to lay the foundations and the infrastructure of a modern state. Those who attack Nehruvian socialism now should remember that but for the state's active participation in capital formation, India even today would have been in the bullock-cart age and on par with Ruanda or Burundi in the matter of development administration different from the old regulatory administrative structure of the British. New welfare legislation was introduced and the judicial system activated to protect the interests of the citizens against the state. These twenty years could certainly be considered two decades of good governance in India.

1967 is the watershed year when defections of Members of Legislatures were arranged through open bribery and United Front Governments (called SVD in Hindi speaking states) were born as coalitions resting on a foundation of quicksand. Suddenly the entire culture of governance changed.

Sardar Patel had created the Civil Services, especially the All India Services, to act as a centripetal force in a country where centrifugal forces are both myriad and powerful. But more important still, he had created the Services within a cocoon of security from arbitrary action so that they could render correct advice, administer impartially and efficiently and act as models of honesty and rectitude. With the ruling politicians needing money to pay bribes to purchase power, an honest and impartial Civil Service was an anathema. The Services had to be broken, by threats, by cajoling, by dispensation of special favours and even by an outright partnership in corruption. One is sorry to state that the politicians had a substantial degree of success in this behalf. This has taken the form of breaking the unity of the Services, exploiting interservice rivalries, harassing honest officers, diffusing rather than decentralising power, breaking the discipline within the service hierarchies by encouraging lateral loyalties and generally playing such havoc with the system that there is hardly any system left. My wife, who was Advisor to the Governor of Gujarat for a brief period in 1996, came back with the firm conviction that the administration there is business friendly and people unfriendly, the police is corrupted beyond redemption by prohibition and made inefficient beyond reclaim by political interference and the district administration had been so paralysed as to leave the state without a delivery system of governance. What is true of Gujarat is, by and large, true of other states also, though there are degrees or shades of difference.

It might be worth considering an analogy with the Armed Forces. Government certainly has the right and the authority to determine the broad contours of defence policy, determine its priorities in the matter of deciding who is a friend and who is an enemy, assign broad tasks and functions to each of the Armed

Forces and then to monitor them to ensure that they fulfil these functions. On this there can be no quarrel. Within these parameters it would be for the Chief of the Naval Staff, for example, to decide how he will deploy his forces and what tasks are to be assigned to each unit or formation. Suppose the politicians begin to intervene at this level and to dictate that Frigate A rather than Frigate B will be deployed in the Ten Degree Channel. Suppose the politicians go further and decide who will be the Chief Engine Room Artificer in a particular patrol vessel. Even worse, suppose the politicians encourage ratings to complain directly against their superior and then insist on a particular posting for which they would have paid a bribe. Can the Navy survive such a situation? Unfortunately on the civil side this is precisely what has happened.

Let us take the example of the police. One often reads stories in newspapers that a certain Chief Minister transferred the DGP, IGP, DIG, the District Magistrate and all ADMs or suspended the Senior Superintendent of Police or Circle Officers of the district. No disciplined uniformed force can survive such an onslaught. It is not surprising, therefore, that the police, whose only real master is the law and whose main job is to enforce the law in accordance with its letter and spirit, is unable to function because it is being forced to obey the politicians rather than the law. One extreme example of this is what has happened in Gujarat recently. When the law and order situation deteriorates it is the responsibility of the executive magistracy and the police to respond and even to anticipate in accordance with law, prevent any disturbance of the public peace, disperse unlawful assemblies, use necessary force to stop rioting, take adequate measures to protect the life and property of the citizens and to bring to book the offenders. It is our experience that whenever the administration has acted firmly riots have been quickly suppressed. In Gujarat the police officers looked over their shoulders, awaiting signals from above and their failure to act in time has resulted in considerable loss of life and property. Lynch law overtook ordinary law in Gujarat. That government was responsible for the failure of the administration is proved by the fact that those officers such as the SSP of Kutch and Bharuch who acted decisively were promptly removed from their posts.

The malaise of bad governance goes well beyond issues of law and order and is much more pervasive and dangerous in the field of development. Policies related to development and the direction and priorities of development have obviously to be laid down by the politicians. Under the decentralised system of administration which is itself under refinement after the Seventy Third and Seventy Fourth amendments to the level of the village panchayat. However, the responsibility for the implementation of the projects is that of the functionaries appointed as civil servants and supervised by the District Collector and the Chief Executive Officer of the Zilla Panchayat respectively. Unfortunately a nexus between the government servants and the elected functionaries has been built up even at this level and there has been no reduction in corruption despite decentralisation. It is almost as if authority is decentralised but accountability is eliminated. As a result of this the development funds continue to be shared between various elected and appointed functionaries and this leakage is adversely affecting the development works proper. It is almost as if the entire system is haemorrhaging.

In our system of separation of powers and the checks and balances, which are a necessary concomitant to such a system, the legislature has a very important role to play, provided that the ministers and legislators understand their true role. The first and foremost is legislation. Legislation requires an ideology and a programme to which the party in power is committed. For example, the Left Front in West Bengal was committed to land reforms and the abolition of the Zamindari system and the rights given to 'Bargadars' (tenants) were at the core of the land reforms legislation in the state.

Having enacted the law there then has to be the political will to enforce it. In Bengal the laws relating to land reforms were implemented because the government and the party were committed to this. They were thus able to prevent the type of fratricidal situation which developed in Bihar. They have been able to prevent both class and caste tension and they have created a new environment of hope in the Bengal countryside which has sharply reduced rural migration into Kolkata. In sharp contrast is the manner in which the Bonded Labour Abolition Act is implemented in MP and other states. This is an extremely well drafted piece of legislation, which clearly identifies bonded labour, prescribes the authorities and the procedure for identifying, releasing and rehabilitating bonded labour and provides for heavy penalties, including imprisonment of up to three years, for those who keep bonded labour, with the trial being summary and the powers of punishment being delegated to the Executive Magistrates. In a Cabinet meeting the Revenue Secretary of MP, who is responsible for administering the law, was told to ask his inspectors to ignore the law. When he expressed his inability to give such illegal instructions he was told that this would result in agriculture coming to a halt in the state. On his suggesting that the state Chief Minister writes to the Prime Minister pointing out his misgivings about the Act and requesting its repeal, he was told that this was not acceptable because after all the law was a fine piece of social legislation. In other words, keep the law on the statute book but do not enforce it. If this brought the law and other laws into public contempt, that did not concern the Cabinet. I cite this example because this is how a general contempt for law is generated, which affects the entire system of the rule of law.

A great deal of criticism is voiced of the role of the All India Services, especially the IAS, for their failure to stem the rot. I am no apologist for the Services, including my own, the IAS. I do believe that the All India Services have not been true to their salt in that they are not prepared to risk their careers by giving correct advice to the ministers or by resisting orders that are improper or illegal. In the changing environment of political amorality many officers in the All India Services have gone beyond the amoral and actually became immoral. For this there can be no excuse, because the Constitution is a shield and buckler and the security given to them by it should have encouraged them to take a firm stand where such action is called for. However, before we finally condemn the prisoner and order his execution, let us once again try to understand the circumstances under which he is working. The present breed of politicians recognises neither rules nor canons of propriety. Therefore, an officer who stands firm is publicly humiliated, transferred, harassed by having false cases foisted on him and generally made miserable. Service homogeneity has been broken by lateral entries and by favouritism in postings and promotions, thus damaging the essential camaraderie and élan of the Services. Pliable officers are only too eager to take the place of an officer who follows the rules. The politicians have also very successfully played the caste card and virtually broken up Service cadres into caste and linguistic groups. What is surprising is not that many officers have broken under the strain, but rather that there are still many of them who follow their conscience, obey the rules, work for the betterment of the people and generally keep aloft the flag of the IAS, IPS and IFS. Some of the younger officers in the Services are beginning to regain their motivation. One hopes that this will help to retrieve the situation.

In the ultimate analysis governance is a function of the desire of those in power to govern rather than loot. One of the major tragedies afflicting us is that with the weakening of the Congress Party we did not see an alternative party strong at national level to take its place. There are far too many political parties, especially those with a regional flavour, which have come to occupy the middle ground between the national level parties. Because the electorate has not been giving any clear mandate to any party these splinter groups have become vital for capturing power and, therefore, they are able to dictate terms, many of them most unreasonable. The message is that if you want to be in power you have to be ready to surrender to blackmail. This is the very negation of governance and opens the door to anarchy. The real danger is not that the Services have declined in morale, morality and commitment to good government. The real danger is that a largely fragmented polity will continue to militate against governance and push us further towards anarchy. This is a trend, which needs to be arrested. For this we need major electoral reforms, which force parties to coalesce, thus forming large, viable national level political alternatives. We need administrative reforms which could protect the Services from undue political pressure, whilst making them accountable to the legislature for competent and honest performance of duties. We need to build a new code of accountability for the politicians and the officials alike, which would force them to perform their functions for the betterment of the people. The details of these steps, however, should form the subject of another discussion.

CHAPTER 6 Who is Afraid of the Big Bad Wolf?

There are two views of civil servants in India: one that they are the real rulers and, the second, that they are the servants of their political masters and have only a subordinate role to play. Votaries of the first view feel that the civil servant is somehow failing the country in not stemming the political and administrative rot that seems to have set in. They feel that if the civil services were to unite the Government would once again begin to function smoothly, efficiently and honestly. The holders of the second view, however, feel that civil servants have not accepted their role of subordination, are devoid of political commitment, do not carry out the wishes of their masters and are responsible for all administrative failures. Between the grindstones of these two extreme views the civil services are being ground into a fine powder, without strength or cohesion.

One fact must be clearly understood. The Indian Civil Services ceased to play the pre-independence role of actually governing this country, on 15th August, 1947. Prior to this date the civil service was responsible both for deliberation and policy formulation as also implementation of policy. Answerability was to a remote Parliament in Britain, and the layers between Parliament and the civil servant in India were so many and so thick that parliamentary authority was very substantially diluted by the time it reached the operation level in India. With independence and the subsequent coming into force of the Constitution, the Parliament and the State Legislatures were located in India, the legislative role passed to them and the deliberative and policy making role to the Union and State

Cabinet. The Indian Administrative Service and other civil services have, since 15th August, 1947, functioned within the new framework. The civil services are not the rulers: rather they are a part of the structure and process of Government.

If the civil servants are no longer rulers they are also not serfs. The civil services are constituted under specific provisions of the Constitution of India, find a mention in it and perform functions defined constitutionally. This is a unique characteristic of the Indian Constitution, for it carries the separation of functions to the finer level of separating even executive functions between the political executive and the permanent one. In a way the permanent executive becomes the Fourth Estate in India, with a subsequent renumbering of other Estates, including the Press.

Constitutionally the services enjoy two sets of separate but complementary safeguards. One relates to the safeguards in the matter of recruitment through an impartial body, the Public Service Commission, the security of service and protection against subsidiary disciplinary action. The second relates to the unique position enjoyed by the civil service under articles 55(b) and 154(1) of the Constitution, which vest the executive power of the Union and the States in the President and Governors respectively, and make these powers exercisable through officers appointed by and subordinate to them. The executive power of the State, therefore, is exercised by permanent officers and not by Ministers. The Minister's powers derive from articles 77 and 176, under which Business of Rules are framed and the business of Government divided between Ministers. The Ministers advise the President or the Governors, with the officers of the Civil Service being a link in that they advise the Minister and at the same time exercise executive functions on behalf of the President or Governor. By no stretch of Imagination can this arrangement be considered onc of the subordination. The relationship is governed by constitutional provisions, and, therefore, each functionary enjoys his own independent status within his own sphere. A civil servant cannot refuse to carry out a proper order of a Minister which would, in effect, be an order of the President or Governor issued on the advice of the Minister. The Minister, on the other hand, cannot stop a civil servant from tendering advice, prevent him from exercising powers vested in him under law, or force him to implement orders which are improper, irregular or illegal. Nor can a Minister prevail upon a civil servant to implement the decisions of Government in a biased manner. The constitutional safeguards available to the civil services are such that in every case where a civil servant has performed his constitutional duty, he has not come to permanent grief. Harassment, frequent transfers, perhaps even a temporary denial of promotion there may be. These however, are short term measures which should not have any permanent adverse effect on any civil servant. In fact the safeguards are a lot more effective than those available to the politicians themselves. In a manner of speaking the protection available to the civil servants is greater than that enjoyed by their counterparts in pre-independent India because, whereas in the former case they are enshrined in the Constitution and are justiciable, in the latter the safeguards emanated either from contracts or from an imperial ethos which insisted upon the protection of Government servants, over where they went wrong to the total detriment of the rights of the individual.

Theoretically there is no reason why any civil servant in India should not do his duty without fear or favour. The civil servants are no Red Riding Hoods, nor are politicians Big Bad Wolves. Both are functionaries on a very human scale. And yet we find that there is a state of constant friction, where it almost seems as if the objectives of the politicians and those of civil servants are diametrically opposite. The goal of Government is the delivery of welfare and this must be the goal of all those associated with government. Why then do we have constant tension?

Where idealism, a definable political philosophy and a strong political will are replaced by a desire to survive for the moment, politics loses cohesion. The present situation in India is that political organisation, ideology and idealism are all weak. Thus, at political levels, a desire to win public favour through the formulation and implementation of welfare policies is replaced by one to curry favour through the distribution of patronage. It is this new political ethos which militates against long-term policy formulation. A prime example of this is a case which occurred in M.P. At the time when the Fourth Five Year Plan was under formulation, the Deputy Secretary in Industries Department responsible for plan formulation prepared a draft of the plan for

Industry. When the file was sent to the Minister it was returned with the remark that he did not want to see it. When the Deputy Secretary personally took the file to the Minister and requested that he might at least try and see whether all his policy objectives were met by the plan, he was told brusquely that the Minister was not interested. As the Deputy Secretary was leaving the room in disgust the Minister called him back and asked him whether the transfer of a particular inspector had been effected. This story illustrates the real malaise of Indian administration bureaucrats formulate long-term policy and politicians responsible for higher level Government decide postings and transfers. This is an utter perversion of the system, and the fact that it is now universal, makes the pill no sweeter.

Patronage extends beyond the corridors of the Secretariat and pervades all levels of administration and political life. The politician at district level would not be interested in a long-term district plan, but his intervention in individual cases would be almost constant. The municipal councillor would not be interested in how the town will develop over a period of time, but would be deeply interested in earmarking in the budget a sum of money which he can expend at his own discretion for the benefit of his cronies. The trade union leader would not be interested in the long-term development of industry, but would be deeply concerned about disciplinary action proposed to be taken against a worker who does not do his duty. In fact in the case of the Railways and Post and Telegraphs department such intervention in cases of disciplinary action has virtually destroyed the hierarchical fabric of these organisations.

The reaction of civil servants to political interference is of three types. One set of civil servants feel that there is money to be made out of extension of patronage and benefit to be derived by going along with the politicians. This group is unfortunately growing rapidly in India. The second group of civil servants consists of these who are utterly indifferent, do the minimum of work, do not actively participate in the patronage by distribution of patronage by the politicians, but try and ensure that they keep out of troubles way. The third and rapidly shrinking group is that of civil servants who feel duty bound to do an honest job of work, to abide by rules, regulations and the like, and say no to persons who ask them to do that which is wrong. This third group is the one under most pressure.

This pressure takes many forms, the least unpleasant of which is browbeating. An example from Delhi is that of a Secretary to the Delhi Administration who, about three years ago, was subjected to considerable haranguing by influential people in order to pressurise him into taking a decision in favour of a party in a case under the Urban Land (Ceiling & Regulation) Act. A weaker man would have succumbed, and it is to his eternal credit that he stood his ground.

A more bothersome method of pressurisation, mainly experienced by officers responsible at field level, is the engineering of complaints in writing, verbally and through the yellow press. This disease is endemic and affects both politicians and civil servants. Utterly baseless allegations couched in the filthiest of language are made against all and sundry, till a stage has been reached where it is almost impossible to distinguish between what is false and what is true. Our reaction, however, has been predictably Indian—we love to pull a chap down. Thus every complaint is subject to harassing enquiries by various agencies, including the police. Where the complaints are made on the floor of the House, contrary to all norms of legislative procedures, the officer is virtually condemned without a hearing. A stage is reached where even the strongest minded officer to give in refrains from taking decisions and joins that group of civil servants who believe, in letting things drift. The growing indecision in Government is a direct result of the feeling of most civil servants that they would not be protected against complaints and that in-action brings more peace of mind than action. What an unhealthy contrast with the situation just five years ago. In early 1964 the then Collector of Betul district of Madhya Pradesh was asked by his Chief Secretary, the legendary R.C.V.P. Noronha of the I.C.S., to make preparations consisted of just one sentence that he was required to make all arrangements and that he was free to take such action as he deemed fit. The Collector probably broke all the rules in the book, plus a number of rules not yet invented, but he set up his camps within one week. After the refugees had been received and settled, by which time the audit people had started to sit up and take notice of irregularities. The collector visited Bhopal and met the Chief Secretary Mr. Noronha who asked him to give a summary of the action taken by him in one typed page. The Chief Secretary's note on the Collector's report read: "Collector, Betul has carried out my orders in taking the above action. Chief Minister may approve". D.P. Mishra was the Chief Minister and he wrote, "I agree with the Chief Secretary". This one single page covered everything that the Collector had done. It is on such mutual trust that Government runs. The whole kit-and-caboodle of spies and counterspies, vigilance people and people who spy on vigilance people, enquiry followed by enquiry, has so vitiated the system that the civil services have reached almost the point of no return in the matter of efficiency, decision making and effectiveness.

Favouritism in postings and promotion and the ultimate threat of an unpleasant transfer or frequent transfers are also weapons used against the civil servants. A few laugh in the face of these threats, but the majority surrenders. What the politicians get is thoroughly demoralised civil service which soon loses its capability even to carry out the whims of politicians. This is perhaps the lesson learnt in Delhi, where wholesale replacement of officers took place first when the Congress returned. It is said that the average tenure of a Collector in U.P. is five months. It is surprising that administration is not at a premium in that State?

The role of a civil servant at the very senior level is not only to advise Government but also to provide guidance and support to their juniors. One outstanding example is that of the late V.K.B. Pillay, then Chief Secretary, Bihar. The P.W.D Minister, in a fit of pique, reverted the Chief Engineer on extremely flimsy grounds. Shri Pillay had the gumption to meet the Chief Minister and had him the collective resignation of all the Secretaries to the Bihar Government. The reversion order was withdrawn post-haste and the Minister duly hauled up. The Chief Secretary was prepared to quit on an issue concerning one of his juniors, and the Chief Minister was magnanimous enough to accept the correctness of his Chief Secretary's stand. One has not noticed a similar stance by these at the top of the civil service hierarchy when, for example, a Secretary to Government was arrested, without any cause, in his own office not so long ago; when Director of the rank of Secretary to Government had to quit the National Academy of Administration on a matter of principle, when a former Chief Secretary to the Government of Madhya Pradesh was placed under suspension on what, prima facie, appear to be untenable charges. No one has noticed any stand being taken when officers remain without posting for months, or when the police and other investigation agencies are used in a politically biased manner. When Shri D.P. Kohli was Director C.B.I., that organisation had a reputation for impartiality unequalled even by the judiciary. The manner in which C.B.I. functioned during the emergency and, subsequently, during the Janata regime, substantially damaged the credibility of the organisation. There is no evidence that the top-most civil servants and police officers in any way resisted the rapid degeneration of this fine force. When one reaches the top, is it not one's duty to stop worrying about one's self? If the fingers were to be pointed at the persons most guilty of causing demoralisation in the civil service, and is afraid that the target would be the topmost civil servants themselves? It is the prinnacle which has crumbled—the base has still strong foundations.

What, then are the civil services to do? The first thing of course, is for them to realise that they owe their existence not to the Council of Ministers, not to politicians; but to the Constitution itself. The Constitution gives them protection, but it also imposes on them certain rights and duties. The principal right is to tender advice without fear of consequence and to implement policy with utter impartiality and in an even handed manner. Nothing, no threat, no intimidation must deter the civil servant from this path. Civil servants who succumb to pressure even in the matters of their fundamental duties tend to come to grief in the long run. The concomitant duty is to the Constitution, to law and to one's conscience. It is the sacred duty of civil servant to resist pressure and to refuse to do what is irregular, improper or illegal. If the consequences are temporarily inconvenient, it is one's duty to bear them cheerfully. In the ultimate analysis the motto of the civil service in India has to be "Who's Afraid Of The Big Bad Wolf".

CHAPTER

7 What Ails Indian Bureaucracy?

—Maharaj Krishan Kaw

Indian bureaucracy is a terminally ill patient. To diagnose all the ailments of this inmate of the Intensive Care Unit would require the combined expertise of a hundred specialists. I will be true to my credentials as a general practitioner and highlight only some of the major illnesses from which it suffers.

Obesity

The most obvious problem with the patient is his obesity. Over the years, successive ministers, secretaries and heads of departments have in their enthusiasm added to the numbers for a variety of reasons. Some of these are:

- Each plan period saw the promulgation of new plan schemes. Most of these had a staff component. The staff liabilities of the previous plan period were shifted quietly to the non-plan, where these kept on piling up from plan to plan. At no stage have we had the courage to do zero-based budgeting. No head of the bureaucracy has the time to look at his tasks today, what organization he would have set up to implement those

The author was a member of the IAS. He held important positions in the Government of India like Secretary, Civil Aviation, Member Secretary, Fifth Central Pay Commission, Principal Adviser (Education), Planning Commission and Secretary, Education.

tasks if he were setting up the department today and then abolish all the other posts. It takes time and energy, it is unpopular and it entails a lot of swimming against the current.

- There is a general notion that if you expand your department, you are a dynamic administrator, whereas if the staff strength shrinks during your regime, you are winding up the department.
- Politicians especially have had this proclivity to employ people in their departments, whether they are required or not, because it is politically expedient to create employment opportunities, especially for people of your constituency.
- Many posts get created because someone somewhere wants a promotion and is not prepared to await his turn. It is not often appreciated that the creation of one unnecessary post to accommodate someone's ambitions has a multiplier effect.
- There are periodic circulars from the departments of personnel, administrative reforms and finance that departments should take a fresh look at their staff strength, indulge in zero-based budgeting or make a cut of 10% or 20% in their overall strength, but these remain pious paper exhortations, as there are neither any incentives nor disincentives attached to such exercises.

Before I proceed to the next ailment, I would like to prescribe some medicines for obesity:

Rx

- We should shift from the present system of budgeting based on inputs to one based on outcomes. In New Zealand, they have a new system under which each Minister has to quantify the outcomes that his Ministry will produce during the next financial year. He also states how much money he requires to produce those outcomes. Once the money is sanctioned, it is up to the Minister and his Secretary to decide what inputs they would use to achieve those outcomes. All the staff is on contract and has to show results or else...
- Pending a major overhaul of the budgetary system, we should have a study of each department conducted by a group of consultants, consisting mostly of the previous secretaries and

heads of departments. It is generally found that bureaucrats improve substantially and suddenly in their objectivity once they retire from service. They should be asked to suggest areas where the schemes and staff can be pruned. The recommendations should be drafted in close consultation with the current incumbents of the top positions in the department.

- There should be a new system under which any diminution in expenditure because of reduction in staff strength would be placed in a discretionary fund, which is placed at the disposal of the department for various initiatives with regard to modernization, computerization, and additions to infrastructure, equipment etc.
- There could also be a scheme under which staff in a particular working unit should be allowed to state that they would be in a position to meet their physical targets even with a reduction in their numbers. The saving on account of the reduction should be permitted to be distributed to the extent of 50% among the remaining staff.
- It should be made clear that one of the major criteria for assessing the efficiency of a secretary or head of department would be the extent to which he is able to achieve economy in expenditure on staff. The Cabinet Secretary in the Central Government and the Chief Secretary in the State should take quarterly meetings to assess the progress made by each department.

Proliferation

The second major problem area is that of proliferation of departments, by breaking up of existing departments. This is one of the biggest reasons for expansion in staff strength and inefficiency. The reasons for proliferation are the following:

- There are political compulsions, especially in coalition governments, where ministerial berths are to be found for a large number of aspirants and dissidents. Existing ministries are broken up into fragments to satisfy such ambitions. This is equally true in respect of officers in different hierarchies wanting to be accommodated in higher assignments.

- Sometimes posts are created just to clear a whole batch of officers who need to be promoted together.
- Very often such proliferation takes place because of something that happens in the Central Government. Suppose, a department of youth services and sports or rural water supply or non-conventional energy sources is created in the Central Government. This is a signal for similar departments being set up in every state of the country right down to the district and village level.
- One important reason is the recommendation of some international conference or the Report submitted by an international organization like the World Bank or IMF. One of the major problems in the Departments of agriculture and rural development was created right under our noses, when a World Bank expert said that agricultural extension should be separated from supply of agricultural inputs. We got an army of extension officers and workers whose only task was to visit a village and advise them to shift to better varieties of seeds and chemical fertilizers. The World Bank had labelled this the T&V (Training and Visit) System. All over India, these chaps were referred to as the Touch and Vanish System. What a massive wastage of funds! This also broke up the organizational unit of the development block in the villages. The World Bank insisted that the Touch & Vanish artists should be exclusively in the agriculture department and should have nothing to do with the Block Development Officers.
- The modus operandi by which these bodies persuade our officers to accept their reports is by dangling the bait of foreign travel before them. An officer will sell his soul if he can thereby wangle a trip abroad, especially to the USA. Most of the World Bank agreements entail a prolonged visit by a team of officers to Washington to negotiate the terms of the agreement with the Bank.

The solutions to these problems are quite complex and are bound to be highly unpopular. It is utterly unlikely that any political party in its right mind will in these days of coalition politics go for the solutions I am suggesting. However, if we mean business, these are the steps we have got to take:

Rx

- The Constitution will have to be amended so as to incorporate the recommendations of the Sarkaria Commission. That Commission made a set of far reaching recommendations about how the ideal size of the Council of Ministers should be determined. These need not be repeated here. If the recommendations are implemented fully, no political party can have an unwieldy Cabinet.
- There should be a conscious decision by the political class that they would not fall in the trap of experts who make facile recommendations about demonstrating the importance attached by the Government to a certain subject by creating a separate department for it. The fact is that a subject can receive greater emphasis only when it is part of a larger whole. One example that readily comes to mind is that of sports. Sports and Youth Affairs used to be a part of the Ministry of Education. Then it was separated out. Today, there is very little sports and youth affairs going on in the schools and colleges of this country, because the budget has been shifted to this newly created department. Ironically, one of the first decisions of the department was that it would cater only to non-student youth!
- Government should take a policy decision that all agreements with international bodies will be signed in New Delhi. If we want to give Government-funded pleasure trips to our officers, let this be done openly, on the lines of the Leave Travel Concession scheme. The British used to give Home Leave to their ICS officers. Today, the private sector allows its executives and their families to take a trip abroad at company expenses. It is one of the recognized perquisites of the executives. What is wrong is to let our officers be psychologically beholden to foreigners for such goodies and allow those foreigners to sabotage our systems.

Ineffectiveness

The third major trouble with the bureaucracy is its ineffectiveness. This was not always so. Over the years, the politicians have transferred all the executive powers from the bureaucrats to themselves. This has been achieved through the following strategies:

- A bureaucrat is kept at a station for a very short while. This extremely short tenure does not permit the bureaucrat to understand the department he is supposed to handle, with the result that he is unable to contribute much to the policies and programmes of the department.
- It is made very clear to a bureaucrat right from his initial service that he is just a cog in the machine, supposed to blindly follow orders. He is not meant to have views of his own on any subject under the sun. Nor is he expected to tender advice, especially advice that is objective and impartial.
- Very serious consequences follow if someone does not toe the line. The bureaucrat can be transferred six times in a year, or be placed in limbo by being kept "awaiting posting orders" for a year or two till he has got rid of his false ego, or he can be placed on the shelf by being posted to a job where he gets his salary but there is no content to the job, or he might be placed under suspension and allowed to cool his hot head, or he might be embroiled in a vigilance case or a CBI enquiry, or he might be involved in sundry matters like income tax raids, false criminal cases and the like, or finally if he is highly inconvenient or intractable, he might be bumped off through a *supari or* some such method.

Rx

This is a very tricky area and there are no easy solutions. In our country, the politicians have tasted blood and it is difficult now to educate them in the fine art of democratic governance. It might be hard to convince them that the minister is supposed to formulate policy and the bureaucrat to implement it. He would not know what policy was and how it was to be formulated. Nor would he like it to be formulated, lest it be held against him when he wants to dole out favours as per his whim and caprice.

The only way some headway can be made is to circumscribe the discretion of the politician while dealing with the bureaucracy.

A suggestion that has been offered is that while the politician should have the unfettered right to appoint any bureaucrat to any office at his discretion, he should not enjoy the same unfettered discretion while removing him from that post. What could be put in place is a forum like a Civil Services Board consisting of retired and serving officials, some members of the Government and the Opposition and some respected citizens like retired judges and so on. The idea is that each bureaucrat should be protected against premature transfer, unless the Government has placed a written case before the Civil Services Board and the Board has given a recommendation in favour of the proposal.

As regards vigilance matters, a beginning has already been made by converting the post of Chief Vigilance Commissioner into a high constitutional office, with little interference from the Government. A similar dispensation needs to be put in place with reference to the setup at the State level, if we have to get rid of the unedifying spectacle of successive Chief Secretaries being sent to jail whenever a new Government takes office, as has now been happening in Tamil Nadu with sickening regularity.

Corruption

The fourth big issue in bureaucracy is corruption. Today, it is difficult to hear about the existence of an honest officer, such is the general reputation of all services. This is because both politicians and bureaucrats have relinquished their traditional roles of keeping an eye on one another. Over the years, the shrewd ones on both the sides have realized that there is no premium in mutual bickering, while both can profit with mutual understanding and cooperation.

Rx

Corruption is not something you can wish away with a magic wand. What we have to remember is that society is an organic whole. Within the same family, one brother joins the private sector. His starting salary may be Rs 50,000 a month. The other brother who joins the government or the public sector starts with Rs 15,000. There is no comparison between the perks. The first brother may have a holiday with family in Europe, a commission on sales or a gift of company shares, while the second brother may have nothing. After 20 years, the first brother may be drawing a salary of a crore a year. These are unheard of figures in the world that the second brother inhabits.

It should be clear to the meanest intelligence that you cannot apply double standards in society. You cannot remove with impunity all the caps that there used to be on corporate salaries and perquisites. If you do, it is an open invitation to public sector executives to indulge in massive corruption.

Let us be clear in our mind. No one is worth Rs one crore to a company. No one needs a crore to live decently. By creating these islands of obscene affluence, we are cutting at the very roots of our traditional value system.

That brings me to the real solution not only to corruption but also all the other ills of the bureaucracy. We have to select the right people and we have to imbue them with the right values. The procedure for recruitment should be such as to induct the best, the people of character, the persons with a mission in life, those who want to serve others, into the civil services.

Training is the other mahamantra that we can use. Values and attitudes should be considered much more important than skills and intellectual attainments.

In this context, we have the readymade structure of five fundamental human values, as taught by Sri Sathya Sai. These are truth, righteous conduct, peace, love and non-violence. These are the kernel of all the religious systems. They also encompass virtues that are purely secular. The beauty is that even one of them is enough to transform the life of a human being.

Suppose I decide to speak the truth. I will then say what I think and I shall do what I say. I will disclose my income and pay my taxes. I will never hide anything wrong that I might have done. At one stroke, all the virtues that we are looking for in our administrators shall be there. Nothing else needs to be done.

So let us do it.

CHAPTER 8

Measures to Combat Corruption in Bureaucracy

—N. Vittal

India is rated as one of the most corrupt countries in the world. According to the Corruption Perception Index 2001 of Transparency International, India is ranked at 72 out of 91 countries. India's relative position can be seen from the index below:

1. Finland
2. Denmark
3. New Zealand
4. Iceland
5. Singapore
6. Sweden
7. Canada
8. Netherlands
9. Luxembourg
10. Norway
11. Australia
12. Switzerland
13. United Kingdom
14. Hong Kong
15. Austria
16. Israel
17. USA
18. Chile
19. Ireland
20. Germany
21. Japan
22. Spain
23. France
24. Belgium
25. Portugal
26. Botswana
27. Taiwan
28. Estonia
29. Italy
30. Namibia
31. Hungary
32. Trinidad & Tobago
33. Tunisia
34. Slovenia

35. Uruguay
36. Malaysia
37. Jordan
38. Lithuania
39. South Africa
40. Costa Rica
41. Mauritius
42. Greece
43. South Korea
44. Peru
45. Poland
46. Brazil
47. Bulgaria
48. Croatia
49. Czech Republic
50. Colombia
51. Mexico
52. Panama
53. Slovak Republic
54. Egypt
55. El Salvador
56. Turkey
57. Argentina
58. China
59. Ghana
60. Latvia
61. Malawi
62. Thailand
63. Dominican Rep.
64. Moldova
65. Guatemala
66. Philippines
67. Senegal
68. Zimbabwe
69. Romania
70. Venezuela
71. Honduras
72. India
73. Kazakhstan
74. Uzbekistan
75. Vietnam
76. Zambia
77. Cote-d'Ivoire
78. Nicaragua
79. Ecuador
80. Pakistan
81. Russia
82. Tanzania
83. Ukraine
84. Azerbaijan
85. Bolivia
86. Cameroon
87. Kenya
88. Indonesia
89. Uganda
90. Nigeria
91. Bangladesh

The fact that more countries are perceived to be less corrupt than India is really a matter of concern for every patriotic and sincere Indian. Corruption in India is a vicious cycle which involves political corruption, business corruption and criminalisation of politics.

I have been asked the question: "Between politicians and the bureaucracy, who is more corrupt?" My answer is that the bureaucracy is more corrupt. This is because the number of bureaucrats in the country runs into about 8 million and the politicians who are in power and who can afford to be corrupt are much less in number. Secondly, politicians have only a limited window of opportunity depending upon when they are in power and between elections. A bureaucrat continues for nearly three decades in power.

The basic causes for corruption in the bureaucracy can be traced to one of the following five factors:

- Scarcity of goods and services
- Red tape and delay which encourages speed money
- Lack of transparency in systems and procedures
- Legal cushions of safety created under the healthy principle that everybody is innocent till proved guilty
- Tribalism or brotherhood among the corrupt. When two people are close to each other we say that they are thick as thieves and not thick as honest men. Corrupt people protect each other.

The system of bureaucracy we have evolved has built in factors which encourage corruption. The very guarantee of tenure under Article 311 of the Constitution of India provides an enormous security blanket to the civil servant. We have added to this security blanket additional layers of cushion thanks to the various judicial pronouncements and organisations like the Central Administrative Tribunal (CAT). As pointed out by Arun Shourie in his book *Courts and Their Judgements*, the impact of courts on administration is to create paralysis in decision-making. This has aided building up a culture of inefficiency and non-implementation of policies. After discussing the judgement of the Supreme Court especially in the context of emergency and the *ex-post* changes in the electoral laws made by the Parliament during the emergency, he observes:

In a word, just as the Supreme Court was a legitimizer of ex-post changes in electoral laws to overturn an electoral judgement against the ruler, just as it was a legitimizer of cruel arbitrariness in ADM, Jabalpur, it became just as much a goad to, just as culpable a legitimizer of the socialist rhetoric, of the lax regimes and other regulations whose consequences we rue to this day.

As far as administration is concerned, the consequences have been two-fold, each fatal even by itself.

In practice, all those admonitions for ensuring 'fairness', 'non-discrimination', for eschewing 'arbitrariness' have reinforced the tendency in the civil service to play safe. They have led the administration to tie itself firmly to rules of thumb. Pay increase, "Parity across the board" Promotions go strictly by years the man has put in—the consequence was put to me graphically by a person who has himself held senior positions in Government. "This is the only place in which by the sheer efflux of time an ass becomes a horse." Even when evidence is staring you in the face that the bidder will not be able to complete the contract within the artificially low rate he has quoted in his tender document, go by H1, L1 rules of thumb—lest someone take you to court, lest someone put the CBI on your tail.

Once again, the point is not that the judiciary has been solely responsible for bringing administration to this pass; courts have not interfered with allocations that the Planning Commission makes to the States for their Annual Plans; yet, more than 95 per cent of the amounts allocated each year are formula-based. The point is that the courts, instead of helping lift a weak political class out of the morass of mechanical rules, have contributed to pushing it deeper into the swamp.

Second, the courts have helped drive merit completely out of governance. By straining so much in favour of 'equality', 'fairness', 'non-discrimination', courts, as much as our politicians and intellectuals, have helped make mediocrity—indeed, non-performance—the norm. Merit, excellence have become dirty words—words that prove that the interlocutor is an elitist, one who has no sympathy for the downtrodden, one who is bent upon perpetuating privilege and inequity.

The consequence of this denigration of merit and excellence, as of rights-mongering, the consequence of reducing administrators to regurgitating rules of thumb has been to paralyse governance, to induce administrators to spend their days going through the motions of doing things rather than actually doing them.

Many a time the implementation especially of policies relating to maintenance of law and order leads to very bizarre consequences. Shri Arun Shourie has drawn attention also to this aspect.

Mr. Jagmohan, who saved the Valley for India at a critical time, was soon put in the dock. In Assam, the Army is repeatedly asked to step in as the negligence and worse of politicians give the terrorists the upper hand. The situation has but to be brought in hand, and that very Army is made the butt of condemnation by the politicians. A policeman in that state who is killed by the terrorists is soon forgotten, his family is packed off with a compensation of Rs. 25,000, while the terrorists who have killed that very policeman are given a lakh each if they "surrender", they are given a Maruti each, they are assured jobs, they are allowed to retain their weapons.

And where our forces have defeated the terrorists most decisively, the Punjab, the situation is the worst. Mr. KP.S. Gill, who rebuilt a shattered and infiltrated Punjab Police and who, by personal example as much as by anything else, led that force to defeat terrorism in Punjab and thereby saved Punjab for the country, is today beleaguered and set upon. The Punjab Police itself, rather the officers and men in that force who fought the terrorists, are just as much in the dock; almost 1500 cases and writs are being heard against them; about 50 of them are in jail or have been suspended from service—not because they have been convicted, but because investigations are yet to be completed and their trials are yet to begin; scores of them have to troop every other day offering explanations to courts where authorities scold them, and hurl pejoratives at them.

Do you remember the young officer who was gunned down in the stadium in Patiala when he was out for his morning run? What were these assassinations—'genuine encounters' as distinct from the 'false encounters' in which terrorists are alleged to have been killed? But not one 'human rights organization' talks of the killings of those officers. Not one 'human rights organization' files a writ requesting the courts to direct the CBI to trace the murderers of these officers and men, and have been prosecuted. No court does in this regards what courts do so routinely on other matters—that is, take cognizance of these killings suo moto.

But there is more than just double standards, much more than mere forgetfulness. There is a hankering to forget, an induced amnesia. When the country was faced with terrorism, so many were prepared to countenance anything anyone did 'Just get rid of them', they said, 'Do whatever you have to'. Now that the forces have made the place safe for us, they have erased from their minds every memory of the beast that they had clamoured the forces vanquish. They have erased from their minds what these brave men have done for the country at the risk, nay the cost of their very lives.

There are several reasons for this induced amnesia. First of course is our addiction—to money, to goods and the rest; now that the danger has been pushed aside, we again have no time from our pursuits. Next, we exercise memory of the sacrifices of these valiant men so that we may not have to do anything for them in return. Most of all, we erase their sacrifices and the risks they have borne so that we do not have to do anything comparable for the country. In fact, to ensure that we do not have to follow their example we convince ourselves that what they did was actually wrong, that it ought not to have been done. The writs and all, the readiness with which sections of the media and others believe everything that even the most questionable source puts out so long as it is against the persons who saved our country, the fact that we accept as normal a policy under which, while the family of the policeman who has been killed should get Rs. 25,000, the ones who have killed him should get a lakh each—all this fits a pattern.

When I was Additional Chief Secretary (Home) in Gujarat, I faced a peculiar situation in the Nadiad Police Station. There were two SHOs, one who was considered to be pro-Muslim and one pro-Hindu in one police station. This came about because the government transferred one of SHOs and he went and got a stay. The government posted another person against the same post. As a result the whole discipline suffers and when discipline suffers, implementation becomes the first casualty. Shri Arun Shourie has also drawn attention in his book *Courts and Their Judgements* to this aspect.

Delays in courts, as well as the punctilious standards that the courts have laid down for natural justice, etc., for what is required in obedience to Articles 14 and 21 disable governments just as much. As is the case on matters we have encountered earlier, the courts are not the only ones that are responsible, for the resultant torpor. They are not even primarily responsible. The Executive is. But I do wonder whether judges today are even aware of what the cumulative effects of their progressive rulings has been on the functioning of the governmental apparatus— there is just one word that describes it precisely: paralysis. That cases in which governments get entangled take as long as the generality of cases is just apart of the problem. Over the years judgements have added one requirement after another that must be fulfilled while doing something. Each requirement can be justified in itself, I have little doubt. But the cumulative result has to be lived to be realised. Nor has the result come about only from specific criteria that the courts have prescribed. The general tenor of rulings, and their tilt have helped create an environment in which it is safer to pass files around than to take a decision, in which it is prudent to go through the motions of doing things than to actually do them. It is almost impossible to describe how palsied the structure has become. Only when one is thrown into the process does one realize the state to which affairs have fallen.

The Central Administrative Tribunal and its Benches were meant to be a substitute for the courts. Appeals from their decisions were to lie only to the Supreme Court. They were not to be bound by the Code of Civil Procedure; they were to be guided by the general principles of natural justice. The idea was that government servants and governments would swiftly settle the matter, that both would shun lawyers and legalistic stratagems and dodges: the petitioner was given the freedom to appear in person, governments were given freedom to be represented by officers rather than legal counsel. The Tribunals were specifically given the authority to decline requests for that plague of Indian courts— adjournments. The cases were to be settled within six months.

Step by step the Tribunals have become clones of courts. In L. Chandra Kumar, the Supreme Court declared that, the specific provision of the law notwithstanding, appeals against rulings of Tribunals would be heard by High Courts. Adjournments have become the order of the day. Both governments and employees routinely engage legal counsel. The counsel proceed as is their wont .... The Committee on Service Litigation reported, "Apart from delay that generally occurs in the Ministry and Department in filing counter-reply to the applications filed by the government employees in the Central Administrative Tribunal, to a great extent the delay is attributable to the inefficiency of the Government Counsels. It is found that they do not take enough interest in handling Government cases. The Ministries and Departments have generally to pursue the matters vigorously with the Government Counsels to ensure timely filing of the replies, etc., in the court and the Counsels on their part in most cases are largely incommunicative...". The familiar tale. Step after familiar step. Each contributing his accustomed bit. The familiar denouement ....

The system which we have evolved by which people can escape accountability is also a factor that encourages corruption in bureaucracy. How does one measure the level of corruption? The level of corruption in any organisation depends on three factors: individual sense of values, social values and the system. As CVC, I have been trying to tackle the issue of corruption in bureaucracy by drafting a three-point strategy:

- Simplification of rules and procedures so that the scope of corruption is reduced
- Transparency and empowerment of the public
- Effective punishment of the corrupt

On the issue of simplification of rules and regulations, the best case I remember is the issue of the hawkers in Delhi which was reported to me on 18.6.2001 by the activist, Madhu Kishwar who runs the Organisation, Manushi. According to her ' the five lakh hawkers in Delhi were paying a monthly bribe of Rs. 40 crores to the police and the municipal authorities in Delhi. I took up the matter with the Chief Minister and the Urban Development Minister and also participated in the Jan Sunvayee organised by the Manushi. The matter was reported in the media and came to the notice of Dr. Pradipto Ghosh, Additional Secretary in PMO, He took my letter to the CM where I argued that while in the context of economic liberalisation, a person who wants to set up an industry does not need any licence, why should a poor man who wants to sell vegetables or run a cycle rikshaw need a licence. The licensing system should therefore be abolished. Based on my letter and further discussions with me, a concept paper was prepared by Dr Ghosh and presented to PM. The PM personally intervened in the matter on 23rd August 2001 and wrote to the Lt. Governor suggesting a scheme for abolition of licensing for hawkers and cycle rikshaw pullers and also a system for better regulation. It is perhaps a commentary on the state of affairs that the PM's directive is yet to be fully implemented.

Computerisation of Banks is another system improvement I was able to push through to check corruption. When I became CVC only 10,000 out of 65000 branches of the public sector banks were computerised. Today 74% of banking business in the public sector banks is computerised. I must thank the bank managements and unions for their positive cooperation on this issue.

While it is important to punish the corrupt, it is equally important to protect the honest and innocent public servant. I therefore issued a total ban on any action being taken on anonymous/ pseudonymous complaints on 29.6.1999.

Another initiative I took in the same spirit was to suggest that CVC must be consulted before suspension of public servants on the grounds of corruption. Unfortunately government have not accepted my suggestion. This needs to be pursued further.

The second element of my strategy was transparency and empowering the public. The step I took of publishing in the web site of CVC, names of charged officers found guilty after a departmental inquiry and against whom major penalty was recommended, became an exercise in serendipity. It was the first example of use of Internet to fight corruption. This attracted worldwide attention. The Harvard University called me to make a presentation on e-government on 19th October 2000 in the

Centre for International Development. 93% of the respondents to a *Hindustan Times* poll said that they welcomed CVC's step. 83% of the respondents to an *Economic Times* poll said that it was a good deterrent measure. 70.5% of the people who responded to a *Pioneer* poll said that it was a good anti-corruption measure. The website became an useful instrument not only for publicising the names of persons who have been found guilty but also to follow up with the disciplinary authorities, action for implementing the decisions regarding punishment. The computerisation of CVC's data highlighted the fact that in September 2000, there were 170 cases where even after completion of inquiry and major penalty recommended, no action was taken for more than five years. I took up the matter with the disciplinary authorities and pointed out that if even after five years no action was taken, it could only mean that either the department was inefficient or there was an attempt to protect the guilty. This had a good impact and the cases of delay came down.

The second element of my strategy was empowering the public. For this, CVC published on the Independence Day 2001 the *Citizens' Guide to Fighting Corruption* which spelt out what *the* citizens can do to fight corruption. They can adopt a four-point plan:

- The first is to participate in the Vigilance Awareness Week, which is being observed on Sardar Patel's birthday on 3 October for a week every year from the year 2000. From the year 2001, 13 lakh NCC cadets are also participating in the Vigilance Awareness Week. This week is used to sensitise public about the negative consequences of corruption and show that the corruption is anti-economic, anti-poor and anti-national.
- The second action point would be for citizens to participate in suggesting to CVC how rules and procedures can be simplified. CVC can use its powers for giving directive for changes in rules and procedures. State Governments are not within the purview of CVC and CVC can at best be an empowered post office in the process for bringing change.

- The third element of the strategy for the citizen is to give information about those who have got black money or benami property so that the CVC can ask the income tax or CBI to conduct raids. From July 2001 this scheme was introduced and more than 900 applications were received of which 64 have been sent for scrutiny to the Income Tax Departments. Three raids have been conducted with positive results.
- The fourth element of action for a citizen would be to participate in the trapping of the corrupt public servants with the help of the police.

The Citizens' Guide to Fighting Corruption also pointed out four agencies which can be used by the citizen to fight corruption. These are: (i) judiciary in the courts through Public Interest Litigation, (ii) agencies like the CVC, (iii) media, both print and electronic, to create public opinion, and (iv) direct action through NGOs like Lok Satta in Andhra Pradesh. *The Guide* was widely welcomed.

The third element of the strategy is effective punishment. As mentioned earlier, the website and follow up action has been used to speed up disposal of cases. It is a matter of satisfaction that 97-98% of the advice given by CVC for punishment is accepted by the disciplinary authorities. Those 2% of the cases where action is not taken, according to CVC advice, are reported in the Annual Report of the CVC, which is placed before the Parliament.

This 3-point strategy seems to have brought an overall improvement in the effectiveness of CVC as an agent for fighting corruption within the government. If the CVC performance is measured against the overall ranking of India in the Corruption Perception Index of international agency like the Transparency International, we have not made much progress. In 1998, India was ranked at 68 out of 85; in 1999 it became 73 out of 99; in the year 2000 it was 69 out of 90, and in the year 2001 it was 72 out of 91. The position of India remains more or less the same though I had an ambitious goal of seeing India ranked at 40 in the Corruption Perception Index.

We have made some improvements in the system so far as fighting corruption is concerned, but a lot still remains to be done.

These are mostly in the area of legislation. The CVC Bill itself has not yet been passed. In the Bill the attempt being made to introduce Single Directive is a retrograde step. This clause must be removed. In any case, it is likely to be struck down by the court if anybody re-approaches the court with a Public Interest Litigation that this provision is unconstitutional and violates Article 14 of the Constitution.

The Corrupt Public Servants (Forfeiture of Property) Act, which the Law Commission had recommended to the Government on 4th February 1999, still remains to be enacted. The legislative measures which I had suggested (para 17 & 18), also remain to be enacted.

As I see it, corruption in India is the result of a vicious cycle involving political corruption, bureaucratic corruption, criminalisation of politics and business corruption. The root cause of corruption in India is political corruption. Our entire democracy is based on corruption. Every political party needs funds and they collect funds in the form of black money. Black money is the oxygen for corruption and corruption is the oxygen for black money.

I would suggest the following strategy:

- Black money, which is at the root of corruption, in politics, business and bureaucracy, should be effectively eliminated. This can be done in a three-phased programme:

Phase I. Three months

(i) Implement the Benami Transaction Prohibition Act 1988

(ii) Amend Prevention of Money Laundering Bill to cover Income Tax, Customs, Excise & Sales Tax

(iii) Enact Corrupt Public Servants (Forfeiture of Property) Act as suggested by the Law Commission and pending with the government from 4.2.1999

(iv) Amend the Income Tax Act on the principle of zero exemption. Exempt all incomes upto Rs. 2 lakhs per annum. Levy a flat tax rate of 20% on all incomes above Rs.2 lakhs.

(v) Amend the Customs and Excise Acts on the principle of zero discretion.

Phase II. Three months
Introduce an amnesty scheme under which within a period of three months, all those who have black money can declare the same and regularize the same by paying an income tax of 21 %.

Phase III
Effectively implement laws passed in Phase I so that black money is practically eliminated.

- Hold the National Convention on Ethics in Government on the lines suggested by Dr C.P. Srivastava in his book, *Corruption—India's Enemy Within.*
- Enact the CVC Bill after taking into account the comments of the CVC on the Parliamentary Committee's Report on the CVC Bill.
- Amend the Representation of People's Act so that the candidates against whom serious criminal charges have been framed in a court of law are prohibited from contesting the elections till their name is cleared in the courts of law.
- For all sensitive posts in Government and sensitive organizations like banks, PSEs etc., introduce the pattern, which is now prevailing for selecting the Director CBI. This will mean that neutral committees of experts will select the panels for filling up the sensitive posts. The government will appoint candidates to the sensitive posts from these panels. Once a person is appointed to a post, he will have a fixed tenure for three years

In order to check corruption there is need to encourage whistle blowers. The Law Commission has recently drafted in consultation with the CVC the Public Disclosures Act for this purpose. This law needs to be also enacted urgently.

As Central Vigilance Commissioner, I tried to discharge my duties to the best of my ability following the strategy mentioned above. The fight against corruption is a long drawn one. I have also indicated some of the points on which action has to be taken. I hope Central Vigilance Commission will one day emerge as a major instrument to fight corruption and improve probity in public life in our country.

CHAPTER

9 Excessive Controls and Bureaucracy

—C.N. Parkinson

I will start with the word "Bureaucracy". The word is French which does not mean that the French invented it. Originally "Bure" was a cloth and eventually a writing desk covered with Bure, a coarse woollen cloth. It came to mean an office or a government department and above all, Bureaucracy is associated with a desk and I am sure, you all realise that you can't administer without a desk. This is essential, you can't begin, you have to have in front of you, a wooden structure usually a bit flatter on top or on the side. You have to have an 'in-tray' and you have to have an 'out-tray'. In the middle some people have a third tray labelled 'LBW' which might be a term in cricket or possibly stands for 'let the fellow wait'. You also need a waste paper basket and once you have this minimum of equipment, you can then begin to administer as a bureaucrat.

Papers arrive in the 'in-tray', and if you are administering, you bring them out of the 'in-tray', put them in front of you, sign them, some people even read them but the essential thing is to sign them, and put them in the "out-tray" or sometimes in the waste paper basket, as the case may be, and that is the central process of administration.

Text of a lecture delivered at a special felicitation meeting of the Indian Chamber of Commerce and Industry, Calcutta.

Government by Bureaux

Now, Bureaucracy means a government by bureaux, by officials sitting at desks, a government in which authority is divided among numerous offices, all of them adhering to inflexible rules of procedure. We come to think of Bureaucracy as a form of rule in which complex and time wasting protocol prevents effective action. We come to think of the Bureaucrat as one who insists upon rigid adherence to rules, form and precedents. The word may be French but the form of rule goes certainly back to ancient Egypt and still more, perhaps, to the ancient Far East. If any one people invented and perfected Bureaucracy, it will probably be the Chinese. As against that, the Germans might claim to rank among the leading bureaucrats of the present age.

There are six characteristics of Bureaucracy and I will run through them at tedious length. The first point about Bureaucracy is that it is highly centralised. We should note from this point that the most highly centralised countries in the world are probably Great Britain and France, most other large States being divided into self-governing provinces. Thus sub-divided are the United States, Soviet Russia, China, India, Canada, Australia, Germany and even the Netherlands. Two countries are undivided and over-centralised to the point of lunacy. These are respectively Great Britain and France.

Faceless Officials

Now, the second characteristic of a bureaucratic government is that its appointed officials are impersonal, nameless and faceless. Each clerk writes in the name of the government. There was a time in my life when I wrote an occasional letter which began, "Sir, I am commanded by the Army Council to bring the following matter to you attention . . . etc. etc." It was, of course, like official documents often are. My documents were a lie because the Army Council knew nothing about the matter concerned and incidentally nothing about me either. I am not certain that they ever met and if they did, certainly it wasn't to consider this sort of letter. Nevertheless, this is what is the form of words which was designed to make the recipients of the letter forget about me and think of a mythical assembly of the great and the good. The letter conveying the decisions signed by one officer, on behalf of another who is his deputy or someone more senior who possibly or someone eventually represents Her Majesty the Queen. The effect on the recipient is daunting because he doesn't know, to start with, to whom his reply should be addressed or whether it should be seen by anybody. He concludes, and perhaps rightly, that he is addressing a system, not a person; that the officer who signed the letter is not an individual but a small part of a complex machine. It is the essence of a Bureaucracy to leave us without any idea as to who the rulers are.

Distinct Departments

The third characteristic of a Bureaucracy is that its officials are divided among departments which are distinct from each other, contrasting in attitude and often mutually hostile. Before you build a house you need planning permission and you have to approach severally the planning authority, the district engineer, the water board, the electricity council, the regional architect, the telephone council and the parish council. Some of these authorities are apparently at war with each other. Others are unaware of each other's existence. This is the way these things function.

When you alter the plans of your house to satisfy the rules administered by the district engineer, you spoil the elevation already approved by the regional architect. Altogether you can't win. Your drive entrance is acceptable to the highway planners but does not please the parish council. We are all probably familiar with the situation when a water pipe is laid by the water board, the trench being filling in and the surface of the road made good. A month later the road is closed once more by the electricity board. It is dug up, the trench is then filled in and the surface made good once more, and it goes on the same bit of road dug up repeatedly. In many countries all these authorities are distinct and there is no chance at all of using the same trench by previous agreement—this never happens—still less of the load having a service pipe in which all services might have been contained from the beginning. On a higher level the co-ordination is probably worse. The welfare department gives a pension to a man who has just deserted from the air force, the home department expels the alien which the foreign ministry wants to question. We thus think of Bureaucracy as a system in which co-ordination is minimal and ineffective.

The fourth characteristic of a Bureaucracy is that the officials applying inflexible rules which are often opposed to mere commonsense. To give the official wide powers of interpretation in the application of laws, regulations and decrees would expose him, it is thought, to both temptations and personal attack. He might, on the one hand, accept bribes or show favour to his friends and relatives. He could, on the other hand, make enemies, being branded as a tyrant by all who have been disappointed in their applications. So to safeguard his position we narrowly restrict his powers.

Quoting Chapter and Verse

All he says to us is 'planning permission is refused because your application is contrary to sub-paragraph 17 of para 691, section 190 of the Act of 1951'. He doesn't say that proposal is undesirable; that isn't under discussion. It is contrary to some clause of some Act passed by somebody at some time. He gives no opinion about the rightness or wrongness of what is proposed. He merely points to a regulation and hides once more in the anonymity of his department. There may seem to be good reasons for giving him his narrow task of interpretation. It is arguably inevitable that he should be put in that position. But what is unfortunate is that legal phrases don't cover everything and that strict adherence to law can be ridiculous or even tragic. We hear of the ambulance racing to the hospital with an emergency case only to be told that the patient cannot be admitted to that hospital but must be taken somewhere else even when this may mean his dying on the way there. 'I have no power to make an exception' is the formula used and this is quite possibly true. We think of Bureaucracy as a system under which officials can thus avoid taking any responsibility.

The fifth characteristic of Bureaucracy is that the procedures as laid down are actually appallingly complex. There are forms to be filled in, rules to be observed, technicalities to be understood and documents to be drawn up. The merchant who has goods to export cannot even pretend to understand the clearances and permits which must accompany the shipment. He hands the task to a forwarding agent who does nothing else. Complexity grows with the size of the organisation but it is also the tendency for complexity to become more complex.

Thinking of forms to be filled in reminds me of two which are favourites with me. One was presented to me at a university in the United States where I had been teaching for about six weeks, and at that point it occurred to some Bureaucrat to ask me who I was. I suppose they knew nothing about me and presented me with a form which started "Who are you? Are you a graduate?" And finally question 27 reads as follows: "Give the names and addresses of your parents even if deceased." At that time when I first had this form to fill in both my parents were dead and I need hardly tell you that I filled it in as follows: "The allegiance fails (no telephone number)". Another form which may come in the way of any of you if you wish for a visa to enter the United States, one of the questions you are asked to fill in—and this is No. 54—reads ás follows: "Do you mean to upset the Constitution of the United States?" And most of us content to reply "no", although I have heard of people who have filled in "sole purpose of visit" and have got in nevertheless.

The Anarchist

But the beauty of that particular sort of question seems to me to centre upon the picture of some anarchist who is heading for USA. His suitcase is filled with explosives and he has every intention of blowing up the White House and everyone inside it. But faced with that form he says, 'I can't tell a lie'. It is a beautiful thought, isn't it? I feel myself that people with suitcases full of explosives would not really be daunted by a question like that. They would probably attempt to deceive us but it is nice to think that there might be in the world an anarchist who couldn't tell a lie when faced with that paragraph.

Any way let us go back to the whole business of forms and they become more complex as time goes on because anyone who deals forms to be filled in always thinks of more questions to ask so that he can show how efficient he is by lengthening form and elaborating it so that all become more complex. One cause of this complexity is the desire of the expert to protect his personal knowledge adding to the mystery rather than attempting to explain. Another cause of this is the overstaffing of the civil service—not in India but in other countries—leading to the creation of work to justify the numbers employed. Any question on our census form will thus become more complicated as time goes on, providing more work for the department concerned. Complexity thus in this way becomes more complex and we can all recognise in this an aspect of Bureaucracy.

Delay Becomes Denial

Now, we have had five characteristics of Bureaucracy. All of them come together in the sixth characteristic which I am now about to describe, and that is the characteristic of ineffectiveness due to lack of purpose and lack of speed. Carried to its normal conclusion, delay becomes denial, centralisation becomes frustration, departmentalism becomes inaction, inflexibility becomes idleness and complexity becomes decay. Slowly and majestically the whole machinery of Government grinds to standstill. Little is attempted, nothing is achieved and even the simplest problems prove insoluble. A good example of this is to be found in USA where the constitution was designed for different kind of society but it was so drawn up as to make reform practically impossible. The difficulties in which the American executive, legislature and judiciary have been placed a year or two ago by what was called the 'Watergate Affair' was not due to the wickedness of individuals but to the obsolescence of a whole system of Government. It was the organisation that was at fault. The framework is weak, the ideas are bad in principle and the Bureaucracy is revolting in its complexity. The whole cumbersome machine drifted into the war in Vietnam which was futile from the outset and from which it proved almost impossible to withdraw. There have been successive blunders in foreign policy and the internal problems are endemic and seemingly insoluble. Beyond all these flounderings in the mud stands the central fact that the system is at fault and the means for changing the system are for all practical purposes non-existent from which, ladies and gentlemen, you will assume perhaps rightly that I shall not be applying for a visa for the United States in the near future and you would conclude that if I apply, I probably should not get it. I have been rather rude but not specifically really about the USA. Because much the same can be said about so many other countries also.

Six Characteristics

Here then are the six characteristics of Bureaucracy. They are first, the disadvantages of excessive centralisation, impersonality, departmentalism, rigidity, complexity and finally incompetence. To find a remedy for these evils which I have described so tediously and at such length, we must replace each of them by its opposite, thus introducing delegation, responsibility, co-ordination, flexibility, simplicity and effectiveness. The habit of each Central or National Government, and this is especially true, I think, of socialist governments, is to make each regional government a mere agency for the execution of central policy. The purpose of any anti-bureaucratic movement would be to take whole areas of administration and make them a purely local matter in which the Central Government would have no say at all. Socialist or anti-socialist legislation should have much the same effect to make everything strictly regional, and I may say that this is a very good aspect of Government in the USA.

There are some further aspects of administration which are purely a State matter. One, for example, is education. In education the federal Government has no say at all. It could advise if it wanted to, but each State Government can go its own way and largely does. It stops, in other words, at the stage of provincial capital and if there is to be decentralisation, the condition of it must always be that you cannot decentralise, well, say in health. While there is a health department of the Central Government, in decentralising it, it is essential that Central Department must be wiped out, not with bomb but with a suitable decree which dissolves it completely and ends it.

I have tried to describe the faults of Bureaucracy but we have to realise at this point that the situation will never be static. That the situation is bad is no proof that it will not get worse. On the contrary Bureaucracy has its own self-induced dynamics. By its own nature. It must tend to expand and proliferate. By its own nature it must become more complex as time goes on. Some 25 years ago, I suppose, I discovered and published the law of proliferation by which any organisation is governed. I since came to realise that this growth has more than one cause, and one cause that we should know is that in any organisation there is an uneven flow of work due to a variety of causes—climatic, religious, seasonal, legal, political, whatever—so that the work is not a level flow, it is up and down and this is known to most people in business that there will be this fluctuation in the work load and, of course, the tendency of the manager, the people at the top, is to staff the organisation on a scale to meet that peak pressure of work and this leaves people under-employed during the slack period.

A Good Manager

But a good manager does not like to see people idle, nor do the employees like to be idle beyond a certain point. Most people are worried if they are idling more than half their time. Up to half their time they seem to be very happy, beyond that they get worried and the result is first that tasks are invented to keep people occupied and if they are not invented people invent tasks for themselves and so keep themselves occupied. The result is when the next peak of activity is reached, the staff are all busy and new staff must be recruited. These in turn will be idle when the work slackens and so the numbers rise from year to year for ever. At the same time the devices used from year to year for ever. At the same time the devices used to make work become more elaborate and complex. The records become more detailed, the statics more involved. It is also apparent that each department or branch has a life of its own. It is not a structure, it is an organisation. It is something with a will to grow, a will to survive, a will to expand. It will never abolish itself, of course, nor the evil, if there is one, which it may have been designed to abolish. Now, we all know that governments other than those of exceptional wisdom as to be found in India, concern themselves from time and time and try to abolish all human failures, all examples of human folly or wickedness.

Plethora of Legislation

People are to be made good and sensible by legislation and the result is, in most of the world a diarrhoea of legislation. I can say that word, the difficulty is to spell it and this is the first test of entering on a medical career; if you cannot spell diarrhoea, you better give it up and decide to be a chartered accountant. But we have a diarrhoea of legislation throughout the world accompanied by similar diarrhoea in the creation of committees and the world is covered by Acts of Parliament and covered by committees and between them they create mountains of paper.

Now, one of the common things is to set up a branch of Government to deal with some particular evil. Such a one may be, for example, pornography. Now, nobody in the world knows what pornography is but we set up a department of Government—an antipornographic department. Now, the certainty about that, apart from its being a likely source of corruption, is that the department will perpetuate pornography as well as itself. Well, it is bound to. People are not going to take themselves out of job. That position is rather like the rat-catcher. There used to be in Government this important officer known as the rat-catcher. He has been replaced by a rodent control officer, who, of course, has to be paid a great deal more. The rat-catcher history brought into clear rats out of the warehouse was always ready to carry out a picturesque and dramatic campaign. He was always careful to leave two rats behind of opposite sexes when the task was completed. He did not want to drop himself out of the job, he wanted to clear out the rats again next year, and so it is with particular departments to deal with drugs or pornography or whatever it is. They will always perpetuate the things that they have been designed to suppress. We may and must deplore the cost of Bureaucracy but the expense involved is actually the least part of the mischief.

Trimming the Civil Service

Now, the next reform needed is to have the number of civil servants and in some few instances double their salary. British administration used always to be at its best in India and people in India, if they have read that, must have realised how bad it must be in Britain. I do not know, but at least to India all the best British administrators were always sent and the rest almost as good used to be sent to the Sudan. The best people available were divided between the two, and you all remember, the whole Indian sub-continent used to be ruled by the Indian Civil Service which numbered approximately 1000–1200. In fact, when India became independent in 1947, a thousand of them, that is all there used to be. What made for a certain efficiency then and what would make for efficiency now is to have a sufficient number of decision-making officers and the least possible number of clerks. With a smaller number of people there are fewer steps between the foot and the summit of the administrative pyramid and that means reaching a quicker and possibly wiser decision at a lower cost. The point is the shape of pyramid. Now the average civil service pyramid has the unnamed people down at the bottom and right at the top is the wisest and the best man of the whole lot who is the chief. Yes, he is the wisest and the best. We have to agree to that, and that is the shape of pyramid. Flatten it out and that to my mind is a better shape of the pyramid. There are more people in it ready to do something and fewer people ready merely to push papers around. So the shape of the pyramid is, to my mind, an important thing.

Another general reform, of course, is that wherever there is a committee, it should be replaced by a single man. Committees are a pest; they are a nuisance; they are altogether something to be put down by rat poison or by whatever means may occur. In the Christian Rules of Conduct known as the Ten Commandments, familiar perhaps to many people who even are not Christians and apt to be forgotten by many people who are, there are a number of rules saying, "Thou shalt not commit murder", "thou shalt not commit adultery" and so on. It rested with my wife to introduce the Eleventh Commandment added to the other ten and this was at a time when I had been serving on many committees and the Eleventh Commandment read: "Thou shalt not commit". And so I offer the Eleventh Commandment for careful consideration by people in India the rule "thou shalt not commit."

Sans Sub-committee

If there is a job to be done, detail someone to do it, do not form another committee and do not let that form a whole series of sub-committees, working parties and all the rest of the rabble. Keep the thing down to something that is workable. How long does it take to receive an intelligent reply because some government departments reply with a postcard and say, "the matter you have raised is under consideration." That is a lie, it is not under consideration, nobody is taking the slightest notice of it and no one could care less about what you have proposed or put forward. So let us wash out these obvious lies and come to the actual time it takes to receive an intelligent reply from a department. If the delay is considerable, and in some countries it would be, it is not because the point is being discussed in solemn conclave by wise and good men who are wrestling with the problem. Nor is it because the department is overwhelmed with the business because we must remember, after all, that it would take us as long to do the work next month as it would do this month. It is just the same thing. You postpone the decision, you are not postponing the amount of work to be done. The delay is due above all to overstaffing and bad organisation. But what is our remedy? Now, of course, the obvious remedy at the moment is for every one in India to acquire and read and digest and memorise works published by myself in conjunction with a friend of mine in Bombay—one of them produced a few days ago called 'The Realities in Management'—and this is obviously the first step but it is not the sole sort of thing that we should indulge in.

Use of Television

And one idea that often occurs to me, I think, that we might make better use of television and radio. Why should we not have radio question time each evening at the same hour. We might ask, for example, why have I received no reply to my application of such a date and the department would be invited to reply and explain why there was a delay and thus put the idle official into the witness-box. We use television and radio for entertainment. Is not it the time that we put them to some practical use?

I began with the plea for decentralisation that a less centralised government would give better service to the individual but decentralisation should have another and possibly more important result. If the Central Government were relieved of all responsibility for matters of mainly local interest, it would have time to consider at length and at leisure the matters which are of national and international concern. Many legislators today are appalingly overworked, over-burdened, with a whole stream of necessary or less necessary legislation. They are quite unable to deal with the business that is laid before them. While time is wasted on nonsense, there are matters of moment deferred from one session to the next. Many decisions are taken on proposals which have been hardly discussed-and that by the way is how Britain came to adopt the metric system. I am sure many people have wondered why Britain after sticking to 12 pence in the shilling for centuries, when every one else was playing with decimals, finally chose to adopt the decimal system at more or less the exact moment when decimals have obviously become obsolete. I am sure every one here realises that this is the world of the computer and no computer in the world has any interest in the decimals. It is a serious thought there when you think that decimals were invented by the Romans because they were obsessed with the number 10 and they got to the number because they miscounted their fingers. The fingers are actually 8 as any Indian would know but the

Romans thought it was 10 and they got obsessed with the number 10, and this is the background of decimals which were wished on us by the French Revolution. Now, we have this beautiful situation when the whole lot is obviously washed out as obsolete and that is the moment when Britain chooses to decimalise its coinage. I do not know whether this is tragic or funny but I leave it to you to decide. I may say and remind you that the sacred number in India is, of course, 8 and this comes by counting the fingers right and realising that the thumbs are not fingers. That brings you to 8 and 8 is the sacred number, of course, in India by tradition. It is a better number than 10 any way and it is not quite as good a number as 12.

Lot of Nonsense

Be that as it may, an awful lot of nonsense comes in and it is the result of over-centralisation, bad organisation, the over work which must result and the haste with which the work is so often finally bungled. Over-centralisation means a congestion of business at the centre and this is a disease from which many countries are suffering. There is a current and growing revolt against the present type of democratic and more or less socialist government. Politicians, I think, are none too popular at the present time. Perhaps the most extraordinary feature of the present age is the contrast between our technical progress and our political stagnation. There are no new ideas seemingly in politics and the practice so far from progressing is obviously slipping back so that the word 'stagnation' is an understatement. We have forgotten seemingly the earliest lessons. We are taught, as for example, a very early lesson in history which reads: never pay blackmail to any one. That is a perfectly good precept which earlier people learnt at earlier period of history. It is still a good principle and one to be remembered when the next case of hijacking comes to our notice. Never pay blackmail to any one and we stick to that and we might say that if we do that least we are not slipping backward but we still lack progress and our problem at the moment seems to be not one of progress but one of survival.

Most Efficient

Once I tried to discover which is the most efficient country in the world and I set a sort of competition in which countries were judged on a purely arithmetic test, the figures being provided by their own returns made each year to the United Nations. Of course, a test of efficiency excludes many other forms of excellence, I was not testing musical or poetic achievement. I was testing efficiency in administration and that can be measured. It can be measured by life expectation, by crime statistics, by the number of traffic accidents, by the number of people in prison, by the number of policemen in relation to the population, the number of days lost by industrial disputes. All these add up to a picture of efficiency or otherwise and I awarded the prize finally on, I repeat, arithmetic grounds, the first prize to the Netherlands and I told this afterwards to Prince Bernhard who started with surprise. He could not imagine that the other countries could be less efficient than his. But they were and the second country was Finland judged by whatever test I was able to deploy. I think that the awardage here of such an award would be rather a good idea and I think that each year it might be rather good to have a wooden spoon or some other body prize awarded to the country that comes out least efficient of the lot. If some countries would like to do some work in order to gain the top, others might at least do some work to avoid being at the bottom.

I have bored you sick and I think the least I can do is to explain to you why I am stopping at this point. Well, I am stopping because of an experience of only last year and the experience came from Brussels. In Brussels, particularly, every one you meet is an ambassador. This is the common sort of occupation in Brussels and you can assume any one you meet is an ambassador till you hear otherwise. One such ambassador in Brussels was told one day that on the following Tuesday he will have a speech to make to the Chamber of Commerce, the Rotary Club or some other body of opinion. He did what any great man does in the circumstances. He sent for a junior member of his staff and said, "I have a speech to make on Tuesday afternoon, write for me the speech," and the youngman, well trained, said, "Your Excellency, how long should the speech be?" And the ambassador said, "The speech should last one hour". On Tuesday morning the young man came back and presented the ambassador with a typed script and said, "Your Excellency, here is your speech for this afternoon's meeting." And the ambassador put it in his pocket and went off to his meeting where the speech lasted two hours leaving both the speaker and the audience exhausted. The ambassador came back to his embassy in rather a bad mood. He sent for that young man and he said to him. "And what do you mean by giving me a two-hour speech when I told you to provide me with a speech for one hour." The young man, white-faced and trembling, said, "Your Excellency, it is a one hour speech, I gave you two copies."

CHAPTER

10 Reforming Indian Bureaucracy

Reform measures are to be tailored to the Indian circumstances, Indian ambience, Indian culture and the Indian ethos. Secondly, the reform inputs need to have a holistic perspective. Segmentary approaches are bound to falter.

Public Point of View

For public, government is a employer. Government of India is one of the best employers in the world. Government jobs have security even after retirement. To discourage craze for government jobs, private employment should also have pension system. Secondly, educational system may be made vocation oriented rather than white collar job oriented as it is at present. Government employees should be accountable for inefficient transport system, frequent power cuts and water shortages. At some stage, they should be held liable in terms of pecuniary penalty or fine for suffering or inconvenience caused to public or clients. The government employees on the seat should be held personally liable for their negligence over and above permissible limit of error or negligence. A stringent view should be taken against late-comers on duty. Delay in decision making should be made punishable. They should be given exemplary punishment for corruption and for amassing property beyond their known or disclosed sources of income. In government, commission should be punishable as much as there are no citizens' charters. Modern public grievances redressal machineries set up are quite ineffective. Their decisions don't percolate down to the public.

From Technology View-point

Technology can be harnessed to provide efficient administration through use of computers, fax, electronic typewriters, xerox, video-conferencing, electronic devices for overseeing security measures and punctuality etc. India is the super-power in the field of Information Technology yet it is not being properly used in India. The I.T. companies work mostly for the western clients. It has been demonstrated that use of computers has checked corruption in railway reservation and these have been successfully used for reducing delays by way of on-line revision of draft letters and by providing readymade storage facilities. At least, the officers have become out of clutches of lower machinery of clerks and others. It is high time that traditional senior bureaucrats including political executives should use the modern devices more freely and frequently. Super computers can be used to tackle large examinations, compilation of income tax details, collection of tax, admission in schools, storage and issuance of millions of land records in rural India, fixing of court cases etc.

From Judiciary's View

The Judiciary in India feels that the bureaucracy in India works arbitrarily and capriciously. They work under pressure from their bosses. Therefore, they give unrestricted stay orders, injunctions and sometime pass strictures against government servants and even hold them liable for contempt of court. As executive is not discharging its due role, the judiciary has walked in to protect public interest through Public Interest Litigation (PIL). The government cases are not being prosecuted properly by government lawyers. The Judiciary also gets raw deal from the executives. Therefore, the judiciary should also show its powers.

From Legislatures or Politicians' Point of View

The legislatures complain that the proposals for bills are not forwarded by the executive in time. The debates in Parliament and State legislatures are not given due attention to.

The sub-committee of the Legislatures are not attended with due seriousness by officials and due follow up action is not taken by the executive. On the other hand, grassroot level politician is very much aggrieved against the administration because they don't pay proper heed to them or provide solution to their grievances, of public or on behalf of public. The senior bureaucrats live in ivory towers and street level bureaucrats or inspectors are drowned in corruption. There is no machinery for redressal of their grievances. Now, the panchayats have taken over most of the grassroots bureaucracy. There is some satisfaction among the grassroot politicians. But they do not have patience. They want to dabble at every level. Now, they are not able to dabble with panchayat administration as everything is as per decentralised way of working through committee system or passing the resolutions. Thus, the politicians remain an unsatisfied lot and therefore they find heaven in interfering in transfers and postings of staff and officers. The bureaucracy provided administrative guidance to business and industry. Talented young persons have been joining the services but their performance is not up to the expected level.

View of Bureaucracy Regarding Reforms

The senior bureaucrats feel that they have virtually no control over their juniors due to rampant interference by their political masters. They are the isolated ones. They are being asked to perform without resources being placed at their disposal. They do not get salaries as compared to the ICS during pre-independence days and as compared to their counterparts in private sector. They do not get perquisites as compared to persons in private sector or even a portion of what judges of High Courts get or even in comparison with members of legislatures. They are not being duly compensated for their round the clock duties. They are not compensated for their merits too.

The lower level bureaucrats blame their senior colleagues and also the government for inadequate compensation. They have no facilities for their children's education, their treatment and treatment of their families. They have to go from pillar to post for depositing their electricity bills and arrange for ration of their families. The senior bosses don't listen to their suggestions. They are virtually alienated by the organisation. They are not being provided transport facilities to come to office and leave the office late after office hours. The lower level functionaries in bureaucracy have lot of grudge against the panchayat and municipal representatives who are less educated as compared to them. The police in bureaucracy always complains of unwarranted interference by the politicians in their day to day functioning. The lower level functionaries also seriously complain of violent behaviour of public with them while they are in office. They also complain of draining out of precious government resources for the personal gains or interests of the politicians in power i.e ministers and senior bureaucrats in the name of VIP visits or VIP arrangements.

Thus, bureaucracy is generally not prepared for reforms. An imposed agenda of reform on conscious bureaucracy cannot be readily successful. Thus, the problem is quite complicated.

International Scenario

The World Bank implemented a number of civil service reform projects—seventy-six of them in developing countries. The result was not good. There was no discernible reduction in the wage bill, there was no efficiency gain either. Industrialised countries with civil service reform have been more rewarding. While the reforms in New Zealand and the U.K. are of transformative nature, those in Japan and Singapore have been incremental. In Singapore, after the British rule for 140 years, the corrupt Singapore Civil Service was converted into a efficient civil service by reduction of 27,000 posts and by transferring many government jobs to the private sector. The bureaucracy of Japan built up Japan from the debris of the war, to the third highest economic power in the democratic world.

The experience is some join 'career service' for the status and prestige it confers on them, which compensate for the not very competitive salary. The USSR fell because the political leadership could not control it once the bureaucracy got involved closely and directly in production, commercial and trading activities.

The expenditure on bureaucracy in USA is of high order in percentage terms too.

In pre-reform Brazil, the economic crisis that drained away the resources of the State, also drained its authority and the administration was no longer in position to check smuggling and evasion of regulations. In Ghana, before the reforms, the State was unable to mobilise resources for funding essential expenditure; it could not even deliver basic health and education services.

Approach to Reforms

If immediate steps are not taken to reform the bureaucracy in India, the expenditure on it will have steep rise. It will be busy to manage itself always. And in the long run, it will not be able to run its normal sovereign functions like maintenance of law and order, regulation and land management. Thus, the civil service in India is to be geared up to play a proactive role in the society.

1. *Comprehensive Institutional Approach*. The comprehensive approach seeks to correct patrimonial distortions, the goal being to create capacity in the civil service both in terms of governance and quality of service delivery. It seeks to

(a) clear the way for growth: this calls for a consensual public/private balance in terms of which the state has responsibility for sovereign functions, provision of physical and social infrastructure and creating an enabling environment for the private sector to develop;
(b) seek effective popular participation in the decision making process;
(c) devolve and decentralize functions and power to the local authorities so as to build synergy and partnership between the central and the local/traditional governmental institutions;
(d) strengthen the civil society; and
(e) design system of public sector performance measurement on four concepts – economy, efficiency, effectiveness and quality of service.

2. *The Enclave Approach*. Reform is limited to building and reinforcing the organization, managerial and technical capacity

of the existing institutions to improve their performance and productivity.

3. *The Hybrid Approach or Middle Path Approach.* In this approach, comprehensive component is bottom-up instead of top down. It takes into consideration the whole of economy.

Weaknesses or Inadequacies of the Bureaucracy

1. Bureaucracy's instrumental role is often subordinated and it emerges as an end in itself.
2. The gap between the administration and the citizen is widening. Bureaucracy has been somewhat insensitive to the needs of the latter and has lost credibility.
3. Bureaucracy has become a slow moving and dull witted giant.
4. Frequent confrontations between several levels of bureaucracy like police vs civil services or teachers vs civil service, bureaucrats vs technocrats paralyse the entire machinery.
5. The public services have become prisoners of their own procedures and precedents. Negative thinking appears to prevail. This leads to inaction rationalized in various ways.
6. The public services are proving increasingly inadequate to the new tasks and challenges. Even in the maintenance of law and order, bureaucracy often finds itself ineffective. In the economic field, its performance has generally been poor. It tries to cure today's ills with yesterday's remedies.
7. The generalist tradition still dominates. On the contrary, need of the day is specialization.
8. Bureaucrats generally take decisions by hunches and intuitions and not by trained and deep insights.

Remedies

(i) A more strategic result oriented (efficiency, effectiveness and service quality) orientation to decision making.

(ii) Focussing attention on the matching of authority and responsibility as a key to improving performance, including mechanism of explicit performance.

(iii) Greater accountability and transparency through requirement to report on results and their full costs.

(iv) Scrapping nexus of bureaucrats, politicians and criminals leading not only to a breakdown of the total system but also to a sense of cynicism amongst the citizenry.

(v) Adopting of innovations and evolving suitable mechanism to eliminate corruption at both political and administrative levels and strengthen citizens' grievance redressal system.

(vi) Improving the system of delivery at the cutting edge of administration by replacing the existing archaic bureaucratic procedure by absorbing some appropriate precepts inherent in the philosophy of New Public Management.

(vii) Making improvements in the working atmosphere of the government institutions and officers to reflect a new work culture and a changed administrative behaviour incorporating the principles of transparency, responsiveness, accountability, participative and citizen friendly management i.e. fostering of new work culture within bureaucracy.

(viii) Greater representation of the middle class at the highest echelons of bureaucracy and the underprivileged sections of the community.

(ix) Re-examination and change of administrative procedures lessening number of laws and Acts with a view to simplify and rationalise them.

(x) Political will for reforms dissociated from short run political advantages and social discipline.

(xi) Task and performance oriented training programmes: Multiple point training to fight obsolescence.

(xii) Performance audit for promotion.

(xiii) Open entry for stipulated tasks at certain levels.

(xiv) Creating competitive environment within and between public service organizations.

(xv) Flexibility to explore alternatives to direct public provision. which might provide more cost effective policy outcomes.

(xvi) Replacement of highly centralised organisational structures with decentralised management integrating with the new 'Panchayati raj' and municipal institutions, where decisions on resource allocation and service allocation and service delivery are taken close to the point of delivery.

Concretising the Performance of the Indian Bureaucracy

An attempt can be made to concretise the present status of the Indian bureaucracy as per assigned factors as follows:

(i) *Macro system.* The macro system is averse to good bureaucratic rule. There is lot of pressure from lower ranks to violate rules or procedures, peers, friends and families exert pressure to earn money at whatever costs generally and the political executives have to run their political parties for which money is required. To them, party interest is uppermost. Thus, the poor bureaucrat is hapless. He cannot withstand all these pressures unless he is made of strong will or is a yogi or a superman. But some bureaucrats around 20% have done so. Therefore, we can assign 'inadequate' category to this factor i.e. 2 marks.

(ii) *Leadership.* Leadership is cracking down. The staff or officers' unions and associations exert pressures from lower ranks whereas the political executives support the unions or associations for their political gains. A demoralised bureaucrat thus resorts to easy tactics and become part of the system. The lower level bureaucrats are not prepared to accept his leadership by virtue of his post or position as because he had misused the same in the past for his personal gains. Thus, two things are left for him to command obedience. First is his technical or specialised knowledge or skill and second is his conduct in front of his colleagues and the subordinates. Some of the bureaucrats, around 4%, have shown leadership as they are free from vices or corruption and are professionally competent. The Department or organization cannot run properly without their contribution. Most of the bureaucrats are highly educated and are well informed. Therefore, even the most conscious employees or subordinates owe their allegiance or loyalty to them. Thus, this factor can be given 'So-So' category with strength 4 i.e. total marks 10.

(iii) *Organizational capacity.* The organizational strength though, cracking down under corruption, favouritism or nepotism, yet the bureaucratic system is only a stable system in the Indian polity and change of government at the Centre or in the States does not destabilize the running of government.

Thus, we can fix following grading to the sub-components:

		Grade	Marks
(a)	Competent personnel (except those who are recruited on the basis of ulterior motives)	8	8
(b)	Appraisal System	8	2.4
(c)	Internal Coordination & MIS	8	1.6
(d)	Transfer, Recruitment, posting & promotion policy	4	2.0
	Total marks assigned		14.0

(iv) *Financial strength.* The financial strength is bad at present. Only the Central Government is financially sound. State Governments and local bodies, who have most of the bureaucracy, do not have funds even to pay off salaries. As Central Government is financially sound which has about 40% of the employees, we may take this factor in the 'So-So' category and assign 8 marks as this factor has 20% weightage.

(v) *Quality of service.* Quality of service is good but it becomes of little use because it is received after its efficacy or usefulness is over. The measure of progress and prosperity of a country can be measured against promptness of service. A work is done in USA and Japan within two hours (for example telephone connection). The same is done within two weeks in China, which is done in India in two months. In least developed countries (LDCs) like African countries, it is done in two years. One should be happy, if it is done at all because either they don't have resources and even if they have resources, they don't have technical competence to use those resources.

Thus, India suffers a lot due to bureaucratic delay. Let us assign strength to the sub-components;

(a)	Training, retraining & research (it is improving gradually and is adequate)	4
(b)	Public Information System 'So So'	2
(c)	Clients' satisfaction 'very inadequate or poor'	1
	Total Marks	7

(vi) *Technological innovation.* There is resistance from the old school and political executive to innovations yet it is taking place. Computers have already occupied all offices in India.

We can thus, give 'So So' weightage to this factor and can rate it as 2.

Summarising above, we arrive at the total Performance of the Indian Bureaucracy as follows;

$$IB\ (T) = 2 + 10 + 14 + 8 + 7 + 2 = 43\%.$$

Thus, the performance of the Indian bureaucracy is even less than 50% but is above 'So-So' category. Bureaucracy thus requires a lot of improvement in all fields.

Conclusion

No amount of planning or conceptualisation can help implementing bureaucratic reforms unless there is a strong 'political will' conveyed through political statesmanship and has to start with willing cooperation from the radical elements in the bureaucracy who are not less devoted to the public cause and public welfare. If the bureaucratic reforms are implemented in proper spirit and direction, the dream of 'welfare of all' can be achieved by all governments in the world irrespective of their ideologies.

CHAPTER 11 Why India Needs a Strong and Impartial Civil Service?

—M.N. Buch

India is a federal republic under Article 1 of the Constitution, as also Article 246 read with the Seventh Schedule of the Constitution, which gives the legislative jurisdiction of Parliament and State Legislatures. Nevertheless, this federation has strong unitary features, with residuary powers of legislation vesting in the federal Parliament. In Germany and the United States, residuary powers vest in the Lands and the States. Many people try and explain away the strong unitary features by referring to the Government of India Act, 1935, which has been substantially carried forward by the Constitution. They thereby forget the famous speech made by the late Sardar Vallabhbhai Patel in the Constituent Assembly when he pleaded for the inclusion of articles creating the All India Services in the Constitution.

Sardar Patel reasoned that India, because of its diversity, its multiple languages and ethnicity, its melange of religions and races and its past history had strong centrifugal forces which, unless countered, could lead to the break up of the Union. He, therefore, advocated the creation of countervailing centripetal forces, which could both create a strain of national unity and hold the Union together when under pressure from breakaway forces. Our Constitution, therefore, has a number of such unifying structures built into it. The states, within Article 1 and List 2 of the Seventh Schedule, enjoy a degree of sovereignty because they have exclusive areas of legislative competence. However, the

Governor of each state is appointed by the President under Article 155 of the Constitution. Under Article 156, he holds office during the pleasure of the President and is accountable only to him. This accountability achieves special significance under Article 356 of the Constitution, when it is the Governor who advises whether or not there is a failure of constitutional machinery in the state over which he presides.

Another unifying force is the judiciary. There is a hierarchical link between the courts ranging from the lowest court of civil judge class II and magistrate II class, as also the executive magistracy, going all the way up through the district and sessions court, High Courts to the Supreme Court. There is no separate federal and state judiciary and any judge can try any case both under state laws and under federal laws. In the United States, the state judiciary is completely separate from the federal judiciary and each tries cases respectively under state and federal laws. It is only at the level of the Supreme Court that both judicial streams come together. The Indian system ensures uniformity of justice and the creation of unifying forces within the Union.

The Armed Forces, the Comptroller and Auditor General and other similar institutions are also a binding force. However, the uniqueness of the Indian Constitution lies in Article 312, which creates the All India Services, which man the senior posts in both state and federal governments. We do not know of any other federation in which a civil service holds posts under both types of government, though the ultimate cadre controlling authority is the union government. Sardar Patel argued very strongly and vehemently, to the extent of threatening to quit if his proposal was not accepted that India needs a strong and independent civil service which, while faithfully carrying out the policy laid down by the elected representatives, would nevertheless be impartial in implementation and fearless in rendering advice because of the security of service that it enjoyed. It is in this context that the Indian Administrative Service, the Indian Police Service and later the Indian Forest Service has been created.

What is the job of a civil servant? Under Articles 53 and 154 of the Constitution, the civil services help the President or Governor to exercise the executive powers of the state. Because the President or Governor is required to exercise such power only on the aid and advice of his council of ministers under Article 74 and 163 of the Constitution, in effect the civil services are there to exercise executive power as directed by the ministers. About this there is no doubt in anyone's mind. Trouble arises when the ministers decide to exercise the executive power themselves and the civil servants are reduced to the level of clerks. The ministers will naturally exercise their powers in a partisan manner because they have a political constituency which they have to please. Democratic government under a system of laws, however, requires that laws and rules are administered without prejudice and without showing undue favour to anyone. There can be no partisan application of laws, rules or policy. That is why we have strong civil services which are, theoretically, accountable to the law for its application and to the ministers for their conduct and their impartial functioning. However, as things have now developed, the civil services are being decreasingly rendered ineffective and politicians have begun to whimsically apply policy and to implement it in a highly partisan manner.

Under normal circumstances, such a situation leads to a regime of favouritism and disfavour. Unless a citizen falls in line with the political requirements of the politicians temporarily in power, he cannot expect a fair deal from the state. Therefore, in order to curry favour he bends over backward to please the politicians. Since nothing pleases the politicians more than a hefty bribe, the next phase is the introduction of a regime of corruption in addition to a regime of favouritism.

However, the worst effect of the emasculation of the civil services is felt during an emergency, whether it be a natural or man-made calamity or it be a law and order situation. The law is clear. If there is a breach of peace, violation of law or a situation of collective violence, the Code of Criminal Procedure and the Police Act enjoin the executive magistracy and the police to take preventive action, including the arrest of the likely trouble makers, corrective action such as deployment of adequate police force and coercive action, which includes use of even lethal force to disperse unlawful assemblies. This has to be followed by punitive action in which perpetrators of crime are arrested and arraigned before a court of law. The executive magistracy and the police are not to seek orders from anyone because they derive their powers from the law and not from the ministers. Similarly in a calamity the lowest executive officer is supposed to take immediate remedial measures and neither budgetary constraints nor issues of jurisdiction should hinder him. However, neither the executive magistracy nor the police actually follow the law because they await orders from above in an act of abdication of their lawful functions.

Two of the most shameful examples of the above are the 1984 anti-Sikh riots and the 2002 Gujarat riots. In 1984 after the assassination of Mrs. Indira Gandhi, the police, especially the Delhi Police, stood by as a mere spectator whilst rampaging mobs slaughtered thousands of Sikhs. Whether in exercise of the right of private defence or in performance of his duties under the Code of Criminal Procedure and the Police Act, every single policeman from constable upwards is required to intervene the minute he sees an offence being committed. Murder is the most heinous offence of all in the Indian legal lexicon. Despite this, the police did absolutely nothing (the American vulgarism, Sweet Fanny Adam, is the expression which comes to mind) and stood by watching the fun. No policeman was punished for this gross dereliction of duty.

In 2002 when communal riots wrecked Gujarat, one found a very similar administrative paralysis, with a few honorable exceptions. The Police Commissioner of Ahmedabad permitted two ministers to take over his control room and ensure police inaction for three days. In Vadodara, the Police Commissioner did not activate his force for a number of days. The honorable exceptions were the Collectors and SSP of Bharuch, Junagadh, Bhavnagar and Kutch. They were all transferred for their pains, without arousing any great public protest. It must be understood that the inaction of the executive magistracy and the police has resulted in thousands of innocents being killed, which is a heavy price paid for establishing political supremacy over the executive even in the matter of implementation of laws.

A regime of favouritism coupled with a regime of corruption, in which the bureaucrats are abused morning, noon and night as servants of red-tape, obstructers of development, bumbling, officious nincompoops, has totally demoralized the civil services. They have become partisan, ineffective and corrupt. The partisanship has even reduced their efficacy as a binding force of our nation. This has degraded the administration to such an extent that one wonders if there is any administration left at all.

The civil services must follow the rules and implement them. If the rules hinder development, let the policy makers, i.e, the elected representatives, change the rules. But for heaven's sake do not give the civil servants the discretion to decide whether or not they will implement policy, the law and the rules. That opens the twin gates of inefficiency and corruption. India must insist on a restoration of the civil services of a type envisaged by Sardar Patel so that each government servant does his duty and there is never a repetition of Gujarat.

CHAPTER

12 Role of Civil Service—Then and Now

—P.C. Alexander

We take many things for granted in our country; our democratic system is one of them. But if in today's world of life presidents, one party elections and managed press, India retains its democratic institutions in full vigour and health, we owe this largely to Jawaharlal Nehru who not only laid the foundations for our democratic administration but also trained a whole nation in the practice of democracy.

I thought it would be appropriate that I talk to you today on the "Role of Civil Service—Then and Now". As one who started civil service career immediately after our country's independence, I can speak with direct knowledge on the evolution of the role of civil service over the last three and a half decades. I can also claim to speak with some special knowledge of the decision making processes at different levels in the civil service at the Central Government as I had the good fortune of serving at every level of civil service at the Centre—Under Secretary, Deputy Secretary, Joint Secretary, Head of a Department, Additional Secretary, Secretary of a Department, Secretary of a Ministry and now Principal Secretary. Since I was one of those selected for the Central Pool of service in the old days, the normal rules of tenure did not apply in my case and thus I could get the unique

---

Text of a talk delivered on November 14, 1983, at the Lal Bahadur Shastri National Academy of Administration, Mussoorie.

opportunity of participating in the process of decision making at all levels of civil service in Delhi.

Deterioration in Standards?

At the very outset, I would like to deal with the general allegation that there has been serious deterioration in standards or quality in the present-day civil service compared with the civil service in the pre-independence days or the early days of our independence. This allegation about deterioration in standards is, of course, made not about the civil service only but about every sector of activity in India. I think it is part of our national trait to decry always the present and eulogise the past. Older people in our country are fond of believing that things were neat and good in their days. The younger generation of course is not convinced that things were all that good or great in the past. I will attribute this complex to the inability of the older generation to understand the changes that have taken place in the last three or four decades and to make the necessary mental adjustments. The people in the West have to a large extent succeeded in making these adjustments, but we, in this part of the world, have yet to make an honest effort at understanding the fundamental changes that have taken place in the last few decades. People of my generation were closer to our parents' generation than our children are to us in value systems and general approach to life. We inherited with ease and pride the value systems of our parents and flattered our older generation by imitating them. But the world during the last few decades has changed radically, and an altogether new generation has grown up which does not take anything as good or great merely because it is old. We are now living in the age of instant communications, computers, space-shuttles and guided missiles and the world is no longer the same it was before. The world has moved much more fundamentally in the last 40 years than it did in the previous 200 years. If both the old and the new generations make a sincere effort in understanding the implications and importance of these changes, there will be better understanding of each other and less complaints about deterioration in standards or quality.

When people speak of deterioration in standards, the dimension of numbers is generally highlighted. We start with the assumption that large numbers mean lower standards. But we should not forget that if there are large numbers in civil service today, it is because of the need for a larger civil service and also because larger numbers have become eligible to enter the civil service. Higher education has now become accessible to classes and communities which never had such opportunities for generations in the past, and as more people get the benefits of education more become qualified for civil service as well.

If only half a dozen people used to be selected in a year to the Indian Civil Service in the years before independence, the base for selection was also very small. Today if 120 or 150 are selected to the IAS every year, we should also remember that this selection is made from over 50,000 candidates who take the preliminary examinations. There were many brilliant men in the old civil service, but we should not come to the conclusion that all those who entered the civil service were necessarily the very cream of the educational system then. In the days when examinations for civil service were held in England, only those who could afford the expenses of travel to England could take such examination. Some of the very best in universities were financially very poor and were, therefore, not able to take the examinations. Numbers by themselves do not make any difference in standards. Take the case of university education. In my batch of B.A. (Hons)-M.A. in my university there were only six of us. From a small base of those who passed the intermediate examination, only six were eligible for admission to this course. Today the number for the same course in my university may be a few hundreds. Can I claim that because I belonged to a small group of six, my university degree was necessarily better in quality than that of those now who take their examination in large numbers? The relevant point is the size of the base for selection. I have mentioned the above arguments to rebut the general complaint about deterioration in standards in the new generation of civil servants and also to point out the fallacy that there is a correlation between standards and numbers. While I maintain my position on these two counts, I must confess that I am getting uneasy about certain distressing trends in the civil service today. As an old member of the service it is my duty to alert you about the danger signals that I see now; I shall come back to this later in my talk.

Comparison between the Civil Service in Pre-independence Days and now

Any comparison between the role of civil service in pre-independent India and that in current times is somewhat unfair because of the vastly different nature of the responsibilities and duties of civil servants then and now. The civil service in pre-independence days was a law and order and revenue-oriented service. The civil service today is a development-oriented service. The skills required for civil service in pre-independence days were the relatively simple skills of administration. Today the civil servant has to cope with the whole range of development problems and has THEREFORE to acquire considerable degree of knowledge and skills in development administration. Negotiations for trade agreements, participation in international discussions in forums like UNCTAD, IMF, World Bank, etc. export promotion, management of Public Sector Undertakings, planning and management of development programmes, family planning programmes and a variety of other tasks which the civil service of today has to discharge are quite new and highly complex demanding great versatility and competence on the part of the officers.

Another most important difference between the civil service then and now is that today the civil servant has to work within the parameters of a full-fledged democracy which means a vigilant press, an alert public and watchful legislatures. The civil servants of pre-independence days were responsible only to executives who were mainly super civil servants nominated by the Viceroys or the Governors and who had no accountability to the people. In a democratic system of government the civil servant is really the servant of the people whose will is exercised through the elected representatives of the people. The whole concept of administration is different from what it was before. Many do not realise the significance of the change because the old designations and titles continue—Sub-Collector, Collector, Joint Secretary, Secretary, etc.

Civil Service and the Political Executive

In a parliamentary system of government there can be no doubt as to who is responsible for governing the country; it is undoubtedly the political executive responsible to the elected legislature. The Secretary in a Ministry or the Head of a Department exercises powers only on behalf of the political executive and subject to the policies and guidelines laid down by it. This may appear to be a difficult system to operate, particularly in a country which does not have a long history of political executives exercising power, but thanks to the great traditions built up in the early years of our country's independence, the system has worked smoothly and satisfactorily.

It is difficult to define as to what should be the ideal relationship between a Minister and his senior civil servant. In an ideal relationship, the Minister should have full confidence in the competence and objectivity of his Secretary and the Secretary in turn should have respect in the judgement of the Minister.

It is not necessary that in a parliamentary system of government the Minister concerned should be a great expert in the subject he handles. We have read in books on British parliamentary practice that there have been very successful Chancellors of the Exchequer who could not even understand the place of a decimal point in a budget document. What is important is that the Minister should have sound judgement and the correct instincts to know what is in the ultimate interests of the people. The Minister should bring to the tasks of administration the concerns and responsibilities he has to the people who have elected him. He applies his judgement on various issues on the basis of the mandate he carries, and the public for all the actions of the civil servants who work under him.

The main duty of the civil servant is to present before the Minister clear options for a decision. In this task he should follow the highest standards of objectivity without being influenced by his individual views or preferences.

It will, no doubt, be very advantageous if a Minister combines in himself political strength with expertise on the subject he handles. It was indeed our good fortune that in the early years of independence we had some senior Ministers belonging to this rare category. The names of Jawaharlal Nehru, Vallabhbhai Patel, Govind Ballabh Pant and C. Rajagopalachari come to my mind in this connection. Take the case of Panditji as Minister for External Affairs for 18 years. When we started our career as an independent nation we did not have even a handful of people who had experience in diplomacy or even great knowledge on foreign affairs. Panditji literally trained the hard core of our foreign service officers and laid down the basic ground rules for our foreign relations which remain valid even these days. I have heard from people who had worked directly under him that as and when cables and messages from our missions abroad or foreign leaders reached his table, he used to dictate the replies to them and even indicate the level at which a reply should go. I have been told that he even dictated the briefs for the important delegations which were to attend international meetings or to take part in bilateral negotiations unaided by any notes or background papers from the Secretariat. He was indeed a one-man training centre for the first generation of foreign service officers and diplomats in our country. Similarly, we had stalwarts like Vallabhbhai Patel and Govind Ballabh Pant in the Ministry of Home Affairs whose administrative abilities and sound political sense commanded the admiration of all those who worked under them.

We were equally fortunate in the early days of independence to have another category of Ministers who, though not having much political standing of their own, commanded respect from the civil service as well as Parliament by their professional competence and knowledge of the subjects handled by them. The names of Gopalaswamy Iyengar, John Mathai, T.T. Krishnamachari and C.D. Deshmukh come to my mind in this connection.

There was a third group of Ministers in the early days of independence. Some of them had spent 14-18 years in British jails, and their services for the country's freedom more than compensated for any inadequacies in their experience in administration.

In a parliamentary democracy the civil servant has to accept the unquestioned primacy of the political executive as the whole system functions on this principle. It is not for a civil servant to question the credentials or competence of a Minister. A question often asked is what a civil servant should do if he is compelled to act against his own conscience or against law. This is often a hypothetical question and I do not think that there will be many cases of civil servants being "compelled" to act against their conscience or against law. If however such situations arise in a civil servant's career, he should have the courage to stand up for law and honesty and to suffer the adverse consequences, if any, for taking such a stand.

Some Distressing Trends

The basic principle of civil service in a parliamentary democracy is its non-political character. But this should not mean that a civil servant should be devoid of political sensitivity or social consciousness. "Committed Civil Servant" is a much abused phrase these days. But what does it really mean? It does not mean commitment to a political party or a leader. It only means commitment to the tasks that have been entrusted to the civil servants. In fact, if there is no such commitment, the civil servant becomes a mere wage earner. In our system of administration the success of programmes like family planning, national rural employment programme, the integrated rural development programme, housing for Scheduled Castes and Scheduled Tribes, or supply of drinking water to rural areas can succeed only if the civil servants responsible for their implementation are really a motivated group and have genuine commitment and faith in what they are doing.

Unfortunately, there is a lamentable lack of involvement on the part of some officers in what they are doing. Administration without involvement becomes routine and ineffective. It will be a sad day for the civil service and indeed a sad day for development administration in our country if civil servants take their tasks in a routine way without involvement.

Another distressing trend in civil service which I have recently noticed is the creeping cynicism about the tasks one is called upon to do. I am told that even some new entrants to the civil service are falling victims to a tendency to be hypercritical and cynical about everything. There may be many things wrong or unpleasant in what we see around us. But if we senior civil servants, who have the major responsibility for ensuring that everything is done correctly and well, start blaming others for the mistakes and shortcomings that we see around us, we are being dishonest to ourselves. If the premier civil service of the country loses faith and conviction and indulges in cynical criticism of others, what can you expect from others at lower levels of responsibility? I can only remind the senior civil servants of the Biblical saying: "If the salt loses its savour wherewith shall it be salted?"

A new trend in civil service which has come up during the last three or four years is a tendency to dilute the responsibility for decision making. Even when there is no need to refer a file to another Ministry or officer for comments and views, many civil servants now indulge in the special art of pushing files vertically and horizontally or raising queries not directly relevant to the subject in an attempt to involve others also in the decision making exercise. Some civil servants seem to be trying to take "insurance cover" for protection from future enquiries by involving as many others as possible in the process of decision making. In spite of the sad experience of the recent Inquiry Commissions, my advice to the civil servants is to take decisions which they consider right and sound without bothering about the consequences of such decisions on a future date. If we have confidence in our own objectivity and integrity, we should not have any fear for taking decisions or recommending decisions based on such principles. There may be bona fide mistakes in the decisions, but what is important is the objectivity and integrity behind them.

Reluctance to meet the members of the public is another trend which I have noticed in recent years. In a political system like ours, where the Government's role has become very crucial in a wide range of activities which affect the life of the people, the civil servant should consider meeting members of the public as their sacrosanct duty.

CHAPTER 13

All-India Services: Decline, Debasement and Devastation

—P.S. Appu

A professionally competent and politically neutral bureaucracy is a sine qua non for the smooth and efficient functioning of a democratic polity. Thanks to the foresight and vision of the founding fathers, our Constitution provided the framework for a splendid administrative structure. The All India Services, particularly the IAS and the IPS, constitute the very core of India's administrative fabric. These Services owe their establishment to the vision and determination of Sardar Vallabhbhai Patel. He hoped that with the ironclad guarantees incorporated in the Constitution, the Services would resolutely stand by the Constitution and the law even under the most trying circumstances. He also expected that they would play a pivotal role in holding together a country of great disparities and diversity and provide a uniformly high standard of administration at the Centre and all the States. For some two decades the All India Services, by and large, functioned as envisaged by the founding fathers. Then the decline started, first slowly, and later at an accelerated pace. The nadir was reached in Gujarat in recent weeks. The IAS and IPS have been laid prostrate. The once superb administrative structure lies in ruins, reduced to a shambles. Evidently these

Services no longer serve the purpose for which they were established.

I shall describe the process of decline and the causes for the degeneration. I shall discuss at some length the developments in Bihar and then briefly deal with the country as a whole.

Bihar

It was our singular good fortune that a number of able leaders, who had a clear understanding of the tenets of democratic governance and could distinguish between right and wrong, became ministers both at the Centre and in the States when India became independent. Some of them had a hand in shaping the Constitution. They all had a clear understanding of the proper role of ministers and top civil servants in a parliamentary democracy. By and large, civil servants gave frank, fearless and well-considered advice. Ministers took decisions bearing in mind the advice that the civil servants gave. Where the Minister did not agree with the Secretary, the former would record his reasons and overrule the Secretary. However, such instances were few. It was well understood that the Minister was responsible for making policy, the civil servant's role being restricted to tendering advice. Implementation was the domain of civil servants and ministers seldom interfered with implementation. The system worked smoothly with reasonable efficiency. I had no personal experience of the functioning of the Central Government in those days. But I had the opportunity to watch from inside the working of the Bihar Administration. I shall briefly describe how that administration functioned in the decade of the 'fifties of the last century.

I joined the IAS in 1951 and I was allotted to the Bihar Cadre. After a few months' training in Delhi I reached Bihar in January 1952. During the next ten years I held charge of two sub-divisions, spent three years in the Home Department, first as Under Secretary and then as Deputy Secretary, working directly under the Chief Secretary. From 1958 I was Collector of Darbhanga for some two and a half years. During my first ten years in Bihar the state administration was in fine fettle, functioning smoothly and efficiently. That was the administration which the distinguished professor of Public Administration Paul Appleby assessed as one of the twelve best in the world. I witnessed the gradual decline of that administration during the period 1962-1970 when I worked as Secretary to Government, first in the Health Department and then in the Finance Department. From 1970 to 1975 I was on deputation to the Government of India. In August 1975 I returned to Bihar. The Administration had degenerated further when I was away in Delhi. My second spell lasted about three years. During that period I held in succession the posts of Finance Commissioner, Resource Commissioner and Chief Secretary. Despite my best efforts I did not succeed in making much improvement during my tenure as Chief Secretary. I left Bihar finally in 1978. During the next two decades Bihar acquired the reputation of being one of the worst administered in the country.

Period of Good Governance and Modest Progress

Bihar was a stronghold of the Indian National Congress before independence. After independence the Congress continued to be the dominant party and it ruled the state for two decades without break. Group rivalry rooted in caste conflict was a significant feature of the Congress party in Bihar before and after independence. The implacable antagonism between the two dominant upper castes of Bhumihars and Rajputs was at the core of the infighting in the Party. Chief Minister, Srikrishna Sinha, a Bhumihar, had wide support in the party cutting across caste lines. Next only to Rajendra Prasad, he was the tallest leader and he did not depend on other ministers and legislators for his survival. His rival, Anugrah Narayan Sinha, a Rajput, was decidedly number two in the Cabinet. He enjoyed wide support among Rajputs. A few leaders of other castes also supported him. But he was in no position to challenge the Chief Minister. Furthermore, both men had worked together for decades in the freedom struggle, and both had imbibed the values of the national movement. They respected each other and so they could carry on for a decade without rocking the boat too much.

L.P. Singh of the ICS was the Chief Secretary. He enjoyed the trust and confidence of both the Chief Minister and the Finance

Minister. Singh was a brilliant administrator, extremely hardworking and dedicated. He was an excellent team leader who had the knack of getting the best out of his team. The Chief Secretary was the nodal point of the administration. He was also the Secretary to the Council of Ministers. All important cases had to go to the Cabinet. The Chief Minister's approval had to be obtained through the Chief Secretary for including any item in the agenda for the cabinet meeting. The Rules of Executive Business framed under Art. 166 of the Constitution contained certain provisions calculated to ensure that every department would maintain a uniformly high standard. The first one was a rule laying down that certain cases which need not go to the cabinet, but were otherwise important, should be put up to the Chief Minister through the Chief Secretary after the minister had passed orders. The second one was a rule requiring the Secretary of the Department to submit to the Chief Secretary the files in which the Minister's orders were not in conformity with the law or the accepted policy of the Government. The Chief Secretary had also the power to call for any file suo motu and, where necessary, advise the Chief Minister to overrule the minister. I had seen a few cases in which the Chief Secretary intervened to get unusual orders reversed. Though some ministers resented the practice, they never protested. For the Chief Minister's preeminence was unchallenged. He was much more than first among equals. In later years when Chief Ministers lost their primacy, those very rules proved to be of no avail in reining in wayward ministers.

That was the state of affairs when Paul Appleby visited Bihar in the early nineteen fifties. He found the administration functioning as it should in a parliamentary democracy. The Chief Minister and his colleagues concerned themselves with policy, which was invariably decided on the free and frank advice of the Chief Secretary and his colleagues. Implementation was left entirely to the bureaucracy and ministers seldom interfered. I know from personal experience that even junior officers like Under Secretaries and Deputy Secretaries enjoyed complete freedom to express their views without any inhibition. So the actual practice approximated the ideal envisaged by Sardar Patel in his speech in the Constituent Assembly on October 10, 1949. The Sardar had said, "Today my Secretary can write a note opposed to my view. I have given that freedom to all my Secretaries. I have told them that if they do not give their honest opinion fearing that it will displease the minister, they should better go. I will find another Secretary." Though there were exceptions where civil servants behaved as sycophants, the majority functioned as expected by Sardar Patel. Unfortunately the idyllic state of affairs did not last long.

Both Srikrishna Sinha and Anugrah Narayan Sinha were old men in failing health. The followers of both the leaders strongly felt that the issue of succession should be settled when they were alive. In the General Election of 1957 the Congress was returned with a decisive majority. The followers of Anugrah Narayan Sinha persuaded him to challenge Srikrishna Sinha for the leadership of the Congress Party. The canvassing by the rival groups soon degenerated into a vicious campaign in which they resorted to all manner of foul means, including the promise of office and bribery. Srikrishna Sinha won by a handsome margin, but irreparable damage had been done to the political process in Bihar. The politics of consensus and conciliation gave way to the politics of confrontation and intrigue. The Chief Minister was obliged to fulfill the promises made on the eve of the contest. A number of supporters, including a few non-entities, were appointed Deputy Ministers. They had little power; yet, they soon started interfering in administration, particularly in postings and transfers. L.P. Singh had already joined the Central Government. M.S. Rao, also of the ICS, had succeeded him. Able, upright and experienced, Rao proved to be an efficient Chief Secretary. He did not, however, have the kind of close rapport that L.P. Singh had with the Chief Minister. Moreover, in his declining years Srikrishna Sinha came under the influence of a small coterie of self-seekers. Bihar's administration started to decline slowly. Yet, when the Chief Secretary or some other senior officer brought an improper decision to the Chief Minister's notice, he would intervene and set things right. I remember instances in which Sri Babu rebuked Deputy Ministers who tried to interfere with the power of the Heads of Departments, particularly in the matter of postings and transfers.

I left the Secretariat in the middle of 1958 and worked as Collector of Darbhanga till the end of 1960. Throughout my tenure as Collector I could discharge my duties without any interference by ministers, legislators and other public men. When the District Boards were superseded and put under the Collector's charge, a couple of Deputy Ministers tried to influence me in the postings and transfers of District Board doctors. I told them politely but firmly that I would not accede to their requests. That was the end of the matter.

I could also extend effective protection to upright officers who happened to displease powerful politicians. That was possible mainly because a man like Sri Babu was the Chief Minister. I shall narrate briefly two instances to prove this point. The Maharaja of Darbhanga owned two sugar mills in the district. There were two rival labour unions, one of the Congress and the other of the Socialist Party. The intense rivalry and bickering between the two unions often led to violence and breach of the peace. Both the Subdivisional Officer and the Deputy Superintendent of Police were upright men. I had assured them of my support as long as they acted firmly and impartially. When the local Congressmen failed in their efforts to influence the officers, the politicians started a vicious campaign against them. They complained to the Labour Minister and the Chief Minister. The Labour Minister visited Darbhanga and after looking into the matter told me that he felt that the SDO and DSP had been partial to the Socialist Union. He did not accept my assessment. The Congress leaders intensified their campaign against the officers. A few days later the Chief Minister came to Darbhanga. He looked grim and visibly angry. When we were alone in the Circuit House I asked him why he was angry and what had upset him. He said that it disturbed him that his young officers were favouring parties opposed to the Congress. I narrated the facts and requested him not to reach any conclusion without looking into the matter personally. Suddenly he became relaxed. The tension was gone. He laughed loudly and assured me that there was no question of his reaching a conclusion in haste. In due course, after thorough examination Government came to the conclusion that the officers had acted correctly.

There was a Union Deputy Minister who was rather self-opinionated and was also a bully. He would visit his constituency three or four times in the year and spend several days there. He was in the habit of humiliating in public the Block Development Officers and their staff. Once he made a frivolous complaint against a BDO. He wanted me to place the officer under suspension forthwith. I told him politely that I would look into the matter and send a report to Government. He was not at all satisfied. On inquiring into the matter I found that the officer had not been at fault. I sent a report to Government explaining the facts. The upshot was that the Chief Minister gave a dressing down to the Deputy Minister. Thereafter for several months the Deputy Minister did not visit his constituency. When he came later he behaved normally.

I shall narrate one more small incident. The Chief Minister was scheduled to open a new Community Development Block in Madhubani Subdivision. A local leader of the Congress organized a luncheon in honour of the Chief Minister. He invited all senior officers also to the lunch. He was a muscleman and bully and often he used to terrorize the people. When he came to invite me I told him politely that I would not be able to attend. I discussed the matter with the Commissioner. He told me that he would accompany the Chief Minister. He added that if I had serious reservations I should myself speak to the Chief Minister. Accordingly, I spoke to the Chief Minister. I told him why I would not attend the lunch. The Chief Minister replied that I was free to act as I liked. He added that he did not have a choice. For, as a politician he was often required to associate with all manners of people including some undesirable elements. Looking back I am convinced that it was the presence of a man like Sri Babu at the helm of affairs that enabled officers of my vintage to act impartially and fearlessly. We could effectively deal with wrongdoers even if they enjoyed political patronage. The personality of the Chief Minister is the most important factor for preserving the administration of a state in good condition.

During that period an administrative structure penetrating deep into the countryside was established. The community development programme was implemented with vigour. Natural calamities were handled with competence, communal peace was ensured and law and order was maintained with a firm hand. It has, however, to be conceded that institutional reforms, social justice and democratic decentralization did not get the required priority. Though a good beginning had been made in primary education, the tempo could not be maintained. Yet, on the whole, Bihar remained a well-administered State. Young officers like me could look forward to the future with confidence, hope and optimism.

Onset of Decline and Degeneration

In December 1960 I returned to the Secretariat as joint Secretary in the Finance Department. Sri Babu died soon after my return to Patna. His successors were first Binodanand Jha and then Krishna Ballabh Sahay. Neither of them had a large personal following. Their survival depended on the continued support of powerful group leaders. Neither enjoyed the prestige or authority of Sri Babu. They could not rein in wayward ministers. Civil servants began aligning themselves with individual ministers.

I was Health Secretary for about five years from mid-1962 to mid-1967. Thereafter I worked as Finance Secretary for two and a half years from mid-1967 to the end of 1969. Harinath Mishra was the Minister when I joined the Health Department. A couple of years later Abdul Qayum Ansari succeeded him. Indiscipline was rampant in the Health Department. Intense lobbying to secure plum postings was the order of the day. Ministers, legislators, bureaucrats and other influential people openly pleaded the cause of their proteges. Harinath Mishra was an honest politician. He approved my proposals to bring about some system and objectivity in postings and transfers and put an end to lobbying. But those efforts met with only limited success. Though Mishra was well meaning, he could not resist the pressure from influential politicians. During Ansari's regime, things took a turn for the worse. Doctors succeeded in getting desired postings by resorting to bribery. On the eve oı the General Election of 1967 the Minister sent down over one hundred transfer orders from his camp office. Many orders violated the guidelines. More than one doctor was posted to the same place and in some cases the same doctor was posted to more than one place. If the Minister's orders were implemented the result would have been utter confusion and further demoralization. I refused to carry out the orders and reported the matter to the Chief Minister through Chief Secretary. Chief Secretary supported me and the Chief Minister decided that the Minister's orders should not be implemented. All the doctors who had paid money were naturally unhappy. The rumour was that in the beginning the cost of securing a favourable order was Rs. 5000 to Rs. 10,000. As the election approached and it was felt that the Congress would be defeated, the amount of bribe came down to as little as a couple of hundred rupees. Corruption had become widespread in other departments also. In the Works Departments corruption had existed since a long time in the matter of awarding contracts. Now bribes were freely offered to secure transfers to particular posts, and even for getting promoted to higher posts. The six years following the death of Sri Babu witnessed a sharp fall in the quality of Bihar's administration. Though Krishna Ballabh Sahay was a very able administrator, he could not stem the rot, as he was dependent on quite a few unscrupulous men for his survival. He did not have the authority to check his erring colleagues. Powerful Ministers began functioning as they pleased. Soon several officers aligned themselves with such ministers and avidly helped them in the abuse of power. The administration was in a deplorable state by 1967.

The Congress was defeated in the General Election of 1967. A number of small parties with conflicting goals and ideologies formed an amorphous coalition to run the government. For a while there was some reduction in the level of corruption, but indiscipline continued unabated. The internal contradictions in the coalition led to the fall of the government before it completed one year. A number of short-lived coalitions followed some of which remained in power for only a few weeks. In one extreme case a government was in office for only a couple of days. The decline got accelerated. During those years to stay in power the Chief Minister was obliged to placate every little group, some of them making utterly unreasonable demands. The office of Chief Minister lost its pristine grandeur and authority. In the winter of

1972 while staying in the Circuit House at Saharsa I happened to see the then Chief Minister being buffeted and abused by an angry crowd of legislators and politicians. I could not believe my eyes, for Bihar was the state that some fifteen years ago Sri Babu had ruled with unquestioned authority and supreme dignity.

Debasement

I was on deputation to the Central Government from the end of 1969 to the middle of 1975. When I returned to Bihar in July 1975 I noticed that the administration had degenerated further. As Finance Secretary I found that the finances of the state were in a precarious condition. Financial discipline had evaporated. In an age in which the administration had no access to telephone or wireless the British rulers had included in the Treasury Code a rule (Rule 27) empowering Collectors to draw money from the treasury in anticipation of formalities to meet emergencies like floods, earthquakes, devastating fires etc. To my dismay I found that Collectors had been freely drawing money for all manner of purposes under Rule 27. In one extreme case a Collector had drawn money under the rule to help the Subdivisional Officer of another district to buy a staff car. I am narrating this simply to illustrate that all checks and balances had disappeared. There was no accountability and anyone could do what he pleased. Resorting to a number of harsh measures I could restore a measure of financial discipline. But the administration continued to be in disarray.

Even during the Emergency, contrary to popular belief, there was no improvement in the level of efficiency. In the General Election of 1977 the Congress was badly beaten. The Janata Party, which was a loose alliance of discordant political groups, came to power. The Chief Minister, Karpoori Thakur had known me from my days as Collector of Darbhanga, his home district. When he was Deputy Chief Minister and Finance Minister in 1967-68, I worked under him as Finance Secretary. We respected each other. Soon after taking over as Chief Minister, Karpoori Thakur told me that he proposed to appoint me Chief Secretary. There were five officers senior to me in the Bihar Cadre posted at that time in Bihar. I suggested that he should appoint one of them to the post of Chief Secretary. I also told him that I wished to go back to the Centre. A week later the Chief Minister told me that it was the unanimous decision of the Council of Ministers that I should be the Chief Secretary. I replied that as a disciplined civil servant I had no option but to accept the post. I, however, added that Bihar's administration was in a mess and that I could be effective only if he agreed to certain conditions. These included appointing officers handpicked by me to key posts, substantial delegation of powers and non-interference in delegated powers. Within a few days of joining as Chief Secretary I found that these conditions were not met. Right from the beginning I found it difficult to persuade the Cabinet to fill key posts on the basis of objective considerations. Lobbying for top posts continued to be the order of the day. Ministers were always on the lookout for officers of their own caste or pliable men. Often outstanding officers were overlooked. In a few cases ministers preferred corrupt and incompetent men. Many officers succeeded in evading transfer orders by resorting to lobbying. Inspite of instructions issued from time to time, interference in day-to-day administration, particularly in the matter of postings and transfers continued unabated. Ministers and legislators were taking a great deal of interest in the transfer of even non-gazetted personnel. Heads of Department and District Officers who resisted such interference were bullied and humiliated, politicians made frequent statements denigrating individual government servants and the bureaucracy in general. The morale of the bureaucracy, which had already been low, went down further.

A few unusual incidents made it obvious that all my efforts to stem the rot would be frustrated. One morning I happened to see a news item prominently featured in the local dailies saying that the Director of Public Instruction had been suspended. Under the Rules of Executive Business no senior officer could be suspended without obtaining the approval of the Chief Minister through the Chief Secretary. I had not seen the case. When I spoke to the Education Secretary he told me that he too had not seen any such file. A couple of hours later the Education Secretary reported to me that he had just received a minute from his Minister directing him to suspend the Director and submit a note the same day confirming that the order had been implemented. The Minister had not even bothered to draw up specific charges. I asked the Education Secretary to send the papers to me and inform his Minister. I submitted the file to Chief Minister pointing out that it would be wrong to suspend the officer without even knowing what were the charges against her. The Chief Minister accepted my advice. But when the Minister threatened to resign on that issue, the Chief Minister caved in. The officer was suspended and proceedings were drawn up. Eventually no charge could be proved. I came to know that though the Director was an efficient and upright officer, she happened to incur the Minister's displeasure for the simple reason that she was not pliable. That incident had an extremely bad impact on the morale of the administration.

Soon lack of discipline reached such alarming proportions that ministers and officers started issuing press statements attacking each other. Two ministers wished to occupy the same house, they decided to take the law into their own hands. Each sent his Personal Assistant with a section of armed police to take possession of the house. Finally the District Magistrate passed an order under Section 144 of the Cr.P.C. restraining both Ministers from occupying the house. Newspapers flashed the news on the front page. Bihar's administration became a laughing stock.

When the atrocious behaviour of some legislators came to my notice I asked the Additional Inspector General of Police, Intelligence, to make a secret enquiry. After a few days he reported that there were 44 legislators with criminal records, equally shared by the Janata Party and the Congress. I discussed the matter with the Chief Minister. I asked him why he could not weed out the criminals. He frankly confessed his inability to do anything because most of the criminals enjoyed the support of some of the top leaders of his party.

When I realized that there was absolutely no chance of the administration being revamped, I left Bihar in April 1978. The years since then have witnessed further degeneration and total devastation. In recent years, Bihar has acquired the reputation of being the worst administered state in the country. In my well considered view the top politicians and members of All India Services are equally responsible for bringing about the ruin. For, if at least one half of them had lived up to the expectation of Sardar Patel and resolutely stood by the Constitution and the law, the tragedy could have been averted. Alas, that did not happen! The charismatic Laloo Yadav bestrides the narrow world of Bihar politics like a colossus. He is his own master, and unlike his mentor Karpoori Thakur, he can be ruthless and decisive. He had the opportunity to set things right and pull Bihar up by the boot-straps. Unfortunately, his priorities are lopsided, and conditions have worsened under his stewardship. It is no consolation to the long-suffering people of Bihar that several states have joined Bihar on the road to ruin.

Other States

Though the degeneration started early in Bihar, soon the other states followed suit. In the General Election of 1967 the Congress Party was defeated in several states. An assorted bunch of small political parties and splinter groups with little in common but opposition to the Congress and love of office came to power. Thanks to intense infighting, the situation was not much better even in the states under Congress rule. All over the country, barring a few exceptions, Chief Ministers became prisoners in the hands of conflicting political parties or groups. To survive they were obliged to placate numerous petty politicians. The new breed of ministers with tenuous tenures was on the look out for pliable bureaucrats. There was no lack of unprincipled opportunists in the bureaucracy. Before long, a large number of civil servants aligned themselves with individual ministers and became active collaborators with disastrous consequences for the administration.

After crushing her rivals, Indira Gandhi acquired total control of the Congress Party early in the seventies. Inner-party democracy was snuffed out and free election of office bearers of the party was abolished. The great party of Gandhi, Nehru and Patel with a tradition of vigorous inner-party democracy was reduced to a plaything in the hands of Nehru's daughter. Chief Ministers of some stature and personal following like V.P. Naik and Devaraj Urs were eased out with thoroughness worthy of a nobler cause.

Chief Ministers came to be chosen purely on the basis of loyalty to the supreme leader, totally ignoring the factors of ability, integrity and popular support. Several non-entities and lightweights lacking administrative acumen and political standing were pitchforked into the office of Chief Minister. Those developments had a devastating influence on public administration in states ruled by the Congress Party. The further decline following the declaration of internal emergency will be discussed in later paragraphs.

Government of India

I joined the Central Government in November 1969. After a brief stint in the Ministry of Health and Family Planning I spent the rest of my tenure in Delhi in the Ministry of Agriculture and the Planning Commission as Land Reforms Commissioner. I had no opportunity to observe personally from a nerve centre the functioning of the Central Government. Therefore, unlike in the case of Bihar, my understanding of the decline of the Central administration is based on my observation from the periphery and what I heard from friends or read in newspapers and journals.

Soon after joining the Health Ministry I observed that senior officers were rather reluctant to express their views frankly. Many of them would mould their views to please the superior officer or minister. On one occasion the Secretary did not like what I had recorded in a file. He discussed the matter with me and asked me to take back my note. He wanted me to write another note on the lines suggested by him. I told him politely that I would not revise my note. The Secretary became angry and told me that it was an accepted practice to revise notes after discussion. I told him that I would stick to my stand. Thereafter our relations became strained and I proceeded on leave. After my leave I joined as Land Reforms Commissioner in the Ministry of Agriculture. Concurrently I held the same assignment in the Planning Commission. In that post I happened to work with four Secretaries. I had cordial relations with all of them. Even when we differed, none of them ever suggested that I should reconsider my stand.

At the Centre the decline started much later than in Bihar. For the first twenty-five years after independence the system was in reasonably good shape. During that period the country tided over the perils and trauma of partition. The threat of administrative collapse was averted. The integration of princely states exceeding five hundred in number, attainment of self-sufficiency in food, the adoption of planned economic development and the survival of democracy were the significant achievements of that period.

Decline and Degeneration at the Centre

From around 1973–74 the administration started to decline at the Centre. It was then that some persons in authority ridiculed the concept of a politically neutral bureaucracy and advocated its substitution by a committed civil service. The ham-handed handling of the popular mass movements against the corrupt regimes in Bihar and Gujarat resulted in great public anger and dissatisfaction. The government of Indira Gandhi was fast losing its moral authority. The departure of men of ability, integrity and vision from the Prime Minister's inner councils coincided with the usurpation of political power by a small coterie headed by Sanjay Gandhi. I shall narrate a trivial incident which presaged the shape of things to come. In the years immediately preceding the Emergency, a close friend of mine had been working as the General Manager of the Super Bazar in Delhi. A crony of Sanjay Gandhi started frequenting the Super Bazar and telling the staff how the goods should be displayed. He also added that he was acting on behalf of the Prime Minister. When his meddling became intolerable, the General Manager complained to the Prime Minister's Joint Secretary. The latter put up the letter to the Prime Minister with a note suggesting that the busybody should be warned. The Prime Minister's reaction was unbelievable. She wrote that she was a busy person and that it was not always possible for her to express her wishes in writing. Sometimes her orders would be conveyed verbally by people close to her! Perhaps the Prime Minister did not realize that she was opening the floodgates to the blatant abuse of power and the subversion of the system.

The declaration of internal emergency was a watershed. Prior to the emergency the administration was, on the whole, in a reasonably good shape. Emergency dealt a crushing blow to the administration, particularly at the Centre and in the State of Haryana. A week before the declaration of emergency I had proceeded on leave preparatory to my reversion to Bihar. I did not work under the Central Government during emergency. So my understanding is based on what I heard from friends. As I was on leave, I woke up rather late on June 26, 1975. I came to know about the declaration of emergency from the single sheet issue of the Delhi edition of the *Statesman*, the only newspaper that came out in Delhi on that day. All India Radio was playing some banal music. Switching on the BBC, I gathered scrappy information about the declaration of emergency. I got ready quickly and went to the Agriculture Ministry. I met the Secretary Triveni Prasad Singh and Minister of State Annasaheb Shinde. Both were stunned. Annasaheb told me that the telephone lines of Jagjivan Ram and Y.B. Chavan had been disconnected. He added that probably they were under house arrest. As I was on leave, I could spend the whole day meeting senior officers in the Ministry. I also looked up a Joint Secretary in the Home Ministry who had already started work on a white paper. I spent the next few days gathering information about the manner in which the momentous decision was taken and the persons responsible for the decision.

I was shocked to learn that the emergency had been declared without the Cabinet's approval. Home Minister Brahmananda Reddy heard about it only at the Cabinet meeting held at 6 A.M. on June 26. Cabinet Secretary B.D. Pande came to know only when he was asked in the small hours of June 26 to convene an emergency meeting of the Council of Ministers. Even the Prime Minister's Secretary, P.N. Dhar, was not in the picture. A couple of days earlier the Home Secretary Nirmal Mukherjee had been shifted to the Ministry of Civil Aviation because of the apprehension that he might prove to be inconvenient. In his place a pliable officer from Rajasthan was airlifted and posted as Home Secretary. On the night of June 25 top leaders including Jayaprakash Narayan, Morarji Desai and others were arrested without the knowledge of the Home Minister and other Ministers. The Prime Minister took the ominous decision to declare emergency on the advice of a small clique headed by her younger son Sanjay Gandhi. Siddharth Shankar Ray was roped in to provide legal advice. The President signed on the dotted line. All the checks and balances built into the Constitution crumbled, Parliamentary democracy was annihilated and the Cabinet ceased to be the repository of executive power. Throughout the emergency a small gang headed by Sanjay Gandhi usurped all the powers of the Government of India. An assortment of hatchet men, opportunists and sycophants gained access to the levers of power.

No minister or senior bureaucrat raised any objection to the declaration of emergency or the manner in which it was done. A few experienced deep agony; and a large number felt uncomfortable. But many IAS and IPS officers enthusiastically collaborated with the authoritarian regime. Without any regard for the Constitution and the laws of the land, they executed illegal orders and cheerfully functioned as instruments of tyranny. The impact of the emergency was most severe at the Centre and in the state of Haryana adjoining Delhi.

During the emergency the great institutions of our federal democratic polity, which had already been under attack, were undermined and severely eroded. The important institutions under attack included Parliament and State Legislatures, the Cabinet System of governance, the office of the Chief Minister, the limited autonomy enjoyed by the States, the judiciary, the bureaucracy and the press. The rule of law was dispensed with and constitutional proprieties were cast aside. All checks and balances built into the Constitution crumbled. An extra-constitutional junta headed by Sanjay Gandhi exercised supreme executive power. Mercifully, Sanjay Gandhi's interests were rather limited. So in areas outside his sphere of interest the administration functioned as in the past, with the difference that many officers availed of the opportunity to act arbitrarily.

Among the States the most severe impact of the emergency was experienced in Haryana. That State had already acquired notoriety for arbitrary governance. The emergency provided an excellent opportunity to Chief Minister Bansi Lal to commit unbelievable excesses. IAS and IPS officers who were unwilling to collaborate were bullied into submission. The official machinery was blatantly misused to wreak vengeance and carry out vendetta. In one extreme case a District Employment Officer who did not accede to the wishes of Bansi Lal's son was harassed and imprisoned. The Supreme Court judge who inquired into the excesses committed during the emergency came to the conclusion that Bansi Lal had been guilty of the abuse of power and that he had behaved like a medieval despot.

In the other states also democratic governance yielded place to arbitrary exercise of power. Many civil and police officers availed of the opportunity to act arbitrarily on their own without any direction from political superiors, Throughout the emergency I worked in the Finance Department. Chief Minister Jagannath Mishra was in charge of the Finance Department. He did not pass any arbitrary and illegal order as Finance Minister. During the emergency the distinction between the government and the party in power vanished. Sanjay Gandhi and Congress President Baruah made two or three visits to review progress in the implementation of the so-called Twenty-Point Programme. As luck would have it, I was not required to attend those sessions. In spite of the draconian measures adopted during emergency there was, however, no improvement in efficiency.

Devastation and Breakdown

In the General Election held in 1977 immediately after the lifting of the emergency, the Congress was trounced. The Janata Party, which came to power, was a fragile makeshift alliance of discordant political groups. Though institutions like the Cabinet System and Parliament regained strength, before completing one year in office the government fell under its own weight. Indira Gandhi's return to power in 1980 ensured that the great institutions of our federal democratic polity would not regain their former strength. The next two decades witnessed the exponential growth of the evils of corruption, criminalisation and electoral malpractice. Though early on during his tenure Rajiv Gandhi showed some awareness of the problem, soon he came to terms with the rotten ambience. His successors also did not try to stem the rot. As a result of perverse personnel policies pursued by successive Central and State Governments, public administration became dysfunctional. Governments no longer govern. Law and order has broken down in large parts of the country and some metropolitan cities. Citizens no longer enjoy security of life and property. The primary purpose for which the State was set up is not being served. The Social Contract has collapsed. Communal, class and caste conflicts often leading to rioting, arson and slaughter have become endemic. The magistracy and the police have often been reduced to helpless spectators. Occasionally they have added fuel to the fire by their partisan conduct.

During 1993–95 I had occasion to study the state of the Land Revenue administration in all the states as the Chairman of a Committee appointed by the Government of India. An extract from the report of the committee is reproduced below:

> "In all states routine is neglected and senior officers seldom attend to their all-important functions of field visits, inspections and supervision. Corruption and inefficiency are so rampant that members of the public find that they cannot get anything done without greasing the palms of the functionaries concerned or bringing to bear great influence on them. Well-meaning and efficient Collectors who try to bring about an improvement in the situation often find their efforts frustrated. They are unable to take any disciplinary action against erring subordinates who have access to peddlers of influence. The main reasons for this state of affairs are the pursuit of perverse personnel policies and mindless political interference in day-to-day administration, particularly establishment matters. In several states ministers routinely interfere in the postings and transfers of even low-level field staff appointed by the Collector. The expression 'political interference' does not adequately describe what goes on. In reality what happens is the blatant misuse of public office for pecuniary gain. Touts, power brokers and peddlers of influence are having a field day all over the country. These unhealthy developments have led to thorough demoralization in the bureaucracy, rampant indiscipline and all round inefficiency. It is high time that effective steps are taken to stem the rot and put an end to

this sad state of affairs." (*Report of the Committee on Revitalization of Land Revenue Administration, Government of India, Ministry of Rural Development*, March 1995, page 12)

I shall now briefly refer to a few major events that clearly demonstrate the breakdown of governance and the abdication of responsibility by the All India Services. During the first two decades after independence communal clashes and tension were endemic in many places. The administration was scrupulously impartial. Criminal elements of all communities were firmly dealt with. From the late sixties in several states the lower echelons of the administration, particularly police outfits like the Provincial Armed Constabulary of Uttar Pradesh, started showing bias against the minorities. The serious communal riots of Meerut and Bhagalpur exposed the lethargy and negligence on the part of the civil and police administration. Even so, the Council of Ministers and the top echelons of the administration continued to be unbiased. During the riots in Delhi in the wake of the assassination of Indira Gandhi the administration did not act with speed. Some prominent leaders of the Congress played an active role in fomenting trouble. The administration let them go scot-free.

The destruction of the Babri Masjid was an important climate in the decline of the administration. Though the Hindu fanatics had given a clear indication of their intention, no effective step was taken to protect the mosque. Prime Minister Narasimha Rao temporized and allowed things to drift. Uttar Pradesh Chief Minister Kalyan Singh openly connived in the destruction of the shrine. The top IAS and IPS officers present at Ayodhya failed in discharging their duty. That incident badly tarnished the image of Indian administration; It was shown to be toothless and biased. The riots that followed in Bombay and other places were not handled efficiently. The police did not intervene effectively to maintain public order.

Then followed several incidents that showed the IAS and IPS in very poor light. A case in point is the Fodder Scam of Bihar. Several IAS officers were alleged to have acted culpably and some were imprisoned. Another instance is the role of the top police officers of Tamil Nadu in humiliating Ex-Chief Minister Karunanidhi. In recent years all over the country members of the IAS and the IPS have shown a marked tendency to carry out the wishes of their political masters without pausing to consider if the action was in accordance with the law. Many of them have been behaving like servile hatchet men and not as members of elite services owing unshakeable allegiance to the Constitution, the laws of the land and the principles of democratic governance. It is true that the major share for this sad state of affairs should rest with the new breed of politicians who have scant regard for the Constitution and the laws of the land. They have no qualms about abusing power to garner illegal gains and carrying out personal vendetta.

In recent weeks the State of Gujarat under the stewardship of Narendra Modi witnessed the complete ruin and devastation of the All India Services. Gujarat was a well-administered state some three decades ago. The decline started with the regime of Chimanbhai Patel. He was succeeded by a number of Chief Ministers under whom the downturn gathered momentum. According to M.N. Buch, a perceptive observer of the degeneration of the Gujarat administration, under those Chief Ministers' nepotism, corruption and favouritism became rampant. The interference in day-to-day administration filtered down to postings of even police constables, patwaris and other low level employees. With the coming to power of the BJP, political interference continued in a more organized manner. A large number of RSS and VHP activists were inducted into Class III and Class IV posts, particularly into the police force and the Home Guard organization. The administration became thoroughly demoralized.

Such being the state of affairs in Gujarat at the time of the Godhra carnage, Chief Minister Narendra Modi, a staunch RSS *pracharak* of long standing, faced little resistance in ensuring that the Civil and Police administration remained inert during the so-called Hindu backlash. According to a report published in the *Outlook* of June 3rd, the Chief Minister discussed the law and order situation with the Chief Secretary, the Director General of Police and other senior officers on the night of February 27, a few hours after the Godhra incident. It is alleged that the Chief Minister said that the next day during the bandh called by VHP there would be justice for Godhra and that the police should not come in the way of the Hindu backlash. Narendra Modi is reported to have snubbed the DGP who expressed some doubts. Thereafter the top IAS and IPS officers meekly knuckled under the bullying tactics of a political leadership bent upon violating the Constitution, the rule of law and the basic principles of democratic governance. The All India Services abdicated. Govardhan Zadapiya, a VHP activist functioning directly under Modi as Minister of State in the Home Department took charge of the Ahmedabad Police Commissioner's Control Room. Another minister issued instructions from the State Control Room. For several days inhuman and hitherto unheard of atrocities were perpetrated against Muslims. Eye-witness accounts and videotapes have documented the gory details of barbarous crimes.

The Gujarat riots were unique. For the first time since independence, a Chief Minister and his cabinet colleagues played a proactive role in rendering the law and order machinery inert and permitting Hindu fanatics and gangsters to have the free run of the state for several days. Under the Code of Criminal Procedure and the Indian Police Act, the sole responsibility for the maintenance of public order rests with the magistracy and the police. The law assigns no role to the Council of Ministers in the maintenance of law and order. When the Chief Minister gave an illegal order it was the plain duty of the Chief Secretary and the Director General of Police to ignore that order. They should have instructed the District Magistrates, Police Commissioners and Superintendents of police to take effective steps to maintain public peace exercising all the powers vested in them under the law. It was also the duty of the DGP and the Commissioner of Police to throw the interlopers out of the Control Rooms. Of course, the senior officers ran the risk of incurring the wrath of a vindictive and ruthless Chief Minister. Considering the Constitutional protection enjoyed by the members of the All India Services, the risk was no more than that of being transferred. It was, indeed, a crying shame that no IAS or IPS officer in top positions offered any resistance at all when the Constitution, the laws of the land

and the principles of civilized governance were trampled under the feet.

Summing up

In the preceding paragraphs I have described the process of decline drawing attention to the cause that led to the degeneration. Now I shall briefly recount the important causes that led to the degeneration. The decline of the great institutions of our federal democratic polity was a prime cause. The decline of the Cabinet system and the degeneration of the legislatures also adversely affected the administration. As far as the states are concerned, the most ruinous development was the sharp decline in the stature and authority of the Chief Minister. These developments were a direct consequence of the snuffing out of inner part democracy in the Indian National Congress and the concentration of all power at the top. The mass politics of the early years gave way to manipulative parlour politics. Blind loyalty to the top leader became the sole criterion for the selection of Chief Minister and ministers. Several persons unfit to hold public office were pitchforked into high offices. The period also witnessed the weakening of the Congress Party in several states and the emergence of new political formations with no clear ideology. For long periods unstable coalition governments lacking in cohesion ruled many states. The only cementing force was greed and the anxiety to cling on to power. More often than not a Chief Minister heading a coalition was a prisoner in the hands of self-seeking ministers. Such governments seldom functioned with a sense of purpose.

Another important development since the mid-seventies of the last century was the growth of a malignant syndrome embodying large-scale corruption, criminalization and electoral malpractice. The unhealthy socio-political environment facilitated the emergence of a breed of cynical politicians with no faith in the Constitution and the laws of the land. They looked upon electoral victory as licence to abuse power, help cronies and amass huge fortunes. The total absence of transparency and accountability in our political system facilitated these deadly developments. A few bureaucrats felt uneasy, but the great majority got on to the bandwagon and either acquiesced in the wrongdoing or shared the loot. Long before the Gujarat carnage the country was heading towards administrative collapse. The events in Gujarat simply revealed that for a long time the administration had been rotten to the core.

Conclusion

It is often argued that since the All India Services no longer serve the purpose for which they were established, they should be wound up. This is a counsel of despair. It is certainly true that the bureaucracy being an integral part of the polity, efforts to rejuvenate the administration should be preceded by thorough-going political and electoral reforms and other measures to pull the polity out of the morass. These should also include a war on corruption and criminalization, drastic devolution of powers as envisaged in the 73rd Amendment of the Constitution, transparency in the management of public affairs, and strict enforcement of accountability at all levels. There is little hope of all these things happening in the near future. The recent reaction of the political parties to the modest efforts of the Supreme Court and the Election Commission to introduce reforms shows how difficult it will be to bring about even modest electoral reforms. The political scenario is, indeed, depressing. Even so, there are two good reasons for retaining the All India Services and trying to rejuvenate them.

In the first two decades after independence we had both at the Centre and in the states ministers who had faith in the Constitution, the rule of law and the principles of democratic governance. Unfortunately, many of the ministers and other political leaders of the present day have no faith in the Constitution and the law or in democratic practices. So, there is greater need today than at any time in the past for the All India Services wedded to the Constitution and the law. They can offer considerable resistance to illegal actions of the politicians in power.

Secondly, recent experience in Gujarat confirms the need to retain and strengthen the All India Services. A great deal has been written and said about the devastation and utter failure of the All India Services. Unfortunately adequate light has not been shed on the performance of a handful of fearless officers who stood by the Constitution and the law. When all over the state the Police acquiesced in the nefarious activities of the Sangh Parivar, the Superintendents of Police of Kutch, Bhavnagar, Banaskantha and Bharuch accorded effective protection to Muslims. They exercised their powers under the law and, where necessary, used force against troublemakers. In one case in which a Commandant of the Home Guards, an erstwhile VHP activist, had stabbed an old Muslim woman and her grandson living in an isolated dargah, the Superintendent of Police took drastic action. He drew up a First Information Report, arrested the culprit and sent him to prison. Not only that, he stood firm when a minister and a member of the Chief Minister's staff tried to browbeat him. Of, course he and the other three officers were subsequently transferred. But the four officers have the satisfaction that they did their duty in extremely trying circumstances in Gujarat's darkest hour. I have no detailed information about the performance of all the IAS and IPS officers. In all probability there are others also who discharged their duties fearlessly. These instances prove that it will be disastrous to wind up the All India Services. If only the Chief Secretary, the DGP and a number of senior officers had displayed the same fearlessness and dedication, the Gujarat carnage could have been averted or at least mitigated.

After having watched Indian administration for half a century, I am firmly of the view that the All India Services should continue. The President is the guardian and the Supreme Court the very palladium of our Constitution. But they are beyond the reach of ordinary citizens. It is a civil and police administration fearlessly upholding the Constitution and the rule of law that will enable millions of Indian citizens to enjoy the rights guaranteed under the Constitution. Abolition of the All India Services will certainly lead to a worsening of the situation.

A question that merits urgent consideration is what practical steps can be taken to restore to the IAS and IPS, at least partially, the ethos and élan that existed some four decades ago. Admittedly, noticeable success can be achieved only after the cleansing of the Indian polity by introducing far reaching political and electoral reforms. There is little hope of that happening in the near future. In the meantime we have to be satisfied with small practical steps to improve the morale of the All India Services and bring about marginal improvement in their performance. There is also the pressing need to extend moral and material support to the few fearless officers who perform their duty with remarkable dedication. This matter deserves to be discussed at a brainstorming session to be attended by some knowledgeable people who have not yet succumbed to despair and cynicism.

CHAPTER

14 All-India Services: An Essential Feature of the Constitution

—Dr. P.K. Agrawal

When the Constitution of India was being drafted, the uppermost thing, which was in the minds of the constitution makers, was how to preserve the unity and integrity of the nascent nation at all costs. They envisaged a federal polity with the unitary bias. As per the experience of the history of the country, the country was made slave on various occasions due to frequent in-fightings inside the country and secondly, due to the weak central power. The constitution makers alongwith others made the provision of All India Services in the Constitution of India as a special measure in Part XIV of the Constitution. Nowhere in the world, the services find a place in the Constitution. The All India services were supposed to be instruments of implementation of the broad unity in the country inspite of the diversity of the languages, religions, races, food habits, castes and communities. There was a threadbare discussion in the Constituent Assembly because the predecessor of the All India services i.e., I.C.S. (Indian Civil Service) was an instrument of British Rule for oppression of the people and they perpetuated the imperial rule. Inspite of that, the people who suffered at the hands of the I.C.S. had intrinsic appreciation for their contribution in the implementation of Government laws and executive directions. They thought them essential to preserve the new administration.

After Independence, the legendary Home Minister and the Iron man of India Sardar Vallabhbhai Patel said: "If you want an all-India efficient service, I advise you to allow the services to open their mouth freely. If you are a Premier, it would be your duty to allow your Secretary or Chief Secretary or other services working under you, to express their opinion without fear or favour. But I see a tendency today that in several provinces the services are set aside and told: 'No, you are servicemen, you must carry out our orders'. The Union will go—you will not have a united India if you have not a good All-India service which has the independence to speak out its mind, which has a sense of security...... Today, my Secretary can write a note opposed to my views. I have given that freedom to all my Secretaries. I have told them, 'If you do not give your honest opinion for fear that it will displease your Minister, please then you better go. I will bring another Secretary'. I will never be displeased over a frank expression of opinion. Members of Parliament should support the services, except where an individual member of the service may be misbehaving or erring in his duty or committing a dereliction of his duties if these service people are giving you full value of their services and more, then try to learn to appreciate them. They are men who prefer honour, dignity, prestige and deserve the affection of the people".

According to Shri Nirmal Mukarji (I.C.S.)—"the postulate, that the Constitution is meant to be worked by a ring of service that will keep the country under control, is entirely untenable, if only because it places the bureaucracy ahead of democracy. Equally indefensible is the view that the IAS is needed to keep India united. Things have changed since the Sardar's days and any discussion about All India Services should reflect the change".[1]

After Independence, an assessment was made by an American Scholar Mr. Taubji. He says, "In the light of his practical experience in the field for 16 months' survey, the I.A.S. has performed remarkably well. In addition to providing basic administrative services, it has helped to maintain national integration, and consequently can take some credit for the fact that India has

---

[1] *Economic and Political Weekly*, December, 17–24, 1994.

maintained her nationhood for twenty years. In several states, the Service has conducted the business of the Government when political leaders were so busy competing against each other that they had little time for government. The Service can collect information around which to build policy. And it may even be able to provide some of the social overheads needed to make modernization possible."[2] Shri Ashok Kapoor, I.A.S. in his two articles published in the *Statesman* (1994) proved that it was the I.A.S. who saved the country from going the Pakistani dictatorship way as because the Indian Administrative Service through Secretaries ensured the supremacy of civil rule over the army. The fate of Pakistani administration is in front of all of us today.

In the eighties, the I.A.S. started dwindling under all round pressure. The I.A.S. showed cracks due to intake of over-ambitious personnel from IITs & IIMs in eighties. It may also be a part of all-round degradation of the values in the society. How can All India Services be away from the society? In year 1973, a revolutionary judgment was given by the Supreme Court in case—*Keshav-ananda vs. State of Kerala*,[3] where the Supreme Court laid down that the basic features of the Constitution cannot be amended. Federalism was held as a basic feature. The federal structure of the Constitution includes federal structure in administration also because the government has got three organs—Executive, Judiciary and Legislature. In the scheme of the Constitution, the Council of States was kept out of subject to dissolution. It means there has to be a continuous institution in every organ of the government which cannot be dissolved. On the contrary, it can be said that we can have a system like the spoils system of bureaucracy in U.S.A. which changes with the change of government or we can be a committed bureaucracy like the erstwhile U.S.S.R. which was totally party-oriented. In India, all the organs of the Constitution have to conform to the basic scheme of the Constitution. Chief Justice Sikri says in his judgment in *Kesavananda Bharathi case* "Parliament has not the power to override the constitutional schemes."

---

[2] Taub, Richard P, *Bureaucrats under Stress*, published by K.L. Mukhopadhyay, Calcutta, 1969.

[3] AIR 1973 SC, 1974 SCC 225.

He further says: "The Constitution can only be altered with some special formality and in some cases by a specially convened Assembly".[4]

Therefore, federal institutions must enjoy some immunity. During the Constituent Assembly debates, there was a move to abolish the I.C.S. and other All India services. But it was not agreed to and it was overwhelmingly agreed to continue All India services. The idea was that they will be free from local bias and will give all India face to the Central Government. If state's services replace the All India services, then who will man the seniormost posts at the Centre?

Secondly at the State level, there are many other State Civil Services who will lay claim for the top slots in States. And there will be lot of confrontation and horse-trading which is also visible now-a-days.

Justice Sikri gave a solution as follows:

"Federal institutions, therefore, must enjoy some immunity. But I would regard these as tainted by the perennial fallacy that because something cannot be cut and dried, nicely weighed or measured therefore, it does not exist."

He further quotes that there might be a Service Commission on the pattern of Judicial Service Commission in Sri Lanka which will ensure better neutrality and impartiality of services.

"The appointment, transfer, dismissal and disciplinary control of judicial officers is hereby vested in the Judicial Service Commission. Thus, there is secured a freedom from political control and it is a punishable offence to attempt directly or indirectly to influence any decision of the Commission".[5]

Shri Nirmal Mukarji in his article referred to above opines that I.A.S. shop be closed. But at the same time in his report on Panchayats in West Bengal, he has pointed out major drawbacks and fallacies in the working of the strongest panchayat system in the country i.e., the West Bengal Panchayats. He says: "Why are the Panchayats tending to run out of steam? This became our primary focus and led us into two broad lines of enquiry. On the

---

[4] Ibid, p. 1532.

[5] Ibid, p. 1518.

conceptual side, there is lack of clarity about the objective of the Panchayats, especially about the implications of their becoming institutions of self-government. On programmes, the virtual exit of Land Reform from their agenda has left the Panchayats with a feeling that there is nothing worthwhile left to do". Thus, how can Shri Mukarji bank upon total devolution of power to the elected representatives. Or whether he *means to import another service to administer India*. The ideal solution is to have checks and balances system which is a basic scheme provided in the Constitution throughout. In case of bureaucracy, the checks and balances may function well between the bureaucracy vs. the elected bureaucracy and each should have power to override the other.

Article 368 provides that entry 70 of List I of Seventh Schedule regarding All-India service cannot be amended without a special and stringent procedure of amendment providing for two-thirds majority in Parliament and confirmation of the same resolution by more than half of the States. It seems to be impossible as people have the ray of hope of justice and fairness left in All-India services.

"The services of the state structure are themselves getting increasingly dysfunctional and diminished. In some North Indian States, parallel authority structures and mafia gangs have emerged. In such a situation, there is a pervasive feeling of helplessness, frustration and gloom among the remaining honest civil servants. The system never demanded a high standard of professionalism but at least there was respect for honest officers. Now integrity is a political liability, rather than an asset."[6]

Personally, he further opines: "Political pressure can be healthy if they result in greater demand on administration for efficiency and better services to the people. Pressure properly regulated and wisely tempered, improve the spirit of administration and help to keep it on an even keel. Unfortunately, the main problem is that the politics of the country has itself become divorced from public welfare and is more concerned with narrow sectarian interests."

---

[6] Saxena, N.C. Director, L.B.S. National Academy of Administration.

In conclusion, the All-India services cannot be abolished unless a special Constituent Assembly is convened.

Therefore, it is better not to create another big confusion in the minds of people at this juncture. A federation being a dual polity based on divided authority with separate legislative, executive and judicial power for each of the two polities, is bound to produce diversity in laws, in administration and in judicial protection. Upto a certain point, this diversity does not matter. It may be welcomed as being an attempt to accommodate the powers of Government to local needs and circumstances. But this diversity when it goes beyond a certain point, is capable of producing chaos and has produced chaos in many federal states.[7]

In fact, a modern constitutional diversity does not matter. It may be welcomed as being an attempt to maintain the unity of the country. The Constitution adopts the following three means to maintain administrative and legislative unity:

(a) A single judiciary,
(b) Uniformity in fundamental laws, civil and criminal, and
(c) Common All-India services.

All India services is a powerful instrument of national integrity as was amply reiterated by the Law Commission of India when it suggested for creation of one more All India Judicial Service to cure ills in Judicial System and which was adopted by the Parliament as a 42nd Constitutional Amendment Act, 1976 added to Article 312 by way of Cl. (3). This will also make candidates easily available to man posts of High Court Judges. The Law Commission and the Supreme Court in All India Judges' case have also suggested for the constitution of All India Judicial Service. But only about half of the States and half of the High Courts agreed for creation of A.I.J.S. The experiment of creation of All India Medical Service has already failed before it started. In case of one more All India Service i.e., Indian Forest Service, the federalism is more helpful as ecology or environment does not know the barriers of states or provinces. The pollution anywhere, is pollution everywhere. If one State leaves the dirty

---

[7] Dr. Ambedkar, *Constituent Assembly Debates*, Vol. VII, 36.

water to be used and applied by downstream States, then the problem will be more serious and it will give rise to mutual bickering among States. Any pollution in air cannot be confined to the political boundary of that particular state. Similarly, the radioactive emissions have much more universal spread. The environment is going to be the focus of people's concern in times to come. Then, one more All-India service, Indian Environment Service will become imperative if Indian Forest Service will be unable to address all concerns relating to environment in general. Otherwise in the name of coordination among states, more bad blood will be generated.

The indispensability of All-India services is further demonstrated in tackling insurgencies or extremism where the state's services yield under local fear for their birth and sins. On the other hand, the personnel of All-India services can work more fearlessly. Therefore, in the present-day scenario, All India services are indispensable.

CHAPTER

15 Need of Administrative Law for India

—Dr. P.K. Agrawal

Law Commission in its fourteenth report[1] observed that the function of administration has rather become positive than the negative, which was earlier. The function of the executive or administration now covered most of the affairs of life and society. The direct result of this has been the growth of administrative law. As dealing with the public affairs also requires specialization, it is essential that there should be expert bodies for adjudication of disputes arising out of the decisions of administrative bodies or individuals dealing with administration it is recognised as a specialized wing of the polity and special arrangement has been made for proper exercise of its powers and functions. This is more essential as the principle 'king can do no wrong' is no longer widely applicable. The privileges and prerogatives of government employees are subject to rule of law, statutory laws and the constitution of the country.

In France, Italy, West Germany and a number of other countries, there is a separate system of administrative courts, which deal exclusively with administrative cases. In USA, there are expert administrative bodies that decide many intricate administrative matters. One of world's powerful rulers, Napoleon Bonaparte, was the founder of the 'Droit Administrati'. It is he who established the counsel d'Etat and he further passed an

[1] Law Commission of India, XIVth Report 1958.

ordinance depriving the law courts of Jurisdiction in administrative matters and ordaining that such matters could be only determined by the counsel d'Etat. The system was based on the principle that the government and every servant of government possess, as representative of the nation a whole body of special rights, privileges or prerogatives to be determined on principles different from the considerations which fix the legal rights and duties of a citizen towards his neighbour or another person.

In India, the consciousness about law or knowledge of law has not informed all the citizens of the country though this is the first prerequisite of any law of the land. Though setting up of administrative bodies and separate administrative courts to adjudicate matters will involve lot of expenditure, yet it will be worthwhile if statutory administrative law is enforced in the country, which will also function as code of conduct for the public officers and employees. The power of the administration is to act suo moto and to impose directly on the subject the duty to obey its decisions. But the power is to be exercised within the ambit of law, which protects individuals against administrative arbitrariness.

One good result of this is that an independent body reviews every administrative action. The counsel d'Etat composed of eminent civil servants who deal with a variety of matters like claim for damages for wrongful acts of government servants, income tax, pensions, disputed elections, personal claims of civil servants against the state for wrongful dismissal or suspension and so on. It has interfered with administrative orders on the grounds of error of law, lack of jurisdiction, irregularity of procedure and misapplication of powers. The system is even today working very successfully in France. So also in USA, the system of 'Authorities' exists. There are various Boards, Quasi Judicial authorities or bodies like Environment Regulatory Authority which function like judicial bodies to review administrative decisions. They take decisions like fixing rates for telephone calls, realization of tax, implementation of regulations for keeping environment clean. They are independent from the administration and are not strictly judicial courts. But they have experts of the particular fields who take quick decisions as regards disputes between the public and between public and the State. In India, these types of authorities are gradually coming into existence which operate as administrative bodies as well as quasi-judicial bodies like TRAI (Telecom Regulating Authority of India). TRAI so far, has shown its efficacy by allowing private players in the field and then by fixing reasonable margin of profit to the government undertakings like BSNL and other private telephone giants like Airtel, Reliance and others who were earlier exploiting the public by mutually fixing call-tariff excessively by way of mutual agreement among them.

The public or consumers are very much fed up with delay and corruption in functioning of the government machinery. The public employees take shelter under the executive prerogative telling the public that they can complain to their higher officers who are either not available or if they are available, they cannot act promptly and in a desired manner due to rule bound functioning of the government. On the other hand, the junior officer who has caused grievance to the complainant is readily available in office whereas the complainant cannot be called for hearing. Thus, his case of complaint is heard and disposed of behind his back. It is said that the 'redressal mechanism' in government only acts partially rendering it totally ineffective at the last end of the beneficiary. Therefore, the Supreme Court's decision in *A.K. Kraipak vs Union of India*[2] has, however, held that the ambit of review of the Court even covers purely administrative actions in effect. The apex Court held that "the dividing line Kraipak between an administrative power and a quasi-judicial power is quite thin and is being gradually obliterated. For determining whether a power is administrative power or a quasi-judicial power, one has to look to the nature of the power conferred, the person or persons on whom it is conferred, the framework of the law conferring power, the consequences ensuing from the exercise of power and the manner in which that power is expected to be exercised. In a welfare state like India, which is regulated and controlled by 'rule of law', it is inevitable that the jurisdiction of the administrative bodies

[2] AIR 1962 SC 1110.

is increasing at a rapid pace. The concept of rule of law would lose its vitality if the instrumentalities of the state are not charged with the duty of discharging their functions in a fair and just manner. The requirement of acting judicially in essence is nothing but a requirement to act justly and fairly and not arbitrarily or capriciously".

The Supreme Court in some cases have struck down purely administrative actions and even fined the top executive like the Union Minister for the cases of arbitrary allotment of petrol pumps and Central Government quarters in Delhi. The Supreme Court has even reviewed appointments on the top administrative posts in Govt. of India and in some State Governments. By these decisions, the Supreme Court has won the popularity of the masses. On the other hand, the administrative system is becoming gradually indecisive and inactive. The senior officers are always afraid of review of their actions or decisions by the High Courts or the Supreme Court. The sword of Contempt of Court always hangs on their neck. In such an environment, a permanent civil service who are the decision makers, will not like to fiddle with their careers. As a result, the economic and social developments will come to standstill gradually.

Let us analyse, how this problem can be solved and a healthy balance struck so that administrative actions or decisions become not only just and fair but also speedy. Lack of speed is the only cause why India is still in the comity of developing nations. The senior civil officers are left alone to face courts when there are cases of Contempt of Court against them. Actually the subordinates down the line have no sense of proportion or judicial bent of mind to put up the notes, suggestions or drafts before them so that they can speedily take just and fair decisions.

The solutions are manifold. Some will suggest that there should be proper recruitment methods. Second school of thought will suggest for extensive training, retraining and continuous training upto the clerk level in the bureaucracy for human resource development. This is not feasible at present because training itself will involve a huge expenditure and development of large infrastructures. The simplest solution is to have an 'Administrative Law' for India. Jennings says, "Administrative law is the law relating to the administration. It determines the powers and duties of administrative authorities.[3]

However, these general provisions can always be translated into action according to the situations and nature of the organization where they are applied. Professor Wade remarks that "Administrative law is concerned with the operation and control of the powers of administrative authorities with emphasis on functions rather than on structure".[4]

Prof. Hart says, "Broadly conceived, Administrative law includes law that is made by as well as the law that controls the administrative authority of a government".[5]

Broadly speaking, administrative law deals with composition and powers of different organs of administration; the limits of the powers of administrative authorities; the procedure which the administrative authorities adopt in exercising these powers and the control of all such powers of administration through judicial process and other means.

Freund says that "the main problem of administrative law relates to the nature and operation of official powers, the formal and procedural conditions for the exercise of powers, official and communal liability, the specific remedies for the judicial control of administrative action, jurisdictional limitations or powers and questions of administrative finality"[6] Therefore, administrative law is the science of powers of administrative authorities. And the nature of their powers can be classified under these three heads;

1. Legislative or rule-making.
2. Judicial or adjudicative.
3. Purely executive.

The main consideration of administrative law is the control over the exercise of these powers.

---

[3] Jennings: *The Law & the Constitution*, p.217 (5th Edition, 1959).

[4] Wade: *Administrative Law*, Fifth Edition.

[5] Ibid, 4.

[6] Kesari, U.P.D.: *Lectures on Administrative Law*, Central Law Agency, 11 University Rd, Allahabad, First Edition, Page 4.

Mr. Ramaswami has aptly remarked as following:

> "The administrative authority interferes in all domains of social and economic life, in the fields of industry, commerce, education, transport, banking, insurance and so on. From the constitutional standpoint, there is a large-scale delegation of legislative and judicial powers to administrative agencies. Without such delegation, the working of the administration cannot be efficient or prompt. In administration, there is obvious need for individual action. There is call for speedy determination. There is necessity for direction, guidance and expert advice. A large measure of freedom, is therefore, conferred on government officials for carrying out administrative schemes. Unless there is rule of law, there is the danger that administration would become totalitarian".

Functions of Administrative Law

Administrative law has come to stay. As regards the functions or scope of administrative law, it primarily consists in finding the ways in which administration could be kept within limits, so that the discretionary powers of administrative authorities could not become arbitrary powers. The task of administrative law is to reconcile the field of administrative action and democratic safeguards with the effective conduct of the government. Professor Wade also emphasizes the same idea by saying that the central question in administrative law is how can the legal ideals of fair procedure and just decisions, be infused into the administrative powers of the state. If proper means of control of executive and quasi-judicial bodies and improving the procedures and extending the scope of Judicial review are imposed on administrative process, dangers of its being arbitrary are reduced. And this is to be all and end of all administrative laws. The administrative process consists of carrying on the business of government or regulating the affairs of individuals in the particular community in the interests of all.[7] The administrative process always involves exercise of some discretion within overall policy laid by the apex level. Thus, the functions of Government or their agents i.e., bureaucracy can be classified as follows;

(A) The Executive:
  (i) Taking decisions
  (ii) Inspection
  (iii) Inquiries
  (iv) Licensing
  (v) Enforcement of standards
  (vi) Appeals
  (vii) Conciliation etc.

(B) The Legislature:
  (i) Enacting rules
  (ii) Delegated legislation or subordinate legislature
  (iii) Inquiries

(C) The Judicial:
  (i) Resolution of disputes between two or more parties
  (ii) Quasi-Judicial functions i.e., judicial decisions with administrative discretion involved like in taxation and other matters involving equitable supply of foodgrains, regulation regarding environment etc.
  (iii) Exercise of judicial powers specifically entrusted by the statutes like powers under Section 144 of Code of Criminal Procedure to prevent breach of peace and maintenance of law and order in the society.

Lord Ripon Reid[8] opines observing in *Ridge vs Baldwin:* "Its growth and development in recent times is due to the fact that in dealing with new types of cases, the courts have had to grope for solutions and have found that old powers, rules and procedures are largely inapplicable to cases which they were never designed or intended to deal with".

---

[7] Garner, J.F.: *Administrative Law*, 5th Edition, Butterworth, London, 1979, p. 5.

[8] (1963) 2 All ER 66(76) HL.

Constitutional Background of Administrative Law

Constitutional Law recognizes administrative law indirectly by envisaging few administrative bodies like Inter State Council (Art. 263), Union Public Service Commission (Art. 315) and Election Commission (Art. 329) etc.

Administrative authorities are subjected to the control of statutes and judicial decisions. In India, the administrative and executive acts can be challenged in the following manner:

(a) Subordinate delegated legislation are expressly brought within the fold of Article 13 of the Constitution by defining 'law' as including 'order' 'bye-law', rule, regulation notification—having the force of law. Thus, the statutory instrument can be challenged as involved not only on the ground of its being ultra vires, the statute which confers power to make it but also on the additional ground that it contravenes any of the fundamental rights contained in Part III of the Constitution of India under Articles 32 and 226.

(b) Even purely administrative action will be void if it contravenes any of those fundamental rights which constitute limitations against any State action.

(c) An administrative act whether statutory or non-statutory will be void if it violates any of the mandatory and justiciable provisions of the Constitution. Remedy of violation of such Constitutional rights is distinct from the violation of fundamental rights and is simple one.

(d) Through Public Interest Litigation, the High Courts and the Supreme Court can review any administrative action in broader public interest.

Through PIL, the Apex Court has created a body of jurisprudence, which is the envy of civilized governance in any part of the world. At the same time, this has become uncontrolled and the judiciary has been stepping into many administrative decisions or actions in the name of broad public interest, which is very vague. The guidelines laid down by the Supreme Court in the 'H.D. Deve Gowda case' to strictly entertain petition in the public interest, are more overlooked than followed. Many orders are passed in PILs by the High Courts and other courts without due consideration of financial and administrative implications. As a result, many of the decisions in PILs are just lying unimplemented. On the other hand, these have created more problems to already over-burdened executive who have obligation to the public through the legislative procedure of budgeting and expenditure. If decisions in all PILs are sincerely and faithfully implemented, no money will be left to pay salaries to government employees nor for any development work. The position has become more acute on the ground level i.e., at the District, municipal or panchayat level. It is better that the time of court is not unnecessarily wasted as because they are engaged in doing the primary duty to resolve disputes between the citizens.

The writ jurisdiction of the Supreme Court under Article 32 controls the state action in violation of fundamental rights guaranteed under Chapter III of the Indian Constitution. Moreover, the right to special appeal given under the Constitution against any award, judgment, decree or order passed by any judicial or quasi-judicial authority in India has vested the Supreme Court with extraordinary jurisdiction to scrutinize the quasi-judicial functions of administrative authorities. The writ jurisdiction of various High Courts of various Central and State administrative Tribunals for the enforcement of a fundamental right as well as any other important legal right against the State actions provides an instance of extraordinary safeguard to citizens of this country. Moreover, supervisory jurisdiction of High Courts on all Courts as well as administrative tribunals, specific provision for contractual and tortuous liability of the Government are remarkable modes of judicial control over the administrative actions in India.

Suggested Form of Administrative Law for India

The Administrative Law in strict sense of positive law is not law. It is a conglomeration of constitutional provisions, statutes, decisional law, rules, regulations, circulars, memoranda etc. It is concerned with various kinds of government, local authorities and public corporations of government agencies, both at the

Centre and at the States and locally with the interplay of ideas and control between these several agencies and the relationships between the several agencies and the general public or the private citizens. It is concerned with the preservation of order, the welfare of the citizen and the rights of the individual as against the government of the country and also with the machinery by which such matters are implemented. Thus, the Indian administrative law in the codified form may consist of the following topics of laws:

(i) Natural justice as propounded by the Supreme Court of India and accepted by the general body politic to the country.

(ii) General guidelines issued for the officers and staff while arriving at a decision or making a suggestion in the file or note.

(iii) Law regarding accountability of the bureaucracy for delay in decision-making or omission in decision-making as because commission and omission are equally punishable before law. The member of public bureaucracy should also be personally liable to the government if the government suffers pecuniary loss due to his latches or malafide decisions. He should be asked to make good the financial loss to the government in terms of penalty, fine or compensation paid by government staff or officer. There will also be appellate fora to reconsider such pecuniary fine and penalty, which will consist of bureaucrats only. This will be like a regulatory authority having specialized persons as members. This will eliminate arbitrariness or subjectivity against the government employee. This function can be done by the Administrative Tribunals already constituted. Twenty-first century belongs to information technology. The administration, which could not keep peace, will be redundant.

(iv) The exceptions in the Contempt of Courts Act should be enlarged and classified. Notice for contempt should be ensured to be delivered personally to the contemner or to his personal assistant or Personal Secretary (PA or PS). Motive should be a good defence in criminal contempt. In case of Small Civil contempt, the fines should be realized personally from the contemner if his personal negligence or ill intention is proved over and above the collective decision mechanism. Contempt power should not be used as a response to failure to implement judgments. If it is so, all in chain should be called for contempt including Ministers. As civil servants are liable for contempt of courts, the subordinate judges should also be liable for not following the judgments or orders of the Superior Courts on equal footing. Truth must be made a defence to the exercise of the power of contempt of court as recommended by the Constitution Review Commission headed by Justice (retd) Venkatchallaiah.

(v) A Commission should be set up at the Central and State Level to regulate transfers, promotions and service conditions of bureaucrats to make them fully transparent and objective.

(vi) Infructuous tiers of appeal like many appellate tribunals should be discontinued since the decision of State Administrative or Central Administrative Tribunals are subject to the appellate jurisdiction of the High Court. In fact, the appeal from Administrative Tribunals should lie to the Supreme Court to ensure efficacy of the Administrative Tribunals and to reduce arrears of cases in High Courts.

(vii) Judicially recognized dimensions of Article 21 like the right of survival, right to shelter, right to a clean and healthy environment and well recognized human rights must be made enforceable rights so that bureaucrats at all levels are well aware of ramifications of their decisions.

(viii) Important constituents of right to information should be part of the Administrative Law of India.

(ix) Constitutional Amendment or Bill after passing by the legislatures should come into force within the specified time periods and should be a part of legislation.

(x) The core powers should not be delegated. The appropriate authority should publish draft of delegated legislation at least 30 days before to receive comments and suggestions from the public. This will bring about awareness of the delegated legislation and will generate public debate. And then, it should be placed before the legislature in due time.

(xi) There should be a constitutional body to investigate instances of corruption. All high functionaries including the Prime Minister like in Lok Pal Bill, should be brought within its ambit. The punishment in the form of pecuniary penalty fine through administrative body should be so much in quantum as the corruption will no longer be a profitable venture.

(xii) Apart from body of law, the administrative law should also contain general code of conduct, which will be generally and equally applicable to all members of the public bureaucracy irrespective of their rank or position in the government. This code of conduct will also help to cover unforeseen actions, actions in unforeseen or emergency situations, commissions or omissions by the bureaucrat.

This whole body of law, rules and guidelines will help the members of public bureaucracy to enlighten themselves regarding their rights, duties and decision-making process in the bureaucratic organization which is intricately linked with the progress of the society or the nation. They will treat it like their Ramayana or the Bible. Thus, the chances of their bona fide errors in decision-making will be less. Many of the cases will not go to law courts delaying the matters further for decision. Last but not the least, public will be greatly benefitted by the just and fair decision-making process at various levels of the bureaucracy and will place their faith and trust in the government bureaucracy.

References

Garner, J.F.: *Administrative Law*, (fifth edition) Butterworth & Co (Publishers) Ltd. 88 Kingsway, London, Year 1979, pp. 525.

Kesari, UPD: *Lectures on Administrative Law*, Central Law Agency, 11 University Road, Allahabad-2. pp. 259.

Subrahmanyam Dr. A.: *Constitutional Law of India*, Andhra Law House, Visakhapatnam, (AP), 2003, pp. 252.

Shukla, V.N.: *The Constitution of India*, (6th Edition), Eastern Book Company, 34 Lalbagh, Lucknow-2266001, 1981, pp. 714.

Wade: *Administrative Law* (5th Edition), Clarendon Press, Oxford, 1982, pp. 892.

Magazine/Periodical

Dr. P.K.Agrawal: *Need of Administrative Law in India* (Hindi) published in *Vidhi Sahitya Samachar, (July–September 2000)*, published by Vidhi Sahitya Prakashan, Ministry of Law, Justice & Company Affairs, Govt. of India, pp. 2–6.

CHAPTER

16 Privatisation

—Subesh K. Das

Increased Role of Private Sector

Privatisation is itself an 'umbrella term' used to cover a wide range of different policy initiatives. The most prominently suggested meaning is 'denationalization' or transfer of ownership into private hands. However, the concept is far wider. It covers 'a range of policy initiatives designed to alter the balance between the public and private sectors'. The concept is to be understood by, 'how far the operations of an enterprise are brought within the discipline of market forces' (Cook and Kirkpatrick, 1988). Experts have described various dimensions of privatisation covering a wide continuum of possibilities starting with 'denationalization' to more reliance on 'market forces' (Ramanadham 1989; Ascher, 1987; Vickers and Wright, 1989). The important ones are:

(1) Denationalisation or transfer of an enterprise or its part into private hands.
(2) Disinvestment or introduction of private capital/sale of government shares.
(3) Leasing out an asset to private company.
(4) Contracting out a job.
(5) Charging for services.
(6) Curtailing public services.
(7) Squeezing subsidies to publicly funded bodies.
(8) Introducing private management techniques and ethos in public sectors.

(9) Encouragement of private participation in new public services projects.
(10) Introduction of competition through deregulation or liberalisation.

Denationalization or transfer of ownership to private hands is the extreme form of privatisation. The other forms like disinvestment, and leasing out can be considered as a step towards denationalization. Liberalisation or deregulation ensures competition, which involves existence of several organisations attempting to provide the same or similar goods or services. In relation to public sector enterprises, competition will mean opening up areas to private sector, which were earlier reserved for public sector.

Throughout the world, there has been a change in 'balance between the public and private sector' activities. The ratio of general government consumption to private consumption for the three groups of countries—low income economies, middle income economies and industrial market economies, is showing a decline since late eighties (Fig. 1). In developed countries, privatisation programme has been initiated because of particular social, economic and political circumstances. In the developing countries, the changes have been induced by adjustment programmes advocated by World Bank and IMF. Policy on privatisation has been adopted by different countries at different points of time. In Britain, it was initiated in 1979. Almost at the same time, the World Bank started using 'policy-based lending', with the recommendation that, 'under most conditions, a better result can be achieved by using the private sector/market forces more fully' (Wallis, 1989; 183). In India, the government initiated structural adjustment programme in 1991. Substantial reform policies have been introduced in the field of trade, industrial policies, and monetary and fiscal policies, with the long term objective of making economy more efficient and competitive. A key component of this is reduction in the role of the state by increasing role of the private sector. Though adjustment programme was initiated in 1991, emphasis on the private sector, started much earlier. The ratio of public sector consumption to private sector consumption shares in GDP started declining from the late eighties.

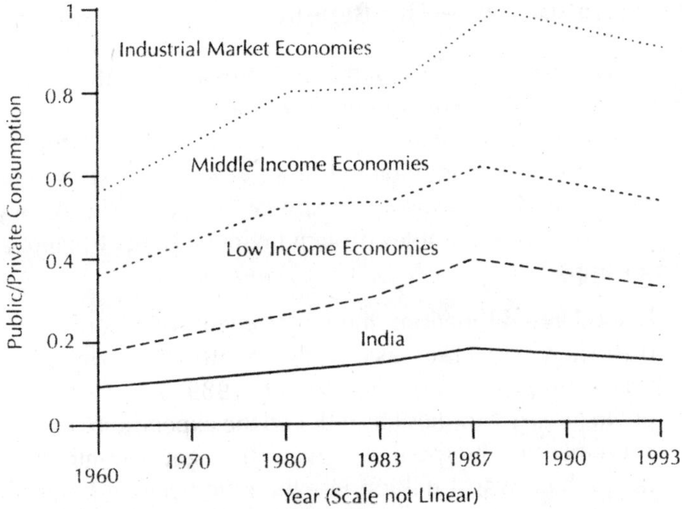

Fig. 16.1: Change in Government Consumption to Private Consumption Ratio in GDP

(*Source:* World Development Bank Report, 1982, 1985, 1987, 1992, 1995; Tables on Structure of Demand)

In the developed countries, the most visible dimension of the change has been denationalization or transfer of public enterprise to private hands, and introduction of private sector management techniques in a public sector. In less developed countries (LDCs) the emphasis is more on cutting subsidies to public sector and deregulation. World Bank's recommendation has also been more on deregulation rather than transfer of ownership (Mosley, 1989; 134). In practice limited denationalization has taken place in the LDCs (Cook and Kirkpatrick, 1989; 28). In India, transfer of ownership and control of state-run units to private ownership and control has taken place in some southern and eastern states. However, no Central Government undertaking has yet been denationalized. Privatisation has been mostly encouraged through opening sectors hitherto reserved for public sector (energy, infrastructure, civil aviation etc.), disinvestment, joint venture, contracting out of jobs, etc. (Ratnam, 1996; 75).

Why Privatisation?—The Benefits

Denationalization reduces budgetary pressure on the governments. Transfer of ownership generates cash from asset sale and stems the drain of finance into the persistent loss makers. Measures like contracting out, curtailing public services, cut in subsidies to publicly funded bodies also give similar benefits. Almost in all countries, there are examples of such financial benefits. Here are some examples:

1. In the United Kingdom, the government sold more than 20 billion worth state assets during the first decade of privatisation (Vickers and Wright, 1989; 22). Contracting out in local authorities has reduced the expenditure on many accounts. In Liverpool, a private firm got a contract at a rate, which was 4 million less than the Council House bid (Farnham and Horton, 1993; 242).
2. In India, disinvestment shares in some selected public sector enterprises raised about 6,900 crore rupees within the first three years of the adjustment programme (1991–94). The subsidy to public sector enterprises was drastically cut. The Central Government expenditure was brought down from 20.3% of GDP in 1989–90, to 16.7% in 1994–95 (*Economic Survey*, 1994–95; 108, 15).

However, the return from sale of assets is a 'once-and-for-all benefit.' The sale or disinvestment of profitable enterprises also forteits the future stream of income for the government. In India, disinvestment was in case of profit making companies. Cook and Kirkpatrick (1989) observed that transfer of ownership has insignificant financial implications for less developed countries. In the less developed countries, the capital market may not be developed enough or private promoters may not be available to replace the public organisations. Imposition of service charges not only increases government revenue, but also adversely affects the poor in developing countries. In Ghana, the Government introduced hospital fees in 1985 to recover part of the cost. In some rural areas, the outpatient attendance dropped by some 50% (Sowa, 1993; 18).

Public organisations are created by government to achieve collective or political goals and to support political objectives and policies. In contrast, private organisations are created by individuals or groups for a market or welfare purpose and are ultimately accountable to owners or members of the group (Farnham and Horton, 1993). While in public organisations objectives are not specified in clear terms, in private organisations objectives are clearly defined and expressed. As privatisation reduces the scope for arbitrary political intervention in the operation of an organisation, it simplifies the objectives of the organisation and improves its efficiency and effectiveness. Evaluation of performance differences between the government-owned, joint sector and private sector of Indian Industry show that, "enterprises owned by the Central Government and the various States in India, while accounting a major chunk of capital investment, are systematically only two-thirds as efficient as private sector enterprises, while joint sector enterprises are also less efficient than those in the private sector" (Majumdar, 1995; M–25). This is in conformity with the economic theory posting higher efficiency levels for the private sector. Private firms need to perform efficiently and effectively to remain in business (Yarrow, 1989; p. 68).

Benefits of denationalization cannot always be claimed in clear terms, particularly in respect of state monopolies. Stelzer (1989) claimed that, "even monopolies are more likely to operate efficiently in the private than in a public sector." But the implications are not always so straightforward. In Britain, most early privatisation involved firms which operated in more or less competitive conditions and they had shown good results. This was followed by privatisation of monopolies—telephone, water and gas—where the position was much less clear (Yarrow, 1989;68; Velijanovski, 1989;26). The all-round benefits from such privatisation programme will ultimately depend on the extent to which it maximises competition and how far the government is able to regulate the functioning of the privatised monopolies.

Competition generates efficiency and ensures consumer benefits. It ensures that customers are provided with goods and services at a price that reflects the opportunity costs of producing them. This is because the spur of profit encourages others to enter markets and provide services. There are many examples of improvement in performance with deregulation. In India air transport has been deregulated, ending monopoly of airlines in the public sector. This has substantially improved passenger facilities and on time performance (*Economic Survey*, 1994–95; 147–148). However, increase of competition is not a simple matter and benefits are often constrained by several complications. It is particularly difficult in case of natural monopolies with extensive market power. Removal of statutory barrier is not always enough. It does not ensure that new entrants can compete in fair terms, specially in view of the market power enjoyed by the incumbent firms. Thus, deregulation measures must accompany a regulatory mechanism to control anti-competitive behaviour like reducing prices below the cost price when rival tries to enter the market. Thus, much will depend on how the regulatory authority can ensure effective competition (Vickers and Yarrow, 1990).

Indiscriminate deregulation may not be appropriate in less developed countries. The economic success of the newly developed countries, shows use of selective protection and subsidisation policies (Cook and Kirkpatrick, 1988). In a competitive environment, the firms with superior managerial skills prosper at the cost of local firms. This leads to industrial concentration in the hands of few firms. We even find this evidence in developed countries. In USA, the airlines industry went through major deregulation during 1981–83. Immediately there was all-round gain in productivity and an overall reduction of fare. Initially the local service carriers expanded their operations, but in subsequent years they could not compete with trunk route carriers and the airlines industry was once again dominated by the big carriers (Dalvi, 1995; 105).

Contracting out of work or compulsory competitive tendering, in areas that were traditionally carried out by inhouse provision, is being increasingly used to reduce cost of service. However, it is still a controversial issue. Supporters of the programme believe that private sector delivery is more cost-effective and efficient than inhouse provision. In contrast, opponents argue that indirect delivery reduces accountability, democratic control (newly elected body has to honour a previous contract), and quality of services. Profit motive sometimes encourages to do the job as quickly and as cheaply as possible. It often leads to increase in nepotism and corruption among public officials. Management at senior level becomes politicised and fails to remain neutral professionally (Farnham and Horton, 1993; 248; Vickers and Wright, 1998; 25). Thus contracting out works smoothly in nonpolitical environment and they arise normally (Ascher, 1987). Most experiences on benefits of privatisation are from developed countries. We cannot make a straightforward claim that similar benefits will accrue in the developing countries. The benefits will depend on the socio-economic conditions and political environment in which the changes take place.

References

Asher K. (1987): *The Politics of Privatisation Contracting out Public Services.* London: Macmillan.

Cook P. and Kirkpatrick C. (1988): *Privatisation in Less Developed Countries.* London: Routledge.

Dalvi M.Q. (1995): Should Indian Railways Be Privatised. In *Economic and Political Weekly.* Vol XXX, No–2. January, 1995. pp. 103–112.

Das S.K. (1986): Social Security for the Unorganised Poor. In *Journal of Rural Development.* Hyderabad: National Institute of Rural Development. Vol. 15, No. 3: pp. 339–255.

Darnham D. and Horton S. (1993): *Managing the New Public Services.* London: Macmillan.

Financial Times (1995, September 30): Interview of Dr Manmohan Singh, Finance Minister of India. September 30, 1995.

Flynn N. (1993): *Public Sector Management.* London: Harvester Wheat Sheaf.

Gill S.S. (1996): Punjab: Privatising Health Care. In *Economic and Political Weekly.* Vol XXXI, No. 1. Pp. 18–21. Bombay EPW Research Foundation.

Government of India (1915): *Economic Survey*, 1994–95, New Delhi: Ministry of Finance, Economic Division.

Government of West Bengal: Department of Labour (1997). *Labour in West Bengal*, 1996. Calcutta: Department of Labour

Mani S. (1995): Economic Liberalisation and the Industrial Sector. In *Economic and Political Weekly.* Vol XXXI, No. 48. November 3014, 1996. Page M–46–54.

Mazumdar S.K. (1995): Public, Joint and Private Sectors in Indian Industry-Evaluating Relative Performance Differences. In *Economic and Political Weekly.* Vol XX, No. 7&8, February 18, 25. 1995. Page M–25–32.

Mosley P. (1988): Privatisation, Policy-Based Lending and World Bank Behaviour. In Cook and Kirkpatrick *Privatisation in Less Developed Countries.* New York: Harvester Wheatsheaf.

Ramanadham V.V. (1989): *Privatisation in Developing Countries.* London: Routledge.

Radygin A. (1995): *Privatisation in Russia—Hard Choice, First Results. New Targets.* London: The Centre of Research into Communist Economics.

Ratnam C.S.V. (1996): *Industrial Relations in Indian States: Delhi:* Global Business Press.

Richardson J.J. (1990): *Privatisation and Deregulation in Canada and Britain.* Dortmouth: Dortmouth Publishing Company Limited.

Sowa N.K. (1993): Ghana. In Adepoju A. *The Impact of Structural Adjustment on the Population of Africa.* London: Hennemann.

Stelzedr I. (1989): *Privatisation and Regulation: Oft-Necessary Compliments.* In Velijanovski C (1989) Privatisation and Competition A Market Prospectus. London: Institute of Economic Affairs.

Stephen C. (1995): Contracting in Local Government: Cutting by Privatisation. In *Public Policy and Administration.* Vol. 10, No. 3, Autumn, 1995. Page 29–44.

Veljanovski C. (1989): *Privatisation and Competition—A Market Prospectus.* London: Institute of Economic Affairs.

Vickers J. and Yarrow G. (1990): Regulation of Privatised Firms in Britain. In Richardson J.J. (1990) *Privatisation and Deregulation in Canada and Britain*. Dortmouth: Dortmouth Publishing Company Limited.

Wallis Malcom (1989): *Bureaucracy: Its Role in Third World Development*. London: Macmillan.

World Bank (1982): *World Development Report*, 1982. Oxford: Oxford University Press for World Bank.

______ (1985): *World Development Report*, 1985. Oxford: Oxford University Press for World Bank.

______ (1987): *World Development Report*, 1987. Oxford: Oxford University Press for World Bank.

______ (1992): *World Development Report*, 1992. Oxford: Oxford University Press for World Bank.

______ (1995): *World Development Report*, 1995. Oxford: Oxford University Press for World Bank.

Yarrow G. (1989): Does Ownership Matter. In Velijanovski C. (1989) *Privatisation and Competition—A Market Prospectus*. London: Institute of Economic Affairs.

CHAPTER

17 State Impunity and the Violation of Human Rights in Relief and Rehabilitation: A Case Study of Gujarat

The state of Gujarat has been torn apart by savage sectarian violence, possibly the most brutal since Independence. There is today widely shared national outrage and anguish, about the enormity of mass brutality which was substantially targeted at women and children from the minority community, and the role of the state authorities who enabled or actively abetted the planned massacre and destruction. This carnage that has convulsed the state of Gujarat in February-March, 2002 involves profound state impunity and violation of human rights. What has been comparatively well documented so far by civil rights activists and a series of people's tribunals has been the role of the state government in enabling the planned carnage, and the complicity and active abetment by state authorities in the mass violence. There has also been some civil society investigation into the deliberate subversion of the criminal justice system, to assist those guilty for the crimes to escape the irresolute arm of the law.

However, what has been much less documented is the unprecedented role of state authorities in wantonly neglecting relief and rehabilitation of the survivors of the mass violence, and even subverting the few non-government efforts to compensate for state failures. Unlike the statutory powers and obligations of state authorities to control public disorders, which are clearly elaborated in the Criminal Procedure Code, 1973 and various police acts, the duties of the state to provide shelter and relief to those devastated, displaced and destitute as the result of sectarian violence, and to help rebuild their lives, including shelters and livelihoods, has not been specifically spelt out in any statute. But it is implied in the fundamental rights to life and equality. In the past, what have never been in dispute have been the obligations of the state in these circumstances, and state authorities have always accepted central responsibility for relief and rehabilitation after sectarian violence. The performance of state authorities has often been lackadaisical, and the outcomes tragic, even spectacular failures, but the *principle* of the centrality of state responsibility for relief and rehabilitation has never been seriously under challenge. The practice of state authorities in Gujarat amounts to impunity and an implied challenge to this principle. The failures of various executive, judicial and civil society institutions to hold the state accountable for this profound and brazen violation of the fundamental rights of its citizens, poses a grave threat to humane, democratic and just governance.

Even four months after the enormous human and social tragedy began to unfold in Gujarat, very little has been done to address even the basic survival needs of the nearly two lakh people economically and socially displaced by the violence. In the immediate aftermath of the violence, there were at least 100,000 women, children and men, 103 relief camps in Ahmedabad alone. An estimated 50,000 people were in similar camps across the state in Gujarat. People were condemned to live as internal refugees in their own land, often their own cities. The violence continued unchecked for nearly three and a half months. Regrettably, there is little evidence of significant state or civil society efforts for long-term rehabilitation of the survivors of mass violence. Even now there is little hope visible on even the distant horizon for the survivors of the mass violence, including around 30,000 people who subsisted in inhuman conditions in the camps.

Backdrop

It may be useful to begin by recapitulating the backdrop of the challenges which confront the government, and indeed the entire nation, in relation to the tasks of relief, rehabilitation and reconciliation in Gujarat. These include the following:

- The mass-violence in Gujarat since February 27, 2002 is in many ways the most brutal and widespread since Partition.
- The violence has resulted in the deaths of nearly 1000 persons, many of them women and children. (Unofficial estimates are more than 2000)
- It has targeted a large number of women and girls with sexual violence.
- Houses and commercial establishments have been looted and gutted across the state, resulting in mass destruction of livelihoods.
- Places of worship have been specifically targeted.
- Nearly one lakh people are in makeshift camps run largely by self-help efforts of the affected communities. These camps mostly lack minimal basic amenities.
- The overwhelmingly large part of the violence has targeted the minority community.
- Communal hatred has been actively fostered in Gujarati society in recent decades, with ghettoisation in towns and cities, and deep distrust infecting even the countryside.
- The state government has done little to manage relief, or to harness the resources required for long-term rehabilitation.

It is against this grim scenario that any strategy for relief, rehabilitation and reconciliation in Gujarat needed to be constructed.

Relief Camps

The principle that underlies the state responsibility in such situations, and the practice even of the colonial government in pre-Independence days, which has been strengthened further by Relief Codes, government circulars and practice after

Independence, is that in any natural and human-made disaster, including riots, the state government is the primary agency responsible to provide relief, succour, security and rehabilitation to the victims of such disasters. It may seek the assistance of NGOs in these tasks, but it cannot be allowed to abdicate its own central responsibility to NGOs. Therefore, the state government must take direct responsibility not only for the food, but also the safety, shelter protection from the extremes of climate, health, psycho-social support to deal with their trauma, sanitation, education and rehabilitation of all the children, women, men and children housed in its camps, and affected by the mass violence.

In Gujarat, the overwhelming majority of camps were set up, and continue to be run, by self-help efforts of the Muslim community. The few Hindu camps, mostly housing people living in Muslim dominated areas who feared reprisal attacks, were similarly run by Hindu organizations, although with more conspicuous state support.

State authorities maintain that it is the culture of Gujarat that NGOs establish and run relief efforts. It is euphemistic to describe the support for most camps as even coming from NGOs, because like the state, the majority of mainstream NGOs which were so active in the relief and reconstruction work after the killer earthquake in 2001, have chosen to distance themselves from healing and rebuilding in this far more politically volatile human tragedy. The result is that in practice, camps are running substantially on the strength of self-help efforts of the affected communities. These self-help efforts even amidst so much adversity inspire great admiration, but this does not absolve the state of its direct and central responsibility that basic living conditions and services are ensured in the relief camps. Tomorrow, if for instance epidemics break out in the camps, state authorities rather than the camp managers, must be liable.

After an average of ten days subsequent to the violence, state authorities commenced the supply of basic rations to the camp, along with a grant of five rupees per head per day to cover costs of cooking, etc. The food is prepared and served in orderly shifts by volunteers from among the camp residents. However, resources are required for much more than just food, in running such populous relief camps of devastated people. Our deep worry remained unaddressed that if resources from relief did not come from the state, donor and aid agencies or NGOs, an impoverished, hapless and gravely threatened community would increasingly find itself thrown into the hands of either the mafia or fundamentalist leaders.

Camp residents, the majority of whom have survived with only the clothes on their backs, need additional sets of clothes, as well as a small allowance for daily expenses. Earlier State Government instructions, dating back to 1985, fixed cash doles for victims of communal riots in camps at Rs.5 per day, and a household kit allowance at Rs. 650 per family. The State Government has raised the household kit allowance to Rs. 1250 per family, and cash doles have been raised to take account of inflation to Rs. 15 per day. However, the State Government has limited this assistance to only 15 days, in contrast to the earlier assistance of Rs.5 that was available for the entire duration of their residence in the camps. The raised dole of Rs. 15 per day per head should also be for the entire duration of the camps. This is to assist the camp residents to meet their daily expenses, and should be provided to them on a daily or weekly basis through the camp management itself. It is important to remember that most of the survivors of the mass violence escaped with no personal belongings. They need some money daily for their minimal personal expenses.

Another matter of grave concern is sanitation. In most camps, the number of available toilets and bathing places in abysmally less than needed, and camp authorities find it difficult to ensure the cleanliness of the toilets. Whereas this compromises the privacy of the residents, especially women, an even far more serious worry is that failures in sanitation, particularly after the rains break out, have the potential of causing epidemics. We need to establish some minimum acceptable ratio of toilets and bathing spaces at all camps, and arrangements for their cleanliness.

Camps, temporary homes to often several thousand children, women and men, are organised mainly in dargahs, schools or graveyards. The majority of residents live in open shamianas.

Makeshift canvas covers were the only protection against the blazing summer heat. However, the survival of the camps and its hapless residents was most threatened by the on-coming monsoons. The camps were low-lying, with tattered canvas covers, no match for the monsoon rains. Activists attempted to alert the state government about the special vulnerability of the residents of the camps during the monsoon rains, and their desperate need for rain-proof shelters. However efforts through the Courts, the National Human Rights Commission and the national media failed to secure state action to construct these shelters.

Finally, three weeks before the outbreak of monsoons, when it became clear that the survivors in the camps would be unprotected from the fury of monsoon rains, a few local organisations decided to build the rain-proof shelters themselves. With volunteers deployed from across the country, rain-proof shelters were constructed with plastic, canvas and bamboo scaffoldings. This massive effort has succeeded in preventing the forced distress dispersal of the most destitute survivors who still remained in the camps.

Civil rights activists and organizations failed to pressurize the state government also to ensure minimal standards of sanitation and clean drinking water, public health and education. Directions of the National Human Rights Commission and outrage in the national media was resolutely ignored by the state government, which refused to provide much more than ration supplies, occasional visits by doctors and grants to run some temporary schools in camps.

It is indeed tragic that such large numbers of citizens are forced to subsist in refugee camps, reminiscent of the camps after Partition, for extended periods. The residents of these camps who are forced to live without work or personal spaces, in very austere physical conditions, long to return to normalcy. But they can be expected to do so, only if they feel secure and have the resources for rebuilding their lives. The neglect of these would prolong their agony, but to force the pace of their exit from the camps without this, would threaten their very survival.

It is urgent that clear and unambiguous statutory instructions are issued and widely publicised, that relief camps can be wound up only after state authorities accomplish the following: (a) full restoration of enduring peace and harmony in the affected areas, so that residents feel secure to return to their normal lives; and (b) full implementation of relief and rehabilitation packages which enable the survivors of mass violence to rebuild and restart their lost shelters and livelihoods, which were devastated in the mass violence. Camps should be shut only when the survivors who have sought the shelter and security of the camps, are voluntarily willing to leave the camps for their homes. Until the voluntary disbanding of camps by the residents themselves, food supplies, sanitation, health care, education and protection against the rains and heat, according to international standards for refugees must be ensured, if the fundamental rights to life and equality of the camp residents are to be secured.

There were at the time of writing an estimated 20,000 people left in around 27 camps in Ahmedabad, and an estimated 10,000 in camps in the rest of the state. They desperately required the following amenities:

- Regular food supplies, which are threatened because the state government has cut off supplies in many camps. Food for infants and children are a special priority.
- Sanitation, drainage, toilets, bathing facilities especially for the women and clean drinking water, all of which are vital to protect public health which is specially endangered in the monsoon.
- Immunization and other public health interventions.
- Fire-fighting arrangements.
- Child care and education facilities and support, with special focus on girl children.
- Clothes and undergarments.

After the monsoons broke out, the state government has mercilessly stopped even the supply of rations to the majority of the camps. The district authorities have served notice to the camp residents that the camps are unauthorized, there would be no provisioning of food or visits by medical teams. The notices pasted in various camps ominously add that the state government would not be responsible if any calamity or *'aafat'* befalls the camp.

District authorities maintain that they want to relocate the camp residents to three large camps. But they are unable to explain how several thousand more women, children and men can be accommodated in these camps, when there continue in these camps sub-human facilities even for the original residents. In the absence of rain-proof shelters and sanitation, crowding these camps further would further mount their distress. The residents themselves are unwilling to be shunted like unwanted cattle. However hard life is in these camps, at least they are close to their old homes and some have been able to find casual work. Virtually unassisted, they have courageously commenced their uphill journey to rebuild their lives. It would be unconscionable for state authorities to make this journey even harder.

However, despite written assurances to both the National Human Rights Commission and the Gujarat High Court, as well as discussions in the presence of the Prime Minister with a delegation of concerned citizens led by I K Gujral, state authorities persisted stubbornly with their pitiless enterprise to close camps and to starve them even of food supplies.

Compensation

The survivors of the mass violence are facing insurmountable difficulties to secure even the meagre compensation that is assured by circulars of the government. Many of these problems are built into the design of the instructions, others are the outcome of openly partisan implementation by state authorities.

(i) *Death Compensation.* The Government of Gujarat has announced a death compensation of Rs. 1 lakh for every person killed in the riots, and the Prime Minister has announced an additional support of Rs. 50,000. The first difficulty here is that this support is available only on the production of a death certificate. However, the overwhelming majority of the victims were so badly burned that they could not be identified. The problem was further aggravated by the turbulence created by the mass violence that separated the survivors from their dead.

In these circumstances, it is not acceptable that the unidentified dead should be legally treated only as 'missing persons', which would mean in effect that the survivors would be eligible for compensations after the lapse of maybe seven years.

Instead, a sympathetic state administration could have developed alternate mechanisms to verify deaths. For instance, an application and affidavit by the next of kin, supported by five affidavits by neighbours or observers, could be accepted. This may be corroborated by documents like the 2001 census, voters' list, ration card or birth certificate. Even if the authorities feel that more evidence is required, death compensation should be sanctioned based on prima facie evidence to the next of kin in the form of bonds that can be redeemed only after the investigation is concluded. However, in the meanwhile, it would ensure that the next of kin is able to subsist on the interest.

Special measures are required to protect the interests of children who have lost both parents and widows, who may be pressurized and exploited by close or distant kin in order to secure the compensation. For the orphaned children, the compensation should be in the form of bonds that would mature only when the child reaches the age of 18. For widows, compensation in the form of 5-year bonds would help stave off pressures for the money from the husband's family.

(ii) *Assistance for Person with Injuries and Disabilities*. In the past, the state government used to provide assistance for medicines incurred due to injuries, based on duly certified medical bills. However, this provision has been deleted and the State Government's assistance is no longer for medical expenses for injuries, but is instead for disabilities. One problem with this approach is that injuries in the mass violence may or may not lead to permanent disabilities. The State Government must provide (a) reimbursement of all medical expenses in injuries including burn injuries, in duly recognised hospitals; (b) compensation of temporary loss of livelihoods in temporary disabilities; and (c) compensation for permanent disabilities as provided for in the government's circular. It is also recommended that certification procedures for burn and other injuries, temporary and permanent disability are completed within the camps themselves.

Every affected family, regardless of whether or not they have suffered bodily injuries, should be given a medical card, initially for six months which would entitle her/him to medical facilities at a clinic or hospital of their choice. The State Government should notify a list of private hospitals which would be bound to give medical facilities (especially specialised services, which are not available in government hospitals).

(iii) *Compensation for Livelihoods.* The large majority of camp residents are impoverished casual workers, artisans, industrial workers, petty traders or members of their families. There are other more wealthy survivors of the mass violence who have lost their business establishments or factories, and they are mostly not in relief camps.

Given that the numbers of damaged business establishments, small and large, run into tens of thousands and are spread across the state, and that the losses amount to thousands of crores of rupees, the challenge of rebuilding the lost livelihoods of the survivors of mass violence is extremely daunting. It would require the mobilisation of enormous resources of government, financial institutions, aid agencies and the private sector.

Existing instructions of the Government of Gujarat, dating back to 1989, provided for financial grants up to Rs. 10000 for riot victims who have lost their earning assets. The new norms recently issued by the State Government provide for assistance up to Rs. 10000 based on actual damage of moveable and immovable earning properties.

This ex-gratia assistance expressly debars the riot victim from seeking loans and subsidies under other schemes of the Industry Department. The ex-gratia relief that riot victims will receive is likely to be much less than the full resources required by the riot victims to rebuild their lost livelihoods. Therefore, the provision debarring recipients of ex-gratia relief for securing benefits of other government schemes must be removed. On the contrary, the State Government should make special efforts to secure the access of the riot victims to receive assistance to rebuild their lost livelihoods, by a convergence of all government schemes in a single window. The anti-poverty schemes of the Ministries of

Rural Development and Urban Development of the Government of India must also be made available on priority for these riot victims. There should also be a floor below which compensation cannot go.

The poorest casual wage labourers who are rendered unemployed because of the mass violence, should be assisted by a Special Employment Guarantee Programme extending to both urban and rural areas, for a minimum period of one year, from the date of the departure of the adult wage workers from the camps. Finally, for non-able-bodied persons without care-givers (old people, persons with disabilities, widows etc.) full social security coverage under existing schemes should be ensured before their departure from the camps.

(iv) *Compensation for Shelters.* An even more daunting challenge is the reconstruction of shelters of almost two lakh persons rendered homeless overnight because of the mass violence. Homes have been looted, stripped bare of their belongings, damaged and burned by marauding mobs.

The Prime Minister announced an ex-gratia assistance to families whose houses were damaged or destroyed at Rs. 50000. Instructions of the state government fixed the assistance up to Rs 50000. Evaluation teams of only government functionaries have tended to work entirely without transparency and empathy, or even technical rigour, and average house compensation paid has been around Rs. 5000.

Surveys by NGOs have found that evaluation teams have fixed housing compensations at very low levels, even well below the already low ceilings. A report of the Citizens Initiative states, for instance, that in Sankalit Nagar, Juhapara, Ahmedabad, of 49 houres burnt completely. 13, that is 27% houses have received compensation between Rs. 1000–2000. 18, that is 9% houses have received compensation between Rs. 2000–5000. 18, that is 9% houses have received compensation between Rs. 5000–10000. Another 18 that is 9% houses have received a compensation which was more than Rs. 10000. One house has received less than Rs. 500. As per the report of an NGO Disha of Wadali Camp in Dahod, most people have received housing compensation of as little as Rs. 200 to Rs. 500.

It would be impossible to rebuild even a mud and thatch hut, let alone equip a house with these levels of 'compensation'. Teams of evaluation of house damage, must include representatives of the riots victims and non-government technical experts, and this must be concluded within one month, because without such assistance, it would be impossible for the survivors of mass violence to move out of the camps into their own reconstructed shelters.

Even these grants would be very meagre given the scale of resources that affected families would require to rebuild their homes. It is possible only if there is a massive mobilisation of housing and other financial instructions, and a single window access to their soft loans organised within the camps themselves. The NHRC instructions had suggested the involvement of HUDCO, HDFC and international financial institutions and development organisations, for augmenting the vast resources required by the riot victims for rebuilding their houses. This does not seem to have yet been done.

Many of the most vulnerable riot victims may be (a) encroachers (without legal title to their house sites; or (b) tenants who are evicted after the house damage. Government instructions must clearly specify that these categories of riots victims are entitled to the same housing compensation and other assistance as other houseowners with legal rights. Unless this is done, the most vulnerable survivors of mass violence would be rendered homeless or would be precariously housed. The government can prevent this only by providing secure land titles for houses to all these vulnerable groups, regardless of their status prior to the mass violence.

One final thorny issue relates to riot victims who refuse to return to their old places of shelter, because of fear. All effort must be made to build confidence of the riot victims to return to their old places of residence, in order to prevent ghettoisation. However, in case they continue to be insistent, the State Government would need to come up with a house-site exchange scheme, under which house-sites in one locality can be exchanged for house-sites of equal value in another locality. In case of relocation, there should be admission in neighbourhood schools without red tape.

Rehabilitation: An Overview

The underlying principle of rehabilitation must be that it is the state government's responsibility to ensure that victims of riots are restored to a situation which is as close as possible to that which obtained prior to the mass violence. This requires a number of things, including:

- Adequate compensation for loss of life, limb, shelter, livelihoods, and temporary disability, dispersed expeditiously and through transparent processes.
- Rebuilding of shelters at the old location, or a new one if the riot victim feels unsafe;
- Rebuilding and strengthening of old livelihoods, or building new livelihoods if the old ones are unavailable after the riot;
- Full medical assistance to those who suffered injury;
- Psycho-social counselling to assist the survivors to deal with their grief, anger and sense of betrayal. There would be special assistance to women who have suffered sexual abuse, and all children;
- Legal assistance to file criminal charges, and in the subsequent investigation, because there can be no healing if justice is not seen to be done.

For rehabilitation of this scale the central and state government, international and national financial institutions, and donor agencies, need to commit substantial resources. The state government should prepare a comprehensive rehabilitation plan, and individual rehabilitation plans for each affected family. There must be a specified time-frame, and there should be no pressure on families to leave camps prior to the full rehabilitation of the family. A quick damage assessment survey is proposed to assess the design of the support. This must be with full participation of the persons affected and living in the camps and outside. Again simple procedures and single window approaches are being proposed. The damage assessment needs to take the impact on family as a unit, and that individual level family change plans are evolved in a participatory manner to cover among other things the livelihood and shelter reconstruction.

Since it would take every family at least one year to rebuild their lives, food and financial assistance should be assured on a monthly basis to every family for at least one year even after they leave the camps. For some groups, like old people without care-givers, it may be necessary to put together long term social security measures.

However, no such effort, either by the central or state governments, or the international aid community, is in evidence. The devastated survivors have substantially been left to their own devices to rebuild their shattered lives, after the payment by the state of niggardly sums of compensation.

Reconstruction of Places of Worship

The reconstruction of destroyed places of worship, at state expense, is an established principle from earlier riots. It is an important component of healing the wounded psyche of affected people. The State Government should (a) formulate; (b) widely publicise; and (c) implement this policy at the earliest.

There is particularly urgency in the context of places of worship which have been buried under roads, over which traffic have begun to ply. The restoration of these places of worship must take first priority.

However, the state government has refused to adhere to these precedents. Several hundred mosques across the state of Gujarat continue desecrated and in ruins, replaced in many places by saffron flags and statues of Hanuman, described by the rioters as *Hullad Hanuman* (Hanuman of the riots). Many of these are historical monuments, an important element of the shared pluralistic legacy of the people of Gujarat.

Independent Monitoring Mechanisms

The foregoing is evidence of enormous state impunity, even in relief and rehabilitation, and determined, wanton, and persistent denial of the human rights of the survivors of the mass violence. It is only if the Supreme Court sets up an on-going independent monitoring mechanism for on-going concurrent review of the relief, rehabilitation and reconciliation efforts in Gujarat, that there is any hope for a reversal of this injustice imposed by the state on a section of its own people. It is suggested for this that the Supreme Court appoints a whole-time Commissioner exclusively for this purpose for one year. The Commissioner would be free to take the assistance of local aid workers, civil rights activists, women's groups, lawyers, doctors and government officials, to concurrently independently monitor the progress and compliance with the instruments of the Court.

Conclusion

The carnage in Gujarat in Feb.-March, 2002, represents an unprecedented challenge to the people of India. If they permit the state to conspire not on in the massacre of a section of its people by mass violence, but also in novel dimensions of silent annihilation through wanton sabotage of all established norms of relief and rehabilitation, our survival as a humane and democratic society and polity is threatened as never before.

CHAPTER

18 Conscience, Character and the Use of Force

—By Harsh Mander

The conscience of the nation has been shaken by the systematic slaughter of innocents in Gujarat, the planned murder, rape and pillage, specially targeting small children and women. With our humanity in tatters—blood drenched, shamed, threatened as rarely before—there is a slowly growing resolve across the country that we must find ways to ensure that this is never allowed to happen again.

To prevent the recurrence of such machinated mass brutality in the future, it is of utmost importance also that all those who are responsible for the current carnage are identified and resolutely held to account. This has rarely happened in the past, instead the nation has seen those liable for such crimes against humanity thrive electorally and professionally, while the devastated victims of sectarian violence are denied even elementary succour and justice. If this is allowed to happen once again in Gujarat, then this is not the last time that our hands will be soiled with the blood of innocents.

There are many groups of people who bear responsibility for the crimes in Gujarat. I choose to focus here on the role of only one of them, the higher police and civil services. The reasons for this focus are that it is a vocation whose central calling is the upholding of justice, of law, order and the protection of vulnerable people. Default in the performance of one's duty by a civil or police officer in a riot is not only the crime of a citizen who turns one's face away from injustice, because of indifference, fear or complicity. It is a crime of much graver magnitude, akin to that of a surgeon who wantonly kills his patient on the operation table.

Until the 1980s, there was an unwritten agreement in our polity that even if politicians inflamed communal passions, the police and civil administration would be expected to act professionally and impartially to control the riots in the shortest possible time, and to protect innocent lives. There were several failures in performance, and minorities were targeted in many infamous riots, but the rules of the game were still acknowledged and in the majority of instances adhered to, which is why the higher civil and police services were regarded to be the steel frame vital to preserve the unity and plurality of the country.

The 1980s saw the breaking of this unwritten compact which has led to the corrosion and near collapse of the steel frame. It became the frequent practice for the higher civil and police authorities to be instructed to actively connive in the systematic slaughter of one community, and to do this by delaying sometimes by several days, the use of force to control riots. Local state authorities complied, and rioters were unrestrained by state power in their mass murder, arson and plunder.

Why is the decisive and timely use of state coercive force—lathis, tear-gas and bullets by police, paramilitary and military contingents—so vital a duty of the state in a communal situation? In every other kind of public disorder—labour, student or peasant protests—the broad consensus across a wide section of liberal opinion is that a democratic state must apply the principle of minimum necessary use of force to restore public order and security, respecting the right of democratic dissent and the expressions of public anger against perceived injustices and grievances.

In situations of sectarian violence, by contrast, the responsibility of the state is completely different from any other. A humane and responsive democratic government must apply in all such situations of communal riots, or violence against minorities or dalits—the principle not of minimum necessary application of force, but instead the responsible but *maximum possible* use of force that the state can muster in the shortest possible time. This is because unlike other expressions of public anger, communal violence targets almost invariably people who are most vulnerable and defenceless. It is fuelled by perilous and explosive mass sentiments of irrationality, unreason, prejudice and hatred, and its poison spreads incrementally over space and time. Its wounds do not heal across generations. The partition of our country continues to scar our psyche half a century after its bloody passage. A whole decade of terrorists in Punjab traced their origins to the maraudings of the 1984 rioters. As I held on my lap a six-year-old boy in a camp in Ahmedabad who described the killings of his mother and six siblings, I felt broken by his pain that can never heal, but wondered at the same time how he would deal with his anger when he grows up. Likewise, the ashes of the horrific burnings in Godhra will stir up their own poison. But it is important to understand that the cycles of hatred did not begin in the railway compartments of Godhra, and they will not end in the killing fields of Gujarat.

It is for this reason that every moment's delay by state authorities to apply sufficient force to control communal violence is such an unconscionable crime: it means more innocents will be slaughtered, raped and maimed, but also that wounds would be opened which may not heal for generations.

Civil and police authorities today openly await the orders of their political supervisors before they apply force, so much so that it has become popular perception that indeed they cannot act without the permission of their administrative and political superiors, and ultimately the chief minister. The legal position is completely at variance with this widely held view. It is unambiguous, in empowering local civil authorities to take all decisions indepehdently about the use of force to control public disorders, including calling in the army. The magistrate is not required to consult her or his administrative superiors, let alone those who are regarded as their political 'masters'. The law is clear that in the performance of this responsibility, civil and police authorities are their own masters, responsible above all to their own judgement and conscience. There are no alibis that the law allows them.

It may be argued that this may be an accurate description of the legal situation, but the practice on the ground has sanctified the practice of political consultation before force is applied. Only to convince the reader that I speak from the experience of myself handling many riots, I could contest this with my own experience in the major riots of 1984 and 1989, where as an executive magistrate I took decisions about the use of force and calling in the army, without any consultation. I could similarly contest this with the experience of many other women and men of character in the civil and police services across the country, who would similarly testify to salutary application of force, to control more difficult communal violence, without recourse to political clearances. There can be no dispute that given administrative and political will, no riot can continue unchecked beyond a few hours.

However, I will not substantiate this with my own experience, or those of older officers. It gives me greatest pride and hope, amidst the darkness that we find ourselves in today, to talk of the independent action taken by a few young officers in Gujarat and neighbouring Rajasthan during the present crisis itself.

Rahul Sharma was posted as SP, Bhavnagar for less than a month when Godhra killings and the subsequent rioting all over Gujarat happened. Following Godhra, he deployed a strong police contingent for the Gujarat Bandh called by the VHP the next day on 28 February. Unlike the rest of Gujarat, the day passed off without much trouble in Bhavnagar. But the next day, Rahul learned that a mob of around 2000 men armed with swords, trishuls, spears, stones, burning torches, petrol bombs and acid bottles, was about to attack a madarssa with around 400 small Muslim boys between the age of 12 and 15. Rahul rushed there with a police force of around 50 people. Seeing that the force was hesitant to open fire on the armed mob Rahul himself took the rifle from a fellow constable and opened fire. As some attackers fell to police bullets, the crowd stopped in its tracks and faded away.

Rahul then made an entry in the logbook saying that he had fired from the constable's gun to save the lives of the children. He also gave an order that any policeman with a gun not opening fire to save human lives from a violent mob would be prosecuted for abetting murder. This gave a clear signal to the police force that the SP meant business, was willing to take full responsibility for his actions and was prepared to stick out his neck any far. This had an immediate effect on his force, and Bhavnagar was a town where more rioters were killed in police firing than innocent victims in actual rioting. For this, Rahul was moved out from Bhavnagar in a mere month of his assuming charge. He is quoted in the *Outlook* as saying, "I'm not one to run away from transfers. I take these things in my stride. Other than controlling the riots, I did no mischief."

In neighbouring Rajasthan, the Superintendent of Police of Ajmer, Saurabh Srivastava, with a young SDM in his first charge and his small force, doused communal fires in Kishangarh on March 1, 2002, which had the potential of inflaming the tinder box of the entire state. They controlled an enraged armed mob of over a thousand men bent on attacking minorities in a pitched battle for over four hours.

Another defence that we are hearing is that the lower police force has become hopelessly charged with the communal virus, therefore it is impossible to deploy it as non-partisan instrument of coercive force to control rioting. It is true that our men and women in khaki work under conditions of great stress, long hours, inadequate facilities and uninspiring training. Even so, whenever commanded by leaders of character, who are non-partisan, professional, fearless and lead from the front, the same forces are known to protect peace admirably.

It is sometimes also argued that the entire higher civil and police services have become politicised beyond repair, therefore whatever their legal and moral duties they today lack the conditions in which they can reasonably be expected to perform them. Once again, I would strongly contest this alibi. I have spent twenty of the best years of my life in the civil service, but always found that despite the decline in all institutions of public life, there continue to be the democratic spaces within it to struggle to act in accordance with my beliefs without compromise. I do not regret a single day. One may be battered and tossed around, in the way that young police officers who opposed political dictates to control the recent rioting in Gujarat were unjustly transferred. But in the long run, I have not known upright officers to be terminally suppressed, repressed or marginalised. On the contrary, I value colleagues, in the civil and police services, usually unsung and uncelebrated, who have quietly and resolutely performed their duties with admirable character and steadfastness. Few in the civil and police services can in all honesty testify to pressure so great that they could not adhere to the call of their own conscience.

It is not that there are no costs, but then if the performance of duties was painless, there would not be many who would fail in the performance of their duties. The costs are usually of frequent transfers, and deprivation of the allurements of some assignments of power and glamour, which are used to devastating effect by our political class to entice a large part of the bureaucracy today.

Today, when I stand witness to the massacre in Gujarat enabled by spectacular state abdication and connivance—or to the national disgrace of people living at the edge of starvation even when godowns overflow with foodgrains—I recognise the cold truth that the higher civil and police services are today in the throes of an unprecedented crisis. The absoloute minimum that any state must ensure is the survival and security of its people, and elementary justice. If state authorities wantonly let violent mobs target innocents without restraint—or let people die unmourned of hunger when mountains of food rot in godowns—and they continue to do this with impunity and without remorse or shame, then basic questions need to be asked. By all of us. Because injustice involves us all.

CHAPTER

19 The Dharmic State

—M N Buch

When the former Prime Minister, Shri Atal Behari Vajpayee, visited Gujarat after the Godhra incident and during the period when violence was at its height in Gujarat, he reminded Narendra Modi, the Chief Minister, of his Raj Dharma. In the *Mahabharata*, in the *Shantiparva* it is stated, "There is no other justification for the king to exist than to protect in every way the people. For protection is the first foundation of all social order." Again and again the *Mahabharata* says that whereas protection of the people is the purpose of creating the king, their protection then becomes his goal and to achieve this goal he is required to subject himself to the discipline of Dharma. In other words, although the king is invested with the authority and power of governance, the true sovereignty belongs to Dharma and not to him. In the *Anushasana Parva*, at page (212.40) the *Mahabharata* states, "Let the king protect his subjects from their fear of him; from their fear of others; from their fear of each other; and from their fear of things that are not human".

I have begun with quotes from the *Mahabharata* because we are governed at the national level and in Gujarat by a political party which, while claiming itself to be secular, also has as a part of its extended family three organisations, the RSS, the VHP and the Bajrang Dal which claim to be the protectors and guardians of Hinduism. The question that I would like to ask the Sangh Parivar is whether it understands anything about Hinduism or, for that matter, its temporal face, Hindutva, as advocated by them. This is a faith whose language, Sanskrit, has no word for religion. In Arabic religion it is called 'Mazhab". Dharma transcends religion because even an aetheist, by his conduct, his acceptance of duty and his adherence to truth, is Dharmic. Panth is narrower than religion and denotes a sect.

The generic term Hinduism covers a spectrum of faiths which completes a global circle of 360 degrees and embraces all faiths. The Hindu scriptures do not have any one book which is revealed by the Almighty and which contains the only truth, or "Ekal Satya". The Koran, the Bible and the Torah are books of revelation which are immutable and cannot be questioned. They create the frame within which the Muslims, Christians and Jews respectively follow their faith and they exclude all non-believers. Not only does Hinduism not have any such a book, but it also has no concept of exclusion of anyone. Anyone who follows his own Dharma is entitled to salvation because Hinduism has no concept of either limbo or ever lasting damnation. They have neither the Bible, nor Shariat, nor Talmud as the ruling guide for the state. That leaves only Dharma as the lodestar to guide the state. It is for this reason that I have used the words "The Dharmic State". I started with the Prime Minister's advice to the Chief Minister, Narendra Modi, to follow his Raj Dharma. It has been amply proved that Narendra Modi failed even to understand what Raj Dharma is, much less follow it. That is why Godhra occurred, that is why Gujarat was torn with strife and that is why Gujarat had Muslims lived as refugees within their own land. Even today the Chief Minister of Gujarat has not realised that, in the words of the *Mahabharata*, "The king who governs always with equality and impartiality obtains Dharma" (*Shantiparva* 69.30).

In Gujarat the excuse given for all that followed upon Godhra is that this retaliation was to be expected in the face of the burning of a train full of kar sevaks. Is lynch law justified in a state where there is rule of law? Is lynch law justified in the Dharmic State? The *Mahabharata* in the *Shantiparva* states, "It is in the nature of the world that many men restrain themselves from wrong doing for fear of punishment of law". (*Shantiparva* 15.6.) This restraint of law was obviously removed in Gujarat with the connivance of government. This is not the attribute of a Dharmic State—this is the definition of anarchy. The real attribute of rule of law in a Dharmic State is, "Neither mother, nor father, nor brother, nor wife, nor priest, no one is above the law . . . . To the king no one is beyond the law of punishment" (*Shantiparava* 121.60). In Gujarat if one happens to be Dr. Togadia, or Mr. Zadphia or Mr. Ashok Singhal, if one happens to be a Bajrang Dali, or a rioter who kills the Muslim and bums down his house, one is above the law. Without hesitation I can say that at least Narendra Modi's Gujarat is not a Dharmic State, not with standing the fact that the Sangh Parivar rules it. Surely Shri K Sudarshan needs to ask himself whether he would like to preside over an organisation whose ministrations have led Gujarat on the path of adharma.

Secularism does not mean paying lip service to a 'panth nirpeksh raj'. It means conducting oneself in a manner which promotes equality and impartiality, separates the temporal from the religious, creates a system of equal laws, respects all religions but does not promote any. The BJP cannot be accused of such secularism, but can the Congress, which governed us for the major part of our independent existence, lay better claims to secular credentials? The foundations of the present state of anarchy in Gujarat were laid by the Congress Chief Ministers, avaricious beyond recall, who succeeded Hitendra Desai. The worst communal riot in the history of Gujarat occurred in Ahmedabad in 1969 under a Congress Government. The 1992 riots in Bombay took place under a Congress Chief Minister. Whereas the Congress has never openly avowed a communal card it has never hesitated in using religion, caste and class as a means of promoting its own electoral interests. In a volatile society such as India one cannot play the communal card and then expect the situation to be normal.

I still remember my days with the Delhi Development Authority shortly after the emergency was lifted and the Janata Government came to power. We had constructed shops in the Meena Bazar area of Jama Masjid and the Payenwala area of Dariba in Delhi to rehabilitate the shopkeepers who had been uprooted from there during the emergency. The majority of them were Muslims. Sanjay

Gandhi told me that we were making a mistake because removal of the shopkeepers during the emergency had eradicated a potential nest of Pakistani supporters. I was horrified to hear this from the mouth of Jawaharlal Nehru's grandson, but it did suggest a mindset which looked on secularism as a convenience rather than an act of faith. My accusation is that if the BJP has created a state based on adharma, the Congress, too, has failed to establish a truly Dharmic State. I make this statement as a Hindu who sees his religion being destroyed by the very votaries of Hindutva, the Sangh Parivar, which lays claim to be the defender of the Hindu faith and I regret that those who claim to be secular have, by their failure to establish a Dharmic State, are putting up no worthwhile resistance to the creation of a state based on adharma. This is the real tragedy of India.

Dear Shri Modi,

As the aftermath of the 1992 post-Ayodhya riots, a number of temples still in use in Pakistan, especially Sind, were destroyed. It is to the credit of Nawaz Sharif, the then Prime Minister of Pakistan, that he ordered the repair of each one of these temples and ensured that they were restored. Here at home we have the recent example of Guru Ki Maseed in Gurdaspur District of the Punjab. Guru Hargobind, the Sixth Guru, built this mosque for his Muslim followers in the seventeenth century. After the partition in 1947 this mosque was taken over by the Sikhs and consecrated as a Gurudwara. Fifty five years later Gurmeet Rai, a distinguished Sikh conservationist, with funds made available by the Sikh community, restored the building as a mosque, the Sikhs voluntarily removed the Guru Granth Saheb to a nearby Gurudwara and restored the building to the Muslims to be used as a mosque. I quote this as an example of how Hindus and those whose faith owes its origin to the Sanatan Dharma should behave. That is the Hindu way, the only true Hindutva.

In contrast we have what has happened in Gujarat recently, where it is alleged that more than two hundred and sixty seven mosques, darghas, idgahs, khanqas and other Muslim sacred places have either been destroyed or converted into temples. The Isanpur Masjid at Paladi in Ahmedabad, the Noorani Mosque in Naroda Patia, Saraspur Mazaar at Paladi, Zafar Row House

Masjid at Vatva, Peer Hazrat Shamsuddin Dargha and the mosque at Mehndikua in Dudheshwar, the Idgah at Kankaria, Mariambibi Mosque, the Hasan Shaheed Mosque, etc., are some examples of historical and religious buildings being desecrated.

Whether or not the Muslims believe that Ram resides everywhere, we Hindus certainly believe that Parmeshwar is to be found at every place of religious worship. When we desecrate a mosque we, in effect, desecrate a temple. Let me tell you a true story based on my own experience. In 1968 I was Director, Tribal Welfare of Madhya Pradesh and I had a pious, illiterate, Muslim driver called Gulshad. I was on tour to Bastar and when we climbed the steep Keskal Ghat my driver stopped at a little roadside temple of Devi of the type one finds at the top of every ghat section of every road in India. Excusing himself he went into the temple—he who was a pious Muslim who offered Namaz five times a day and kept the Roza faithfully during Ramzan. When he emerged a few minutes later, he had a tilak on his forehead and some prasad in his right hand. When questioned Gulshad told me that he had gone into the temple to offer his thanks to God for the safe journey. When I asked him why he went to the Devi temple he said that so far as he was concerned it was an "ibadatgah", or place of worship. In his eyes he saw Allah rather than Devi and he recited the Kalima and the Fateha. As for the tilak and the prasad, he saw nothing wrong with that as they were of holy origin. I narrate this to you because my illiterate driver that day taught me the true value of religion.

It is not enough for the Chief Minister of Gujarat to state that he would hand over the damaged shrines to NGOs to rebuild. It is the duty of the Chief Minister of Gujarat and his government that they help to restore each one of these mosques, idgahs and shrines and to hand them back with respect and veneration to the Muslims as a sign to them that India is as much their country as it is of the Modis and the Buchs. I could write volumes on my inner feeling about what has happened in Gujarat, especially because I am the son of the man who took over Junagadh from the Nawab early in 1948, and, who as one of Sardar Vallabhbhai Patel's officers, was substantially responsible for the formation of the Part B State of Saurashtra. In Junagadh, though the wounds of partition were very fresh indeed, not one hair of any Muslim's head was harmed, despite the fact that my father was an ICS Officer of the Punjab Cadre and had witnessed the horrors of partition at first hand. His heart was full of compassion and not revenge. Can we expect less from the man elected by our people to be the Chief Minister of a State of the importance of Gujarat? Surely you will not allow a civil servant to appear to be more concerned about his people than their elected representative.

CHAPTER

20 Good Governance in the New Millennium

—N. Vittal

When our freedom struggle was on and the British tried to highlight how they had brought good government for running this country, our leaders used to say that good government was no substitute for self government. Well, history has moved on. Now that we have our own self- government, the question is whether we can postpone the issue of having good government any long. As I see it, the difference between the words government and governance is that the government represents the organizational structure for running the country and governance is the manner in which that function is performed.

From a broad perspective, I would consider certain features to be very essential to describe any functioning of a government as conforming to the standards of good governance. The basic requirement for any citizen in a country is a sense of security and opportunity to rise to his full potential and earn an honest livelihood. If a government can provide these three factors, then I would consider the government to be having good governance. In terms of functions, therefore, the first of three essential characteristics of a good governance would be the rule of law. All citizens must be treated equally and their rights must be protected. This also means straightaway that there should be least corruption if not no corruption in public governance. Corruption distorts the entire rule of law.

Rule of law involves, making the rules and regulations and implementing them. The making of the laws for a country depends upon the type of government which a country chooses. In India, we have chosen under our constitution, the rule of the people, the democratic form of government. The three pillars of governance are identified in our constitution, the Legislature, which makes the law, the Judiciary which interprets the law and the Executive, both the permanent bureaucracy and political executive, which implements the law.

If there is corruption, it is obvious that the entire process gets vitiated. We have in our country, the controversy about tainted ministers. Law breakers are elected to positions of power and are becoming law makers in the legislature. A lot of legal quibbling is going on about the fairness of the system. From a fundamental point of view, in any test of governance, a government which allows legislators to break the law and yet became law makers themselves certainly can not be said to have good governance. Applying this, in India today, we do not have good governance.

The process of how corruption vitiates the whole rule of law can be traced through other steps also. The making of the rules or laws is itself vitiated, law breakers are making the laws. When it comes to implementation of the law, two agencies are involved. The first is the judiciary, which interprets the law. The second includes the executive, which implements the law. On corruption in the judiciary, a former Chief Justice of India has gone on record to say that he could vouchsafe about the integrity of only 80 percent of higher judiciary. The inference is that the other 20 percent are of doubtful integrity. Corruption in judiciary distorts the entire legal process of interpretation. Corruption in implementing agencies, especially the police and the agencies concerned with revenue administration, are well known examples of how the entire objective of good governance is vitiated. It is no wonder that India is rated as one of the most corrupt countries in the world. We belong to the more corrupt part of the world and this is really a shame for all of us. A corrupt country therefore, is not a country with good governance. By this test also India fails the test of good governance.

The third aspect of good governance would be whether a citizen can make an honest livelihood and his dignity is respected. As President Abdul Kalam points out, each one of us is blessed by God with some talent or other and we must be able to rise to our full potential. The dramatic achievements of the Indians who go abroad and become Non Resident Indians, compared to that of the resident Indians is a standing example to show that in India we do not have good governance from the point of view of providing opportunities to individuals to rise to their full potential. The per capita income of an Indian is $400 per annum while that of NRI is nearly $4000. When we look at individual achievers we find that Indians who went abroad have achieved distinctions like winning Nobel Prize and so on, whereas, this distinction is yet to come to the resident Indians especially in science, physics, chemistry or medicine.

There is yet another aspect of good governance. From a purely hardware point of view, the total factor productivity of the economy should be high. There should be no wastage. A nation which is low in productivity and wastes its resources is a nation that is not governed well. In that sense also we are not country which can call itself as a good governance. The energy consumption of our industries must be the highest amongst the energy guzzling. It is said that we lose 10% of our grains because of our poor storage. Perhaps, 40% of our vegetables are lost because of poor storage though we are one of the largest producers of fruits and vegetables in the world. The enormous loss in transmission of our power sector is well known. When it comes to productivity, we again fail the test of good governance.

Once we have identified the four factors of good governance, namely, rule of law, elimination of corruption, an environment that provides opportunity for every Indian citizen to rise to his full potential and high total factor productivity of the economy, it is easy to prepare a roadmap for achieving good governance. It will be a long road, but we can make progress continuously, once our directions are clear.

Let us start with productivity, to begin with. It is an objective issue and may not raise emotions. In India, when it comes to economic administration, there has been a perverse equation. What is politically popular and appealing is economically disastrous and vice versa. The 2004 elections showed that the Chief Ministers who talked about good governance and applying information technology in governance and were talking in the modern idiom got defeated. Those leaders who appealed to populist sentiment and talked of providing free electricity to rural areas have come to power. The question is: if we want to really achieve good governance in our country, how to resolve this issue? My suggestion would be, to make all our policies pass a test. Does it improve total factor productivity? By this we may be able to remove a lot of emotion from the political debate on economic issues and able to focus on real results. Now that we have got a decade of reform process, and with the common minimum programme of the UPA government focusing on the common man, it will be possible to come out with innovative suggestions about how every policy decision improves productivity. That may be a standard step you can take to move towards good governance.

We may then come to what I would call the software aspect of the government, namely, the rule of law, checking corruption, and opportunity for every citizen to realize his full potential. So far as rule of law is concerned, perhaps it must be the most slow moving in the world and the most hermetically protected in the world. Thanks to the 1971 Contempt of Court Act, even truth is no defence against the judiciary. This has to change. Unfortunately, there seems to be a lot of problems on the issue of judicial reforms because the judiciary has been claiming primacy on all matters judicial. While this has contributed to the healthy independence of the judiciary, probably, it has also to that extent denied opportunity for people outside the judiciary to influence it by bringing about changes. There is need for encouraging an atmosphere of open mindedness and willingness to reform in the process. The recent bill introduced by Mr. Fali Nariman in the Rajya Sabha was atleast a tentative step in the process.

"We have seen in the past controversy between the union law ministers and the judiciary especially in the matter relating to national judicial commission and so on. Apart from the aspect of the independence of judiciary and issue like corruption etc., the basic system is whether something can be done to improve the productivity and the modernization of the judicial system. Justice Venkatachallaiah, when he was the Chief Justice of India, took a major step in introducing IT in Supreme Court and with the dramatic results. I understand that the pendency came down from 1.6 lakhs cases to about 20000 cases. Can this be internalized and made part of the judicial process. But mere introduction of IT will not help the speeding process. There has to be a relook at the various laws so that at least the basic principles which will help the speedy process are introduced. I would suggest the following:

We must be able to bring in the concept of the sunset principle so that antique laws do not clutter the system and become totally counter-productive. As Shakespeare pointed out, the laws that are formed are like ' scare crows'. But if they are not properly designed and implemented, they become like scare crows, which become virtually nesting grounds for the birds, who find that the scare crows are after all only dolls and not live beings. There is a special need for limiting the number of appeals and also bringing healthy principles like writing of judgements mandatory. What I mean is that if a judge hears a case, he must deliver the judgement within a limited time. He should not be transferred or elevated to the Supreme Court unless he keeps his record uptodate in this respect. In a conversation with a former Chief Justice of India, I learnt that there was a judge in the High Court of Madras who had probably heard more than 50 cases and had not written the judgements and the Chief Justice ensured that he would not be given additional work unless he caught up with the pendency of the judgements. These are simple matters that should be able to bring about an increase in the speed of the system. Further, when it comes to issues like corruption, it is the enormous delay, which allows the guilty to escape."

In fact, I wrote an article called the Vittal's Second Law in *New Indian Express* dated 10.10.2004, to point out that the greater the publicity in the media a case of corruption or fraud gets, the greater the chance that all the guilty will escape. I reproduce the article, which is relevant to our subject here:

"Based on my experience of thirty years in administration, in 1990, I wrote a piece, called Vittal's first law. My law says that in every organization those who work get more work and those who do not work get pay, promotion and perquisites."

Looking at the growth of corruption and criminalisation of politics in recent times, I am now ready with my second law. Greater the publicity a case of corruption or crime receives in the media, greater the chances of acquittal of the guilty. Right now for instance, the Telgi scam estimated at Rs.30000 crores is making the waves in the media. Applying my second law, you can be absolutely sure that nobody will be punished in this case. The same is true of every other case which is getting publicity in the media and which will get publicity in the future.

The reasons for this are simple. We are a country where we have well-established set of rules and regulations. Our constitution is based on the highest principles. The principle of natural justice requires that everybody is presumed to be innocent till he is proved guilty. The guilt has to be proved under the law beyond reasonable doubt. It is this very system of law, which ensures that the guilty escapes. Take for example the hawala case. One of the persons concerned even confessed on the TV that he took three lakhs of rupees from Mr. Jain. But the court discharged him on the ground that such confessions were not covered by the 1877 Indian Evidence Act. No wonder the conviction rate in criminal case in Indian courts is only six percent.

The second reason for the acquittal is the very slow nature of our judicial process. It is said that if our courts were not to take any new case from today, it will take 300 years for all the present cases to be disposed of. The Harshad Mehta scam hogged yards of publicity in the media. Ultimately, before the courts could come to a decision Mr. Mehta himself died. At about the same time in early 90s there was a case of serious fraud involving the Barings Company. Leeson who was accused in that case was punished within two years.

The third reason is that our own system provides generous legal cushions of safety to the guilty. As CVC, I noticed that the corrupt people accumulate a lot of wealth. That very wealth is utilized by them to engage the best among the lawyers and laugh all the way to the bank. I wonder why that it never occurs to any presiding officer in the court that if a person could engage a costly lawyer, he should have made his pile through illegal means. After all cases which receive publicity are those where VIPs or a lot of money is involved. Looking to the repeated use of money power or influence by the corrupt, as CVC I carried a sloka, parodying the old sloka which says that the gods are against the weak. The sacrifice offered to the non-vegetarian gods is not the horse, elephant or the tiger but the humble goat.

Ashnam naiva, Gajam naiva
Vyagram naivacha naivacha
Aja putram balim datyat
Devan duchala Gathoka!

In our system,

Secretary naiva, Chairman naiva
Minister naivcha naivacha
LDC balim dalyab
CVC dulchaha gathaka!

No Secretary to government is punished, no Chairman, no Minister. It is the poor Lower Division Clerk who is punished by the CVC.

There is a fourth reason, why the prosecution in the most publicized cases fail. The investigating agencies, in order to prove the guilt and perhaps subconsciously prove their skills at investigation, always bring in the element of conspiracy under section 120 IPC. This attempt to prove conspiracy many a time backfires.

Finally, there is always the real and all pervasive presence of corruption in every section of our society. This makes it easy for the guilty to escape. So, unless there is a dramatic change in our quality of governance, Vittal's second law is bound to prevail for a long long time."

We must be able to look at these issues and see how we can speed up the whole process of law.

We then come to the issue of corruption. I suggest a three-point strategy to tackle the issue of corruption, especially, the bureaucratic corruption, which is very closely linked with the issue of good governance.

(i) Simplify the rules and regulations so that the scope of corruption is reduced.

(ii) Transparency and empower the public; use of IT can go a long way in greater sunshine into the governmental system and demystify the governmental functioning.

(iii) Above all is the third aspect, effective punishment. As CVC, I tried to ensure that the cases in which the departmental enquiries are over and the CVC has recommended action like major penalty were implemented. Earlier there was no follow up on these cases and it was not unusual for the guilty to escape because of sheer non-action on the part of the disciplinary authorities.

We then come to the remaining aspects of good governance, namely, opportunity for every citizen to rise to his full potential. This would mean that we should be able to have development of healthy institutions and centers for excellence and also a method of identifying talent and encouraging them. For example, I understand, in China, youngsters with sport talent are spotted and nurtured specially. The number of gold medals in the recent Olympics, China is the standing proof of how effective the system is. Why is it we cannot do this in India?

When it comes to science, we should have a method of consciously encouraging people with a bent of mind for science. Our science is really going to suffer in future because over a period of more than 20 years, the number of students taking pure science course is going down as the career opportunities in science and scientific research are not very attractive. Can we not emulate what has been done in the United States through organizations like National Science Foundation and provide adequate resources so that the scientific talent in the country do not lose their opportunity? It is a healthy sign that the liberalization of the economy, the explosion of the satellite television and the plethora of TV channels has given opportunity to lot of young talent to come out so far as the ICE (Information, Communication and Entertainment) sector is concerned. We will have to constantly think in terms of providing opportunities so that the citizens of our country do not lose to rise to their full potential.

At the beginning of the millennium India has an advantage of having a very large population, may be 37 pecent below the age of 35. But this demographic advantage will be lost if we are not able to provide employment opportunities for the youth. It is good that the common minimum programme also talks about employment guarantee schemes. We will have to consciously follow policies which will encourage creation of more employment.

Another aspect of opportunity for rising to full potential is the issue of social justice. We have followed a policy of reservation and affirmative action. But now that the issue of extending it to the private sector is concerned, we have to see what is the best way to nurture the talent and capabilities in weaker sections.

CHAPTER

21 Accountability in Administration

—N. Vittal

Accountability means responsibility. The issue of accountability has become a matter of public debate especially in the private sector in the context of the corporate scandals that have exploded in recent years. Accountability in public administration is given more importance than in the private sector. Public servants are entrusted with certain powers of office, so that they can discharge their duties effectively. But what is the reality? Many public servants are perceived to be corrupt and they do not perform their duties and they are not punished at all.

There are three sources, which determine how accountable a person is. The first is the innate nature of the person himself and his values. Perhaps, the best example of accountability is the love of every mother for her child. The care a mother takes up to her child in sickness and health in bringing up the child is something, which is universally recognized. Mother's love can be seen as an ideal example of accountability. After all, there would have been no progress of the human race, if the mothers had not taken care of their children and nurtured them. If mother's love for the child is taken as the idealized form of accountability, then we can also say that accountability ultimately arises out of individual's sense of duty, a sense of obligation and responsibility, and if this could be enveloped in a feeling of love, then perhaps it becomes an ideal form of accountability. People who perform very well in any organization are those who love their jobs. Accountability and job satisfaction can be considered to be the two sides of the same coin. Hence one spring of accountability is the individual's perception about his job and his own qualities. Some people take seriously every task given to them. There are others who may not do so.

The second factor for accountability, especially in the context of the organization, would be the enforcement of a scheme of reward and punishment. Perhaps, in the private sector, this is more effective than in the government. In private sector, the executives who perform extremely well and bring more profits and help in better performance of their organization can be rewarded over and above their normal compensation. Similarly, if they fail they can also be fired. Apparently, this is not taking place in public administration. Therefore, the second spring for accountability, a system of reward and punishment, does not work very effectively in government. The main reason for this is that we have built a system in Article 311 of the Constitution, which provides a guarantee of protection to government servants. This along with the labour legislation combined with the system of our judiciary, has created a situation where what I would call the 'Vittal's law' applies. A few years ago, I wrote an article called 'The vicious cycle of Vittal's law'. My law says, in every organization, those who work get more work. Those who do not work get pay, promotions and perquisites. This is because of the absence of the system of effective reward and punishment.

There is a third source for accountability. This arises from the codes of conduct expected of professionals. Every profession, be it engineering or chartered accountancy, has its own associations. These organizations lay down for each profession, a code of conduct for their members. These codes of conduct by and large automatically build in an element of accountability also.

In fact, the accountability can also be linked with our unique concept of 'dharma'. When we go back to history, we find that every person in the society is supposed to follow his dharma. *Swadharme nidharamshreya pardharmo bhayavaha.* It is better to die than not perform ones dharma is what Lord Krishna says in Bhagawat Gita. When we talk about accountability, we are basically talking about dharma and accountability of public servants.

I have spent more than four decades in public administration and the issue is whether we are having public servants who are accountable and their accountability is being enforced. Recently, we have had a parallel development taking place in the private sector as a result of the scandals in various multinational companies. Corporate governance has emerged as a major issue. Corporate governance, ultimately, depends on three principles. The first is transparency. Transparency is required to fix accountability. Accountability is for all those who are stakeholders and shareholders in the organization. We can, therefore, see that if we want to improve effective accountability in public administration, we will have to incorporate and bring changes in our system based on these principles.

In the case of the public servant, the public accountability would be for the citizens or the stakeholders in the organization. Because every public organization has a certain clientele the public servant should be accountable to the clientele. So, how do we ensure this accountability? The first step needed is the greater transparency in the functioning of government and public organizations. In recent times, there has been a demand for Right to Information Act. We have an Official Secret Act and it should be balanced by the Right to Information Act so that every citizen knows his rights and has access to information and also knows how decisions are taken on any issue in every organization, especially the public service organization. Thanks to the development of information technology, it is possible to bring in a very high degree of transparency effectively in government and hence the concept of e-governance today is getting greater recognition. Transparency has a great advantage because it is possible to fix responsibility through transparency. Many a time, when decisions are taken in government, one does not know who took the decision. When things go wrong, the observation made by John Kennedy in the context of the Bay of Pigs fiasco becomes very common. "Success has many fathers. Failure is an orphan". We have, of course, bodies like the Comptroller and Auditor General of India which try to fix responsibility in financial matters. Nevertheless, by and large, the audit has been ineffective because it is done much after the event takes place. Post audit hardly has any impact and very rarely we find that any public servant of note has been punished for failure.

Next to transparency, what is needed also is a system by which the present extreme protection given to the public servants is removed. Article 311 needs to be drastically modified so that practically the entire set of public servants can be brought under a contract system. There could be rolling contracts so that the public servant is continuously aware of the fact that if he does not perform well and discharge his duties, his services can be terminated. Terminating the contract is much easier than operating in the present system where a lifetime employment is assured at the joining. The labour laws in our country are also such that once a person is hired it is very difficult to fire him. We have now got a government which is definitely left of center and as a result the protection given to the employees is not going to be diluted. The challenge, therefore, is all the more. How to bring in the sense of responsibility in a situation where the legal rights of those enforcing the accountability are highly unsatisfactory?

Perhaps, we should look at the other two springs of accountability. One would be the professional associations which lay down high standards, so that each person is automatically aware of his responsibility and discharges his function. In fact, some of the professions have recently come under scrutiny, especially professions like the chartered accountants, where the need for global standards or globally applicable accounting practices (GAAP) etc., are issues that are being raised. If we could have a systematic approach of every public servant being guided by the professional associations, probably we would have taken a step towards inculcating a sense of greater responsibility.

Ultimately, the best method of accountability may be to see whether jobs can be made inherently interesting like the example of mother's love we discussed earlier. Can the performance in public administration itself be made into a creative and enjoyable activity so that the sense of accountability is enhanced automatically? Perhaps, here we will have to look at the human behaviour and see how psychology can be effectively used to modulate organizational behaviour. The British system which we adopted after independence was based on a system of mistrust. Is it possible to replace it with the system of trust so that every person feels that he is believed and he could take a decision? Our audit approach is also such that if somebody makes a mistake, he is punished and his career is ruined. This creates a culture by which people do not want to take any decision and lack of decision making itself becomes a virtue. We had a Prime Minister, who once said that not taking a decision itself was a decision! But such an attitude of not taking decisions also encourages a culture of avoiding decisions and pushing responsibilities either upward, downward or sideward in an organization. Indian administration is 'action shy'.

Yet another reason for lack of accountability is that many a time objectives are not clear. If the duties are clearly defined and objectives are clear, then accountability can easily be fixed. That is why we find that even though our administration is generally perceived to be non performing, lethargic and so on, but at the time of crisis like natural calamities or elections we find that the same system works better. It is so because during the time of crisis, the objectives are very clearly defined and hence accountability can be more clearly enforced. Parkinson's law leads to overlapping of functions, and dilutes accountability.

We may have to evolve a strategy for promoting a culture of accountability by understanding the forces which promote it and design our systems and procedures in such a way that these forces are strengthened. Ultimately, what we must aim at is bringing a change in culture. What we have probably in administration today is the perception of power orientation. Every person, however small he is, thinks he has the power and the idea of service is lacking. So how to bring in this change of culture is an issue all of us should think of. Long ago, L. K. Jha observed that we probably made a mistake by calling our public servants as government servants. As a result they became only high priest serving all powerful entity called government and ceased to serve the public, which in a democracy is all the more necessary.

CHAPTER

22 Corruption and the Rule of Law

—N. Vittal

The issue of good governance is becoming increasingly a subject of serious debate in the country. The results of the recent elections have been interpreted ultimately as a verdict of the people on the issue of good governance specifically in two states. What is basic to good governance is the rule of law. What distinguishes a civilized society from an uncivilized one or a society where anarchy prevails is the presence of the rule of law. Where there is anarchy, might is right and the rule of the jungle prevails. What distinguishes a civilized society is that there are orderly accepted rules of law and there is a system of enforcement of the rule of law, which ensures that the principles of freedom and justice are observed. Every principle of rule of law is embodied in our constitution, which provides for an independent judiciary and guarantee fundamental rights and well defined roles for the legislature and the executive. India can rightfully claim to be the foremost country in Asia committed to the concept of the rule of law.

This concept of the rule of law is quite old. We had in the past monarchy but the emphasis was on the king observing dharma and ensuring that all citizens are protected. For the weak the protection is provided by the king by enforcing the law. In recent times, India is rated as one of the countries where there is genuine democracy. The question we have to examine is whether we have in more than 50 years of governing ourselves as an independent country achieved the ideals visualized in the constitution. Do we today have a level of governance in our country about which we can be proud?

Corruption is the use of public office for private gain. It springs from the basic human tendency of greed. We have today in India a society, which has become corrupt. India is rated as one of the most corrupt countries in the world. Under the provisions of Prevention of Corruption Act, 1988, only a public servant can be guilty of corruption. In the private sector, if a similar activity takes place, it will be considered as cheating or a case of criminal breach of trust. If there is one major factor coming in the way of good governance and rule of law in our country, it is corruption. Corruption is like AIDS. Just as the AIDS knocks out the immune system of the human body and leads to early death, corruption knocks out the immune system in the form of checks and balances to ensure good governance and implementation of the rule of law, which results in the society becoming dysfunctional and moving towards anarchy.

The rule of law presumes that first laws have to be made. The legislature makes the law, the judiciary interprets the law and the executive (both the political and permanent executive) implements the law. Laws reflect and crystallize the principles for reaching a given social objective. Corruption defeats the social objectives behind any law. Corruption distorts the whole process of law by misinterpretation. In fact, as Central Vigilance Commissioner I have often noticed that while some honest public servants may be not very intelligent, every corrupt official is intelligent. He is so clever that he is able to misinterpret the law and at the same time cover his tracks. Oscar Wilde observed, "The Thief is an artist. The policeman is only a critic."

Political Corruption and Law Making

We may now examine the dynamics of the rule of law. The framing of the rules and laws and their implementation form the essence of this dynamics. Corruption distorts the rule of law at each stage. We are proud of the fact that we are a real democracy. Our elections are perceived to be generally clean and fair supervised by an independent election commission. Nevertheless, when we go into the details of the operations, we find that our present system of elections does not throw up the right types of leaders. Elections have become a very costly affair. The pervasive presence of corruption in our political system and the use of black money are well known. Our political systems including the raising of funds for elections are not transparent. The enormous growth of black money is perhaps the root cause of the culture of corruption that has come to dominate our political system. Black money is the oxygen for corruption and corruption is the oxygen for black money. As a result we find that our entire process of election itself is based on corruption.

This basic defect in the electoral process starts the vicious cycle of corruption in our country. Political corruption leads to bureaucratic corruption, which in turn leads to business corruption and also criminalisation of politics. Elections have also witnessed not only corrupt electoral practices apart like the bribing of voters but also use of money power and muscle power. It is in the use of muscle power, the criminals come in.

Starting as aides to political powers that be, the criminals in course of time entered the mainstream and the democratic process. The Vohra Committee pointed out how there was a parallel system of governance dominated by the criminals. We witnessed in the recent elections also, criminals contesting the elections from within the prisons. Some get elected and may even become ministers. The justification for such persons becoming legislators and ministers is that under the law that everyone is presumed to be innocent till proved guilty. I wonder whether it is fair to talk about the rule of law when criminals are getting into the legislature and law breakers are becoming law makers under our present system. At the starting point of building the institutions which make the laws namely the legislatures, corruption distorts the whole process by the enormous influence of black money in the electoral process. The Supreme Court has decreed now that every candidate to election will have to declare his criminal background, educational background and his assets. In the recent elections, a lot of valuable information has been brought out by these affidavits. Probably this is the first step towards bringing greater transparency in the system. Some NGOs have also tried to educate the voters about the background of the candidate so that criminals do not get elected to the legislature.

The role of the black money is not only at the time of contesting the election, but even after the elections. If the legislature is a hung one, there is the phenomenon of horse trading when the legislators are bought. Apparently, the danger of such defections was recognized. The first attempt to check it was made by the Anti-Defection Act. Based on the experience of the implementation of the Anti-Defection Act, further attempts have been made to tighten the whole Act, so that if a person elected on a particular party ticket defects, he is forced to go back to the constituency and get elected again. This perhaps, is the process by which we are learning towards building a society where rule of law prevails.

In countries like Britain and the United States, the process of political fund raising is perhaps more transparent. Even in those countries, there are also complaints about the need for a greater fairness and more transparency in the process. What we find in India is the total opacity about the raising of funds for the elections. It is this process which is probably another cause of endemic corruption in our political system. The idea of public funding in elections has been mooted but I wonder whether this itself will solve the problem. For instance, in Germany, there is public funding of the elections, but even then there one of the great Chancellors had to go because of the issues complaints relating to raising of funds for the party. The NDA government had moved a law to remove the restrictions about contributions to political funds. We should aim as a step towards better rule of law and good governance to achieve at least a situation comparable to that prevails in the USA so that we will have greater transparency in the electoral fund raising process.

Corruption distorts not only the composition of the legislatures but also the process of law making and implementation. As Central Vigilance Commissioner I found that the laws we make are somehow designed not to affect those sources which generate black money and the fountain springs of corruption which distort the entire system. Three examples, will suffice. The first is the voluntary disclosure of income scheme (VDIS), which was implemented some years back. On payment of 30 pecent of tax, black money was converted into white. Earlier, the schedule of income tax was such that the taxpayers who had earned a certain high level of income would have paid 40 pecent tax. VDIS gave the impression that those who were honest enough to pay the taxes in the high-income group would have paid 40 pecent and the crooks who cheated the government and collected the black money got away with paying 30 pecent. It appeared as if by curious process, those who accumulated black money were being encouraged and allowed to legalize their activities.

The second example is our banking system, where the names of those who are willful defaulters (a polite word for those who cheat banks after borrowing money, siphon the funds for other activities for which loans were sanctioned and do not refund) are kept confidential. This struck me particularly, when as CVC, I published the names of those who were found guilty of corruption in the departmental enquiries in the website of the CVC. I raised the issue with the RBI Governor as to why the names of willful defaulters of banks cannot be published. The Legal Advice given to the RBI was that because of the provisions in Chapter 3 of the RBI Manual, Article 14 of the Constitution and so on, these names could not be published. It is interesting in our country that the industries become sick but the industrialists do not become sick. This is because we have developed a system by which, it is easy to cheat banks and public institutions and at the same time parade as important members of society.

The third example is the Prevention of Money Laundering Act, which was passed in 2003. Money laundering means handling the proceeds of scheduled crime. Scheduled crime means the crime under the Acts mentioned in the schedule of the Act. Black money in our country is generated by evasion of income tax, excise, sales tax, property tax, etc. In the law that has been passed by the Parliament, the laws which are mentioned in the schedule are the Arms Act, the Indian Penal Code, PC Act, Drugs and Psychotropic Substances Act, and the Trafficking of Women Act. So the basic laws evasion of which leads to the generation of substantial amount of black money in our country are kept outside the purview of the law!

Yet another example is the Central Vigilance Commission Act, which has been passed recently as a follow up of the judgement of the Supreme Court in the Vineet Narain case. In 1989 the government of India issued a directive known as the single directive. The main purpose of this directive was that the officers of the level of joint secretary and above cannot be investigated for corruption by the Central Bureau of Investigation, which is a police organization without the permission / sanction of by the government of India. This was struck down by the Supreme Court in the Vineet Narain case as being violative of Article 14 of the Constitution. A criminal is a criminal whether he is above the level of the joint secretary or below. But this single directive has been again introduced in Section 26 of the CVC Act as passed by Parliament. As CVC, I had written to the government pointing out that this provision should not exist. But still this clause has been included. Apparently this has been challenged in the Supreme Court again. Law making is the first step in the whole dynamics of the rule of law. This example shows how it can be distorted by the impact of the culture of corruption.

Corruption & Implementation of Laws

The second stage in the dynamics in the rule of law is implementation. It is here we find many examples of how the process gets distorted by the culture of corruption. We have already seen how clever corrupt people can misinterpret the law and make the law a source of corruption. Shakespeare realized this in one of his plays, *Measure for Measure,* where he observes that laws are like *scare crows.* The scare crows initially are meant to scare the crows. But once the birds realize that the scare crows are only dummies, they start building their nest on it! Many laws in our country have been examples of the scare crow syndrome. For example, the Urban Land Ceiling Act, introduced during emergency with the noble objective of making available the land for housing the poor in urban areas has ultimately resulted in the law which even gave a tremendous scope for massive corruption by creating artificial scarcity of urban land in the country. Professor Dr. Indiresan has gone on record to say that perhaps, thousands of houses may be available for rent in Mumbai, if only the Rent Control Act is deleted. The Rent Control Act initially framed with the idea of protecting the tenant who is a weaker person has created a situation which is well known in Mumbai leading to *pagadi* phenomenon. The landlords having realized that it is fools who build houses and wise men live in them have therefore, opted to keep thousands of flats in Mumbai vacant than letting them out. This is another distortion created by the rule of law. A third example in implementation is even when the laws are made for removing some evils in the society, they are not implemented. For example, the Benami Transactions Prohibitions Act was enacted in September 1988. Section 5 of the Act says that benami property can be confiscated. One of the common methods of hiding illgotten income to corruption is benami property. This is sought to be tackled by the law. Section 8 of the Act says that government should frame rules for implementation of the law. Even though 16 years have passed since the enactment, the law has not yet been implemented. In 1999, I enquired from the Revenue Department, whether rules have been framed. The rules have not been framed. In fact, there was a news item to the effect that the government wanted to scrap the law. So we find that when it comes to implementation, the law itself can be made counterproductive or not implemented at all. The double effect of corruption in the implementation process of the laws is thus very obvious.

The implementation of the rule of law can be seen from three different angles. The first relates to the implementation of the rule of law so far as basic law and order is concerned. The second relates to the set of economic offences. The third relates to implementation of social legislation. Corruption in the police and the estimate of how a common man has to pay by way of bribes gives an idea about how the entire police machinery can be compromised. The demand whenever there is a major crime to entrust the case to the CBI arises because at the state level police agencies seem to have lost their credibility. One cause for corruption in the police is because police has a monopoly in the maintenance of law and order and investigation of crime. Keeping in view the spirit of competition and market forces, it will be worthwhile to think of introducing a competition to the police forces by setting up a parallel force under the local authorities, which will be manned by the disciplined elements of the population like ex-servicemen. This is an idea, which can be tried. Objections may be raised on the ground that law and order cannot be implemented by multiple agencies. However,

Bombay Police Act visualizes how police forces can be delegated in special circumstances for controlling traffic, etc. Why not extend the concept specially when there are complaints about the police not registering FIRs properly?

The second angle relates to economic offences and these have become increasingly significant in the era of liberalization. Corruption seems to have been getting new avatars and here again corruption can influence policy making and also regulation of markets.

In the area of social administration also, laws which have been enacted have also been not implemented because of corruption. For example, prohibition in Gujarat has been a constant feature and corruption has probably has led to the parallel development of bootleggers.

In the process of implementation of the laws, two players are important. The first is the judiciary and the second is the police or the law enforcing government agencies. There have been many good things said about judiciary and the judicial system. The independence of India's judicial system is well known. In fact, some of the recent initiatives taken by the Supreme Court, especially in matters relating to elections, have brought home the fact that the judiciary can still play an effective role in ensuring that the real spirit of democracy is observed and the citizen rights are not tampered with.

Nevertheless, there are many aspects of Indian judicial system, which call for immediate improvement. One striking aspect of our judicial system is the enormous delay in arriving at the decisions. Justice delayed is justice denied. If this yardstick is used we can say that our judicial system denies justice most of the time to the citizens of our country. It has been said that the number of cases pending in our courts is in the order of thirty million. If the cases are disposed of at the present rate, and if the courts do not take any more new cases from today, it will take 300 years to dispose of the existing cases at the present rate.

The enormous delay in the judicial system by itself causes injustice to be done to a number of citizens. For instance, let us take criminal justice in the country. According to one of the leading lawyers, the conviction rate in the Indian courts is six percent. With such poor conviction rate, there is really no respect for the law in many states. The enormous delay in the system combined with the low conviction rate act as an incentive to indulge in crime. Corruption, therefore, has become a low risk high profit activity in our country. Even though we have the plethora of laws they are not having any deterrent effect at all.

There is also yet another dimension of our law, where improvement is called for. Our laws are based on the very healthy principle that everyone is innocent till proved guilty. Under the Evidence Act, when a matter goes to the court, the prosecution has to prove beyond reasonable doubt that the crime has been committed. The enormous delay in our system and the loopholes provided by which the rich can escape by engaging clever lawyers are a major weakness in our legal system. Although from a broad point of view the Indian judiciary is independent and has really played important role in certain major landmark judgements, when it comes to ensuring that there is rule of law in the country for the majority of citizens, we have miles to go.

Corruption goes directly against the rule of law. In fact, there have been allegations of corruption against the judiciary itself. But any debate about corruption in judiciary is hampered by the fact that under the Contempt of Courts Act 1971, truth is no defence against judiciary. Hence, one has to be extremely careful about making any statement about the judiciary lest one is hauled up for contempt and punished. Corruption helps in distorting the basic objectives of the rules and regulations and thereby sabotages the rule of law.

If we are looking at one aspect of the rule of law where a forward looking state comes up with programmes for the benefit of the poor and the weaker sections, corruption can bring in distortions and defeat the very objective of the government. We have already seen that if in the judicial system itself there is corruption, that can definitely lead to miscarriage of justice and the corruption can come in the way of rule of law being implemented by the legal system. If public servants are corrupt, the policy objectives are lost and to that extent the rule of law is compromised.

Most of the time corruption flourishes in our bureaucracy because of delays, lack of transparency, and the protection given to the corrupt on the very healthy legal principle that everybody is innocent till proved guilty. I will call these as the ' legal cushions of safety'. Corruption in the bureaucracy is also being institutionalized. One of the discoveries I made when I published the names of those who were found guilty in the departmental proceedings in the website of CVC was that quite a few of them were in responsible positions. This brought out the nexus between corrupt political leaders who are in government and the corrupt officials. Cases like the one in which one of the private secretaries of a former Minister of State for Revenue was caught taking a bribe of three lakh rupees or so from a deputy commissioner of income tax for a posting in Mumbai shows how posts can be auctioned. Corrupt officials are willing to pay money for getting what can be called juicy lucrative jobs. The Telgi scam has exposed how the entire system can be suborned to serve the interests of the corrupt. In such a situation, to talk about the rule of law in India may appear to be a totally irrelevant.

Corruption distorts the rule of law but if there are laws which can be effectively implemented, corruption can be checked and the rule of law enforced. The basic law against corruption in our country is the Prevention of Corruption Act. Till the Hawala case in which the Supreme Court pronounced the judgement on 18th December, 1997, there was a doubt whether the term public servant covered only officials but also the political leaders. The judgement clarifies that the political leaders as Members of Parliament and legislatures and holding office like Ministers are also covered as in the definition of public servant. What is more important, the judgement also took a major step in strengthening the institutional mechanism to fight corruption so far as atleast the government of India is concerned.

In 1962 after the Mundra scandal, the government of India appointed the Santhanam Committee. Based on a recommendation of the Santhanam Committee, the Central Vigilance Commission was set up in 1964. This was mostly an ineffective body for a long time and had no real powers. It was basically an advisory body. The Supreme Court in the hawala case gave a directive that the CVC should be made into a statutory body and have the power to supervise the working of the Central Bureau of Investigation and the Enforcement Directorate. This was a major step and today CVC is a statutory body and a certain degree of independence to CBI has also been ensured in the process. The CBI Director is appointed by a committee headed by the CVC and consisting of the Home Secretary and Personnel Secretary. They recommend a panel of three names and from that panel only the Director, CBI, is selected. Similar system is adopted for senior officials in CBI also. Once a person is appointed as the Director, CBI, he cannot be shifted for a period of two years without the permission of CVC. Such restrictions have brought healthy impact on the process of checking corruption, though we have still miles to go. The strengthening of the institution of CVC is a welcome development.

Corruption, Citizens and Society

We then come to the question of how do people perceive corruption. Corruption is respectable in our society because respectable professions indulge in it. There has been a lot of debate about corruption in the media and every time a scandal burst on the scene, the media go to a drill, first there is an expose, lot of articles being written, headlines made and again things come back to normal unless some major scandals break up. There is one aspect of such scandals which should make all thinking Indians wonder. Why is corruption a sustainable phenomenon in our country and why it is in fact respectable in middle class standards? In any debate on corruption in our country, the usual suspects are the much maligned politicians and the bureaucrats. Very rarely the professionals, doctors, lawyers and chartered accountants are included in the debate. There seems to be a conspiracy of silence so far as corruption in respectable positions in our country is concerned.

Having been CVC for four years, I have come to the conclusion that the sustaining life blood of corruption in our country is ultimately, black money which accounts for 40 percent of the GDP according to some estimate. How is this black money created? Black money is created by tax evasion and we find in this that the respectable professions in our country must be playing a very major part in generation of this black money. How many doctors, lawyers and chartered accountants pay the taxes? Probably a lot of financial engineering methods can be adopted to go in for tax avoidance, this has to be perhaps treated on different footing from tax evasion. But the net result is that there is a huge generation of black money in these professions. The study on corruption in different sectors undertaken at the instance of the Transparency International shows that an average Indian pays in all a bribe to the extent of 26000 crores of rupees per year in ten sectors and the most corrupt sector turned out to be the medical profession. This sum works out to about 50 percent of Defence budget of the country. Is there some way out by which the respectable professions will adopt higher standards and start the process of cleansing internally through their codes of conduct and other professional ethics? Perhaps we cannot hope for this because, so long as everybody indulges in the game, the change has to come only from the external sources. This perhaps can be only by enacting laws like the law for confiscation of ill-gotten wealth and law for confiscation of benami property. The Benami Transaction Prohibition Act was passed in 1988. Section 5 of the Act provides that benami property can be confiscated by the governemt. It is a pity that even after 16 years, the government has not found it worthwhile to frame rules under which the 1988 law can be implemented. Therefore, we continue to be a country where corruption flourishes and what is worse, it is respectable because respectable professions are indulging in it.

Is corruption an issue in India? Do people realize that corruption will one day destroy the rule of law? The level of awareness of corruption and its negative consequences depend upon the sensitivity of the people concerned. As the Central Vigilance Commissioner from 3rd September 1998 to 2nd September 2002, I constantly tried to highlight the three negative consequences of corruption, namely, it is anti-economic development, anti-poor and anti-national. I also came out with a publication called "A citizen's guide to fight corruption". Citizens who would like to fight corruption can think of adopting the methods recommended in that handbook.

To begin with, the citizen, if he wants to fight corruption, must himself be honest. We find in our country that there is a sort of schizophrenic attitude to corruption. Every person wants to have his own work done on priority, irrespective of what damage it may cause to the system. Transparency International rates India as 83 in a list of 133 countries for the year 2003 in the corruption perception index. That shows, as a nation we have been rated as a very corrupt nation. Corruption is not only widespread but it has also become a part of the very common man's life.

If we question people whether they perceive corruption to be an issue, the answer is yes. Recently, in the context of the elections, the NDTV 24 x 7 and the *Indian Express* made a study. In that study, corruption figured as a prominent issue in elections. We have seen in 1989, how Rajiv Gandhi was defeated on the issue of Bofors. While in the election time, corruption does figure as an issue even though many corrupt politicians get elected. The only solution to ensuring that corruption is tackled in our country effectively is by increasing greater awareness among the public of the evil consequences of the corruption. This will take a long time.

The level of corruption in any organization or society depends on three factors. The first is the individual's sense of values. The second is the set of social values and the third is the system. Individual's values today are very much affected by the impact of the media where continuously consumerism is being promoted. Further, in our society we do not question how a person earned money. Get on, get honour, get honest, seems to be the operational philosophy of many people. We also have the social evils of dowry and so on which thrive on this consumerist spirit.

When it comes to the society values, we have already seen that by and large there is a tolerant approach so far as the issue of corruption is concerned. That brings us to the system. Does our system encourage corruption? Our judicial system is very slow and the conviction rate is hardly six percent in criminal courts. This means that there is very good incentive by way of our system in checking corruption. If we are able to improve our system and ensure that the corrupt are punished quickly, then probably we will succeed. As Central Vigilance Commissioner, I was adopting a three-point strategy to check corruption. The first is the simplification of the rules and regulations, so that the scope of corruption is reduced. The second is, transparency and empowerment of public. It is good that there are a lot of developments taking place on the issue of transparency. There is a healthy competition among the different states to apply information technology and go for e-governance these days. Greater the application of information technology, greater will be the transparency and to that extent less scope for corruption.

The third aspect is of course is effective punishment. Effective punishment depends upon speedy enquiry and decision-making. We have already seen how slow our judicial system is. Justice Mohan, a former judge of the Supreme Court, has made a suggestion, which is worth implementing. What he suggests is for all corruption cases, there should be a maximum time limit of one year within which the case will be heard and even the appeals disposed of. In our system, so far as the election cases are concerned, there is a time limit within which election petitions have to be disposed of. So, it is possible to make amendments to the criminal procedure code to ensure that all corruption cases are disposed of within one year. To achieve this, all corruption cases have to be treated under summary trial procedure and disposed of in six months. There should be only one appeal provided and the appeal also should be disposed of within six months. In this way, we can ensure that at least the corruption cases are disposed of fast. So far as the departmental enquiry cases of corruption are concerned, instructions already exist that they should be cleared within six months. If the disciplinary authorities pay attention and adhere to this time limit, we could bring a very healthy change for the better and ensure that the corrupt are quickly punished. This will help to go a long way in cleansing the system.

Restrictions for the contributions to political parties are being relaxed so that we may one day reach a stage where the greater transparency in the political fund collection and the financing of elections. In India the political fund collection is opaque.

Conclusion

It is the effective implementation of the rule of law that confers legitimacy on the State. If the rule of law is compromised by corruption, the state loses its legitimacy. Mario Puzo in *Godfather* traced brilliantly how the mafia gathers strength and social legitimacy if the regular judicial system fails. The state loses legitimacy if it is not able to implement the rule of law. We have seen how corruption distorts the entire dynamics of law enforcement right from framing of policies, enacting legislation, implementation by the agencies like the police and the judiciary. Justice delayed is justice denied. Poor implementation results in the state forfeiting its legitimacy. The growth of the underworld and criminals is the direct result of this development. Criminalisation of politics damage further the framework for ensuring good governance and the rule of law.

Every country gets the governance it deserves. We deserve a better governance and rule of law. The first step is making every citizen aware of the need for rule of law. Taking steps to implement the ideas mentioned above is the next step. Here we must draw inspiration from the *Chandogya Upanishad*:

Ya deva Vidhyaya karoti Shraddhaya
Upanishada, Tadeva viryavattara Bhavati

When we apply our knowledge with faith, conviction and deep analysis, our action becomes strong and leads to success.

Index